Border Humanitarians

Syracuse Studies in Geography
Robert Wilson and Donald Mitchell, *Series Advisors*

The series Syracuse Studies in Geography is distinguished by works in historical geography, political economy, and environmental geography but also publishes theoretically informed books across the breadth of the discipline.

Also in Syracuse Studies in Geography

From Rice Fields to Killing Fields: Nature, Life,
and Labor under the Khmer Rouge
　　James A. Tyner

Market Orientalism: Cultural Economy and the Arab Gulf States
　　Benjamin Smith

Remapping Modern Germany after National Socialism, 1945–1961
　　Matthew D. Mingus

Border Humanitarians

Gendered Order and Insecurity
on the Thai-Burmese Frontier

Adam P. Saltsman

Syracuse University Press

Syracuse University Press
Syracuse, New York 13244-5290

All Rights Reserved

First Edition 2022

22 23 24 25 26 27   6 5 4 3 2 1

∞ The paper used in this publication meets the minimum requirements
of the American National Standard for Information Sciences—Permanence
of Paper for Printed Library Materials, ANSI Z39.48-1992.

For a listing of books published and distributed by Syracuse University Press,
visit https://press.syr.edu/.

ISBN: 978-0-8156-3768-4 (hardcover)
      978-0-8156-3763-9 (paperback)
      978-0-8156-5560-2 (e-book)

Library of Congress Cataloging-in-Publication Data
Names: Saltsman, Adam P., author.
Title: Border humanitarians : gendered order and insecurity on the thai-burmese frontier /
      Adam P. Saltsman.
Description: First Edition. | Syracuse, New York : Syracuse University Press, 2022. |
      Series: Syracuse studies in geography | Includes bibliographical references and index. |
      Summary: "Following the stories of exiled Burmese activists in Thailand who struggle
      to end gender violence among refugees, Border Humanitarians offers a critical lens
      to understand the politics of local and global human rights and aid work in contexts
      of displacement and mobility"— Provided by publisher.
Identifiers: LCCN 2021062677 (print) | LCCN 2021062678 (ebook) |
      ISBN 9780815637684 (hardback) | ISBN 9780815637639 (paperback) |
      ISBN 9780815655602 (ebook)
Subjects: LCSH: Women—Abuse of—Thailand—Prevention. | Women—Abuse of—
      Burma—Prevention. | Borderlands—Social aspects—Thailand. | Borderlands—
      Social aspects—Burma. | Refugees—Thailand. | Refugees—Burma.
Classification: LCC HV6250.4.W65 S248 2022 (print) | LCC HV6250.4.W65 (ebook) |
      DDC 362.8808209593—dc23/eng/20220228
LC record available at https://lccn.loc.gov/2021062677
LC ebook record available at https://lccn.loc.gov/2021062678

Manufactured in the United States of America

For Stéphanie

For Amelia and Ralph

Contents

Illustrations, Maps, and Table

Acknowledgments

I am grateful to the many individuals and institutions whose support made this book possible. I extend my heartfelt thanks to the many activists and migrants living in Mae Sot and Phob Phra who participated in the interviews and group discussions on which this book is based. I owe many thanks to the individuals in Mae Sot involved in the projects that became part of this book. I am deeply grateful to co-researchers who have preferred to remain anonymous. In our time together we forged an environment of trust, reflection, purpose, and solidarity. I thank also the Burmese Women's Union, Burma Lawyer's Council, Mae Tao Clinic, MAP Foundation, Overseas Irrawaddy Association, Sana Yar Thi Phan Women's Center, Social Action for Women, Tavoyan Women's Union, World Education, and Yaung Chi Oo Worker's Association. I am thankful to Santi Dusitvorakan, Saw George, Hla Su, Charoensin Intaphad, Sara Kauffman, Khin Thu, Khu Khu, Liberty Thawda, Dominique Maidment, Suttinee Seechaikham, and Akkarat Wantanajai, who provided assistance to the assessment on which much of this book is based. Shane Scanlon and Nyunt Naing Thein from the International Rescue Committee provided important support to this project. I owe profound thanks to Chotayaporn Higashi, whose house we turned into an office, who assisted with research and translation, and who shared her knowledge about the history of the borderlands. I am thankful also to Klo Say Wah, Nu Nu, Shalom, Mu Gay, and Saw George for their help with translation.

In 2019, I received the Worcester State University Faculty Scholarly and Creative Activities Grant to travel to Thailand and Myanmar and follow up on research for this book, which is based on my dissertation, *Surviving Displacement: Burmese Migrants in Thailand's Border Economic*

Zones. I received funding for preliminary dissertation research from the Boston College Center for Human Rights and International Justice and the Boston College Department of Sociology. Dissertation research and writing was supported by a dissertation fellowship from the Boston College Graduate School of Arts and Sciences and a grant from the United States Bureau of Population, Refugees, and Migration via the Feinstein International Center at Tufts University. Funding for follow-up research came from a Ritchie P. Lowry grant and from the office of the dean for the Graduate School of Arts and Sciences.

The Department of Sociology at Boston College, the Feinstein International Center at Tufts University, the Institution for Population and Social Research at Mahidol University, and Chiang Mai University's Regional Center for Social Science and Sustainable Development provided significant institutional support during the years of research. I am also grateful to the École française d'Extrême-Orient (in Paris and Chiang Mai) and the Musée du Quai Branly–Jacques Chirac for providing a space for me to research and write, and to the Thailand office of the International Rescue Committee, which provided multiple forms of support in Mae Sot both in 2011 and in 2012–2013. Special thanks also go to Mary Petrusewicz for copyediting the book, to my editorial team at Syracuse University Press, including Peggy Solic, Mona Hamlin, and Fred Wellner, and to Kay Steinmetz and Meghan Cafarelli—all of whom helped guide this book smoothly through the publishing process.

Throughout the process of writing, May Campbell, Stephen Campbell, Atchara Chan-o-kul, Chakkrid Chansang, Adisorn Kerdmonkol, Saw Khu, Koreeyor Manuchae, Phil Robertson, Geoffrey Aung, Lanna Walsh, and Roisai Wangsuban were extremely generous with their time in responding to my questions and sharing information; I am grateful to them. Thanks to Nor Da, Atchara Chan-o-kul, and Chakkrid Chansang for sharing photographs, some of which I include in the book. I would like to thank the friends, colleagues, and mentors who took the time to read drafts of memos, proposals, transcripts, and chapters and share their honest feedback with me, pushing me to deepen and strengthen my work. This includes Lisa Dodson, Karen Jacobsen, M. Brinton Lykes, Ahjane Billingsley, Zine Magubane, Shawn McGuffey, Mary Beth Mills, Alex Pittman,

Leslie Salzinger, and Graeme Storer. Mary Beth, Karen, Brinton, and Shawn were all members of my dissertation committee, and I am especially grateful for their advice in putting together sound arguments and analyses. As the chair of my committee, Stephen Pfohl provided immense support, reading my work with care, providing thought-provoking feedback, and taking the time to connect with me wherever I happened to be. I owe deep thanks to William Savage, who helped edit the manuscript tirelessly and meticulously. I presented aspects of this book at numerous conferences in recent years, including the American Association of Geographers, the Association of Asian Studies, and the Society for the Study of Social Problems. I am grateful to panelists and audience members for their feedback.

In journeys between Southeast Asia, France, and the United States during the research and writing, numerous people opened their homes to me, giving me a place to stay and keep my belongings. For making me feel at home wherever I am, I owe gratitude to Atchara Chan-o-kul—a mom away from home, Vanessa Dillen, Ron and Shuli Garonzik, David Magone, Juan Pablo Ordoñez, Alexandra Pittman, Laure de Vuilpillieres, Jonathan and Shelley White, and Sarah Woodside. I am grateful to my family—Amelia, Ralph, and Rebecca Saltsman, Jessica and Rodolfo Buonocore—and parents-in-law Annie and Johnny Khoury, who were all incredibly supportive throughout this entire endeavor, offering patience, encouragement, love, and home-cooked meals. I am deeply appreciative of the support I received from my grandparents, Benjamin and Serilla Ben-Aziz, who expressed confidence in my abilities all along.

And finally, my gratitude to Stéphanie Khoury is beyond thanks. She was with me from the very beginning and has always been there to provide a listening ear, a discerning eye, and words of encouragement; she lifted my spirits at the darkest moments, helping me to continue moving forward. Her love and support enabled me to see this project through to the end.

Border Humanitarians

1

Introduction

The Intervention

Our truck drives past sites that have become familiar markers of Mae Sot's heterogeneous center, this diverse town on Thailand's border with Myanmar: first the gate to the Buddhist monastery behind the main road where I see dogs asleep in the shade of the temple; then, amid two-story shops, a row of sagging wooden houses whose sloped rooflines succumb to gravity, remnants of the old face of the town. Turning out of an alley, we proceed onto a hectic road in the Muslim quarter of downtown where the smells of sawdust from lumber yards stacked with milled teak mix with the sweetness of frying roti, motorbike and truck exhaust, and curries with rice noodles hawked from sidewalk stalls. But today, as we sit in our air-conditioned truck, insulated from the sounds, smells, and tactile sensations we pass, seeing the town from behind the window glass makes me feel like a voyeur, turning the place and its people into objects for consumption and "enjoyment" (Benjamin 1998, 95). When we finally weave our way toward the edge of town, we emerge from the tightly packed, block concrete buildings of Mae Sot to roadside dirt lots zoned for construction, intermittent high-walled and windowless garment factories, open fields with goats eating grass and litter, and finally to our destination as we turn off the paved road onto a bumpy ridged track worn into existence by repeated use.

We arrive just outside the periphery of Mae Sot, pulling up in our Toyota Hilux that bears a USAID logo, in front of the cluster of corrugated zinc and woven thatch houses where nearly one hundred Burmese families live behind a set of oxen stables. This is the neighborhood known as Kok Kwai in Thai and Kyuwe Kyan in Burmese, which translates in both

1

languages to "buffalo enclosure." Despite being less than a five-minute drive from the heart of Mae Sot, Kyuwe Kyan is outside the urban space, without road access, and hidden from the view of most residents. Abutting rice fields, Kyuwe Kyan floods severely every rainy season; all houses are on stilts and the water rises to just below the floor. Pieces of wooden board serve as partial plank walkways, and residents who can afford them wear rubber boots to wade up to the main road when the ground is saturated. Additionally, the swampy rainy season brings swarms of mosquitoes, making dengue fever a major problem.

Rather than seeing this settlement as a contrast to the industrial border town of Mae Sot, it should be considered a product of the town's—and the country's—reliance on low-wage and informal migrant labor as well as the socioeconomic fallout of that complex history. Mae Sot is illustrative of its place as a middle-class border city in Thailand, but it is riddled with informal settlements: houses made from found materials crowded into the lots of individual landowners or next to factories, usually behind walls or out of view from the main road.

The settlements are, in this sense, invisible slums maintained at low cost to supply the adjacent Thai households with domestic workers and the factories with wage laborers representing an ethnically diverse population of Burmese who in recent decades have fled war, militarism, and economic devastation in search of refuge and opportunity in Thailand. In this way, places like Kyuwe Kyan are both inside and outside the urban space of Mae Sot. They are so-called "Third World" spaces constructed in a state whose leadership has been vocal about achieving "First World" economic status (Arnold and Pickles 2011). As such, these locales are related to the global trend of constructing and maintaining an idea of a class of flexible and feminized labor in outsourced care and domestic work, piece-rate sewing or weaving, and other forms of supply-chain production that are instrumental aspects of labor's intensification, diversification, and heterogenization in a post-Fordist era (Mezzadra and Neilson 2013, 88; Wright 2006).

There is something ad hoc in the informality of these spaces, as if they sprung up spontaneously in otherwise empty locales. And yet everything about these habitations is deliberate: they are often in enclosed spaces,

1. Mixed urban housing. Mae Sot, Tak Province, Thailand, June 2021. Source: Atchara Chan-o-Kul.

their boundaries are the boundaries of the landlord or factory property, they are built or allowed to be built by landlords who cleared and leveled their land, and in many cases these settlements developed over time— Kyuwe Kyan, for example, has grown slowly over a twenty-year period. While this pattern reflects a kind of urban fragmentation that is common to the sprawling growth of cities in Southeast Asia (e.g., Harms 2011; McGee 1991), Mae Sot's variegated settlement pattern derives from its topography, its proximity to decades of war and displacement in Myanmar, and its role as a peripheral economic space in a global economy where an imaginary of frontiers as profitable transport and manufacturing hubs is increasingly central. By imaginary, I refer to sets of logics, beliefs, ideologies, and ways of seeing that emerge out of particular political and economic structures (e.g., Brown 2014, 74).

Now, during the dry season, as we get out of the sterile environment of the truck, our senses are hit by all that we had been shielded against: in the foreground is the chemical smell of a slow-burning trash heap—two children are stoking the flames, sending up a pall of engulfing yellow smoke; behind them the heat muffles the sounds of the settlement, giving it an empty, faraway feeling.

Arriving in Kyuwe Kyan, we are stepping into "the field" where we will mobilize the community to take action on a village cleanup campaign that migrants decided on during a community health consultation with an NGO the previous month. I am along for the ride as an observer with this NGO's health team, which aims to improve access to basic healthcare for dozens of migrant settlements like Kyuwe Kyan along the border—many are on the outskirts of Mae Sot, near factories, behind warehouses, adjacent to fields; others are in rural areas in districts to the north and south. As a researcher, I want to know more about this place, about how it and its inhabitants are part of Mae Sot and are also the embodiment of "other" space—that is, space that is alien and marginal. Though our arrival lays bare my privilege and that of the NGO to conduct these visits and observations—to enter the settlement and move about freely—I am interested in the feelings of ambivalence and discomfort that these moments might engender among the migrants and NGO staff alike, or the lack thereof. We unload supplies from the bed of the truck and carry everything to the side of a house where a community health volunteer lives and where this NGO organizes its activities. Unsure of what to do, I watch as the staff and the volunteer put up a plastic banner on the house wall with USAID's logo and the message "From the American People" in large print. They open boxes and remove tins of cookies, twenty-liter trash bags, baskets, gloves, and face masks, arranging them on a table we brought. Soon residents gather and a representative from Mae Sot General Hospital begins an animated lecture in Thai about the importance of maintaining a clean neighborhood, which the community health volunteer translates into Burmese. "Litter, feces left on the ground, and unwashed hands are some of the main ways we transmit germs," she lectured. There are about thirty people sitting or standing nearby, listening to this presentation; others peer through the open windows of their houses or continue with their household work, seemingly oblivious. Then residents and NGO staff take gloves, bags, and baskets and set off through the settlement, collecting bits of garbage lining the pathways and stacked up under houses. The trash heap smolders in the near distance.

Walking slowly through Kyuwe Kyan, crossing the paths of the remaining small groups of youth and elders who are picking up litter, I see Ma Sandi, a program assistant for the NGO, standing behind a house listening earnestly to a middle-aged man with a white-collared shirt tucked into a longyi, a cloth garment, ubiquitous in Myanmar, that hangs from the waist. My eyes catch hers and she beckons me over, eager, or at least willing, for me to hear their conversation. She introduces me to Sayar Htun Lwin, a teacher who lives in Kyuwe Kyan, with whom she has worked over the years.

"The sayar [teacher] and I have known each other for a long time, since we were both working in factories here," Ma Sandi says, referring to their days doing low-wage migrant labor. "We still keep in touch to support the communities." Sayar Htun Lwin is an instructor at a nearby learning center, a school for migrants set up by community and nongovernmental organizations because school-aged migrant children were unofficially excluded from local Thai schools due to language barriers and the costs of education. The two of them are off to the side of the larger group, out of earshot, and they have been talking quietly in Burmese. Sayar Htun Lwin looks from me to Ma Sandi and continues their conversation about a student, which Ma Sandi translates for my benefit. "The father is bringing drugs into Kyuwe Kyan, and yesterday his wife informed me that he was hitting her and the children, but this is not the first time." Though the sayar is not trained to deal with violence of any kind and though he is not part of any official response network, as a teacher he has a unique role in that he interacts on a regular basis with nearly all the families in Kyuwe Kyan. I get the impression he is *the* point of contact when problems arise. And even though Ma Sandi is also not part of the growing NGO-sponsored interorganizational presence for supporting survivors of gender violence among the migrant population, I can't help but notice the ease and sense of familiarity with which she handles this disclosure.

"Let's talk to her and see what she wants to do," Ma Sandi reflected. Then she sighed, "Maybe we'll need to make an agreement between them to stop this fighting. Maybe with the imam." At the time, I took this to be a passing conversation between two friendly colleagues, but as we drove away from Kyuwe Kyan with our trucks full of garbage bags, crossing an invisible border between the peripheral space of the informal settlement and reentering the buzzing urbanity of Mae Sot, this interaction took center stage among the questions emerging out of the day's events.

What, for example, was the value of the intervention I had just observed, and how did Ma Sandi's and Sayar Htun Lwin's management of a gender-violence case fit in amid the official activities of that day? Lectures about handwashing and trash collection days appeared to be archetypical illustrations of what James Ferguson (1994) called the "anti-politics" work of NGOs in development or humanitarian settings. By working to ameliorate only some of the symptoms of deep-seated structural injustices that produced migrant exclusion from Thailand's social institutions, international organizations were effectively depoliticizing the conditions of migrant life and labor there, which in turn is its own form of politics, promoting particular worldviews, discourses, and agendas (Hardt and Negri 2000; Li 2007).

Settlements like Kyuwe Kyan and its residents are largely invisible to the rest of Mae Sot's population as a result of migrants' poverty, undocumented migrant status, informal sector livelihoods, and socially excluded ethnic and religious identities. There are an unknown number of Burmese migrants in the border districts around Mae Sot, but estimates suggest anywhere from 80,000 to 350,000 people, most of whom are believed to be undocumented. There are an estimated 2–4 million Burmese migrants in Thailand; approximately two million of these are legally registered workers who can be officially counted (Harkins 2019; Peeradej 2011). Wages for migrants in the borderlands are a fraction of the national minimum; the cost and effort of becoming registered—and thus semi-legal—is prohibitive; and migrants work long hours on jobs considered by many to be dirty, dangerous, and degrading (Pearson and Kusakabe 2012a). Their movement is restricted, they have a hard time accessing healthcare and the justice system, and they are subject to deportation or abusive treatment by authorities if caught outside their place of work (Pearson and Kusakabe 2013; Pearson et al. 2006). On top of this, they must contend with the widespread notion that such conditions are appropriate for their undocumented status and are a natural dynamic fundamental to regional and global supply chains.

For the same reasons that Kyuwe Kyan residents are invisible to many in Mae Sot, however, they are hyper-visible to NGOs working in this town who aim to empower them, especially women, to be healthy, law-abiding, and responsible individuals. These apparent contradictions reflect, in fact, a point of intersection between the humanitarian mission and the destruction wrought by global capitalism, the legacy of colonial hierarchies, and the exclusionary practices of sovereignty. This NGO's intervention contributed to the idea that the migrant residents of Kyuwe Kyan were responsible for their own welfare, thus removing any accountability for the extreme precarity of their circumstances.

At the same time, there was something outside this interventionist dynamic in what Ma Sandi's and Sayar Htun Lwin were doing. They were off to the side of the community clean-up activity to discuss the case of domestic violence in private, as if they were performing work that was somehow illicit. Their work did not fit neatly into the NGO model of professionalization that sought to incorporate Burmese activists' service provision work into the fold of the Thai state, which had structured migrant exclusion in the first place. I realized that what I had witnessed revealed an alternative form of politics being enacted on the border, a politics of both solidarity and order-making about gender violence that appropriated the resources of humanitarian NGOs but was rooted in relationships and networks that crossed nation-state borders and thrived off of the unique forms of agency and possibility that emerge out of dispossession and precarity. How, I wondered, did the anti-politics work of NGOs intersect with this form of politics that was more situated in migrants' experiences, especially in this borderland space where the transience of migration seems to defy efforts to organize, and where it was hard to imagine a sense of community? How, that is, were border humanitarians, migrant-activists like Ma Sandi and Sayar Htun Lwin, producing gendered forms of order and security out of the violence of their own exclusion?

Building on these questions, this book interrogates the relationship between the kinds of NGO projects described at the start of this chapter and the social and political relations of capital accumulation on the border that have shaped the town into a variegated pattern of visible homes and invisible slums. This means looking at the kinds of networks, practices, and discourses migrants rely on as they navigate precarious life and work in the borderlands to make order out of the disorder of state and market-driven economic structures. It means asking how the enclosures, settlements, and labor camps that are home to thousands of Burmese migrants here signify the multiplication of borders that produce and simultaneously erase difference, rearrange and fracture sovereignty, and impose hierarchies that place greater value on some lives than on others, and that affix people to place and to labor in the most intimate ways. Following the stories of exiled Burmese activists in Thailand who struggle to end gender violence among forced migrants, *Border Humanitarians* offers a critical lens to understand the politics of local and global human rights and aid work in the context of displacement and mobility.

Collaborative Research and Reflexive Ethnography in Humanitarian Intervention

There is much that is ethnographic and reflexive about this book, which is built on nearly four years of research conducted between 2011 and 2019. Writing about migrant communities comes with enormous risks of essentializing and fetishizing both people and landscape in a way that reproduces hierarchies of difference. To write "from the borders," as Mignolo and Tslostanova (2006) direct, is to engage in a form of methodological and analytical praxis, to move iteratively between reflexive interrogation and dialogic analysis in a way that decenters reifying conceptual frameworks (Cornwall and Molyneux 2006). I was in many ways a participant-observer in the stories this book tells. Always negotiating my place within an activist-scholar spectrum, I conducted the research for this project while affiliated with various organizations. *Border Humanitarians* is as much based on the voices of those with whom I collaborated as on my own analytical perspective; indeed, putting these into conversation with each other reveals important sites where we co-produced knowledge and uncovered gaps in my own perspective and understanding, laying bare my own assumptions.

During some of the years I worked in and around Mae Sot as an NGO staffer or research consultant, especially the earlier years, I was a direct participant in the human rights and humanitarian programs that are a focus of this book. In early 2011, working for a university and a humanitarian organization based in the Global North, I managed a research project to map urban displacement in Mae Sot (Saltsman 2011). In late 2011, and for part of 2012, I conducted human-rights investigations for a Global North[1] advocacy group working on refugee policy in Thailand. In subsequent years, I volunteered with a border-based unregistered Burmese community organization to help it secure funding for its projects. Not only did these experiences pull me in various directions according to the agendas of the groups with whom I worked, but they created opportunities to explore the ways that power and privilege intersected in various venues to allow dialectics between different forms of knowledge (Horst 2006).

Much of the research for this book began during my work as a program coordinator with a Global North humanitarian NGO in 2012–13, where I was tasked with running an assessment of gender-based violence (GBV) in migrant communities along the border. This opportunity allowed me to build new relationships and tap my existing network of Burmese and Thai activists and direct-service providers working with migrant-led organizations along the border on issues of gender violence, labor rights, and human rights. I acted as a co-facilitator for the eight-month-long assessment, an action research project aimed at improving humanitarian programming, working collectively with a multiethnic group of Burmese and

1. In this book, unless an NGO is affiliated with the United Nations, an official body of global governance, I do not refer to those operating in multiple countries as "international" or "global" but instead refer to them in terms of their rootedness in the Global North or South, using these terms to signal a one-thirds world (North)/two-thirds world (South) political-economic divide (see, for example, Mohanty 2016). While many Northern human-rights and humanitarian organizations tend to characterize themselves as international, I argue that this identification masks the geopolitical and economic power relations that inform their agendas, discourses, and practices. A Global North/South differentiation is more about global power flows and should not be taken as geographic terms. This way of framing humanitarianism reminds us of the kinds of tensions and hierarchies that are always, though not explicitly, part of the story.

Thai migrant-rights activists and direct-service providers from six border-based NGOs (five of which are, at the time of this writing, unregistered and thus officially illegal in Thailand) and two Global North NGOs (one of these funded the assessment of GBV).

These migrant-rights activists and direct-service providers included people like Ma Sandi and others who were each embedded in their own personal histories of exile, mobility, struggle, and life on the border, as well as their own positionalities—their relationships, worldviews, and social identities—across lines of class, gender, religion, legal status, and ethnicity/ethnic nationality.[2] Some, like Su Hlaing, who identified as Dawei[3] from Myanmar's Dawei region, ran organizations to provide comprehensive aid to members of their community. Others, like Hser Dee, who identified ethnically as S'gaw Karen, were part of larger migrant-led organizations focused on healthcare or labor rights. The GBV assessment group I worked with included five different ethnicities: Shan, Karenni, Pwo Karen, and Bamar—the majority ethnic group in Myanmar—in addition to Dawei and S'gaw Karen, and both Thai and Burmese nationalities. Though co-researchers were open about their ethnic identification, places like Mae Sot and other border areas outside the refugee camps are ethnically heterogenous, and ethnic identifications might even be blurred. As Campbell (2012) demonstrates, the borderlands can be characterized as a transethnic space where migrants come together to forge solidarity based on issues of shared concern, such as labor rights, and such issues are often more salient factors for mobilizing collective action than ethnicity. Following the lead of co-researchers and the many migrants we met, this book engages ethnicity less as an analytical category to understand everyday life and more in terms of how ethno-nationality as a political and

2. In Myanmar, *taingyinthar* (lit. "national races") refers to the 135 official ethnic-nationality categories that the government considers part of its multicultural and multi-ethnic state (Cheesman 2017). I use the terms "ethnic nationality" or "ethno-nationality" to refer to particular political projects in Myanmar that incorporate ethnic identity as a defining feature of their movement.

3. Dawei is one of the 135 officially recognized "nationalities" or ethnic groups in Myanmar.

ideological project has been central to mobilizing certain kinds of order-making and humanitarian aid.

I use pseudonyms for my co-researchers, leaving their organizations unnamed as well, in an effort to shield their identities from any unintended consequences. There were eleven co-researchers in this assessment team (nine identifying as women and two as men)—all working for advocacy or social-service organizations focused on violence against women, women's empowerment, labor rights, and reproductive health. All but two identified as forced migrants from Myanmar; the two who did not grew up as ethnic minorities on the Thai side of the border. Most co-researchers had intimate knowledge of the precarious life and kinds of labor migrants performed in Thailand; most had either worked on, or were familiar with, gender violence in migrant settlements here. All were connected to the various forms of humanitarian intervention targeting Burmese displaced in Thailand.

Guided by the principles of Participatory Action Research, including a commitment to co-designing our approach and privileging knowledge derived from lived experience, our group shared responsibility for coming up with the scope and focus of the GBV assessment. Collectively, we decided to look at how migrants in four settlements—two in Mae Sot town and two in the rural district of Phob Phra, to the south—perceived and responded to gender violence in their area.

Co-researchers collectively interviewed and conducted focus-group discussions with approximately 140 individuals identifying as Burmese forced migrants, including self-identified religious and community leaders, teachers, community health workers, and representatives of women's groups.[4] We engaged in shared analysis and interpretation of what we had gathered, and brought together a broader network of border-based, Thai, and Northern NGOs to discuss the findings and brainstorm humanitarian programming. Despite efforts to structure our work as democratic,

4. Among these participants were a mix of different religious and ethnic identities, including Christian, Buddhist, Muslim, and Hindu. While co-researchers and I did not systematically record ethnic identities from these participants, preferring this identifier to emerge inductively, there were some sites with Karen leaders and others where Islam was a more salient organizing factor.

Map 1. Mae Sot and Phob Phra districts in Tak Province, Thailand. Source: Adam Saltsman.

collaboration is always messy as diverse ways of seeing the world and differing agendas collide in a social field shot through with imbalanced power relations that include the "ever-present histories of colonization and imperial intervention, [and] the hegemonic power of Northern academics" (Lykes and Crosby, 2014, 146; see also Janes 2016). How this group collaborated, navigating our own relationships, worldviews, and social identities—our positionalities—and constructing knowledge about gender violence in the sites along the border where migrants worked and lived, provides a useful and reflexive case study of humanitarian intervention in this space that echoes, deepens, and complicates the rich body of work on the subject (e.g., Daley 2013; Englund 2006; Fassin 2011; Pallister-Wilkins 2019; Ticktin 2011a, 2011b).

I returned multiple times to the Thai-Burmese border and elsewhere in the region to further pursue threads of this research. In 2014, 2017, and 2019 I met up with co-researchers in Mae Sot, and in Bangkok, Thailand, and Yangon, Myanmar, as they relocated and continued on their own professional and life trajectories. I also conducted interviews with dozens of migrants living in labor camps and urban neighborhoods, numerous heads and senior leadership of migrant-led organizations working on gender violence and women's rights, as well as European, American, and Thai representatives of UN and donor agencies, Thai gender-justice advocates, Thai representatives of the Tak Province Chamber of Commerce, and the Tak Special Economic Development Zone Office. At times I worked with research assistants who helped make connections and who helped with Burmese-English and Karen-English interpretation. Some of them feature in this book—rather than thinking of them as invisible intermediaries, I view their voices as part of the story as well. Based on fieldwork spread out over nearly a decade, *Border Humanitarians* brings to the fore the stories of co-researchers, those we interviewed, and multiple other perspectives on precarious migration, humanitarianisms, and the political and economic realities and imaginaries in the ever-shifting Thai-Burmese borderlands.

Although, as the sole author of this book, the work ultimately represents my singular voice, I use the reflexive approach to shed light on the way that ethnographic and humanitarian research like this can be part of what, in Cabot's words (2016, 649), renders forced migrants "ghostly" as scholars and practitioners adapt their narratives to their "representational project and goals." The discourse I examine in the following chapters includes that which I myself helped produce and circulate, only sometimes wittingly. I read in my position the inevitable partiality that any study brings. But instead of seeing this as a limitation, explicitly recognizing positionality is part of my "ethnographic toolkit," as Reyes (2020) puts it, enabling a reflexive lens to include in the analysis my work, the work of my colleagues, and the transnational and institutional knowledges we represented and with which we grappled. This means adopting a phenomenological lens for seeing our work as performative—that is, as a set of practices, discourses, and interactions that together play a role in enacting and reproducing our social reality. Seeing my own work and voice, and that of the others included in this book, as elements in the performative reproduction and contestation of our realities and the borderlands itself opens up new ways of thinking about dispossession, humanitarianism, and the intimate ways our subjectivity and positionality constitute the social space.

Positionality and Performativity in the Production of Border Space

Collaborative research and conversations like the one I witnessed between Ma Sandi and Htun Lwin offer a window into how those with direct experience of displacement and precarious life in Thailand, and those engaged in humanitarian aid work, discuss gender violence and draw on their knowledge, backgrounds, and other available resources to strategize an effective and appropriate response. Telling stories and examining the content of these narratives are examples of "the politics of everyday life," as Daley and colleagues (2017, 4) write, in that they deal with "questions of survival, livelihood, representation, social reproduction, marginalization, resistance, and political life." The individual histories of migrant-rights activists and service providers with whom I spoke, as well as the accounts of how migrants perceive and react to gender violence around them, are sites for the production and articulation of political subjectivities. Subjectivities are fluid and in a state of "becoming" amid the structures and practices of daily life in the border space, including humanitarian intervention, labor conditions, and the everyday work of securing basic needs (Isin 2012; Kallio et al. 2019).

In narrating and analyzing their experiences in the borderlands, social actors deploy gendered identities and ideologies to understand a context, to make meaning, and to regulate behavior or offer interpretations of order. To think about gender in this way means analyzing interaction and discourse as the manifestation of bodies functioning as a "site upon which ideas, ideologies, and politics are performed and made meaningful" (Mountz 2018, 762). This reflects a Foucauldian (1979) use of gender as a concept or set of ideas that are always already under production, produced discursively. In asking how and why migrants, activists, service providers at migrant-led organizations, and Northern humanitarian aid workers frame gender and gender violence in certain ways, I am interested in the phenomenological question of how geographic location, personal history, and relationships all play a role in how we make meaning of our reality—that is, in the situated nature of our knowledge (Hopkins 2018). This means looking at positionality in the context of border humanitarianism, at the ways that one's social and geographic location—embedded within a matrix of social hierarchy—relates to a set of vantage points from which one regards and engages with the world (Massey 1994; Hopkins 2018).

I use the term "gendered border positionalities" in this book to explore how migrant activists, service providers, and others exercise knowledge situated in complex histories of mobility, precarity, resistance, displacement, and humanitarianism to both make meaning of the multiple forms of gendered violence in the borderlands and to rely on understandings of gender to make order in a space of social exclusion and uprootedness. This helps us understand how precarity can be simultaneously made sense of and reproduced as social actors navigate the overlapping forces of dispossession, political exclusion, humanitarian intervention, and capital accumulation. Migrants' discourse linked to displacement, violence, and the resolution of interpersonal conflict on the border both demonstrates and constitutes these gendered border positionalities. The notion of "positionality," as I use it here, is closely related to that of emergent political subjectivities, but whereas a focus on gender and subjectivation suggests an analysis of the ways that migrants see themselves on the intimate level of gender identity, positionality reflects how social actors deploy their subjectivities to make meaning of and structure the world around them.[5]

5. By "subjectivation," I am referring to the ways in which power infuses everyday life as individuals encounter social hierarchy and other social structures. Subjectivation is the ongoing process of inhabiting, perceiving, and enacting one's identity. It refers to

Taken together as interactions embedded in complex matrices of power, and considered as part of a diverse constellation of discourse about gender violence, migrant bodies, and dispossession on the Thai-Burmese border, it becomes possible to see that our group's efforts to make meaning and effect change are also constitutive of the social realities and the spaces in which we were embedded. As Lefebvre (1991, 162) reminds us, "it is by means of the body that space is perceived, lived—and produced." This view supports an analysis of the Thai-Burmese border zone as a "borderscape," a space that is "fluid and shifting; established and, at the same time, continuously traversed by a number of bodies, discourses, practices and relationships" (Brambilla 2015, 19). In this borderscape, discourse, relations, networks, and interaction—mobilized in an iterative fashion— are means for the performative production and reproduction of social space and structures. Power relations inhere and give meaning to space, and through their performative enactment may, ultimately, affirm dominant systems and ways of seeing.

Referring to performativity here builds on the writings of Judith Butler (1993), including later work that explores how precarity and dispossession are conditions reproduced iteratively through discourse and practice (Butler and Athanasiou 2013). Performativity, which Butler (1993, 20) describes as "the power of discourse to produce effects through reiteration," not only takes place *in* space but is "implicated in the production *of* space, which is itself a contested performative process" (Rose-Redwood and Glass 2014, 15; see also Bell et al. 1994). The state as embodied and our subject-positions vis-à-vis the state and market forces in which we are embedded materialize and rematerialize iteratively through discursive practices (e.g., Mountz

---

an ongoing experience of personhood "that includes his or her positions in a field of relational power" and that "is produced through the experience of violence and the manner in which global flows involving images, capital, and people become entangled with local logics in identity formation" (Das and Kleinman 2000, 1). To study how issues like violence, migration, borders, and labor intersect with gender on the level of subjectivity is to suggest an analysis of how the particular power relations bound up in these processes and concepts push individuals and collectivities to consider themselves and to struggle with diverse notions of how to live life.

2004). In this sense, social exclusion on the Thai-Burmese border is a product of the iterative practices of state security officials who commit violence against migrant bodies, as well as of employers who repeatedly construct the notion of "migrant illegality" in their refusal to regularize their immigrant labor force or pay the minimum wage. The border space is regularly reproduced every time migrants encounter the state and are reminded of their social exclusion from its institutions (Rajaram and Grundy-Warr 2007; Kaiser 2014). When migrant-led organizations in Mae Sot and the residents of labor camps along the border share their stories and perspectives, we not only learn about how social actors make meaning of conflict and violence but we also gain a deeper understanding of the generative qualities of violence and precarious life, of the ways that "the logic of dispossession is interminably mapped onto . . . bodies" (Butler and Athanasiou 2013, 19). Such experiences are performative in the way their repetition stabilizes categories and infuses them with meaning, reinforcing both a perception of otherness, or alterity, as Decha writes (2015), and the material consequences of exclusion, including exclusion from basic rights. In this sense, order and the ways in which order is perceived materializes through multiple and heterogenous forms of practice, discourse, and relations at particular moments in time (Deleuze and Guattari 1987).

Arguing that post-developmental spatial arrangements that accommodate global supply chains have led to a multiplication of labor and borders, Mezzadra and Neilson (2013, 251; see also Sidaway 2007) suggest that this heterogenization "entails the production of diverse subject positions and boundaries that crisscross the composition of living labor and insert themselves within shifting assemblages of knowledge and power." That is, a multiplication of labor engenders a multiplication of subjectivities. As new forms of political subjectivity emerge at the intersection of multiple forces of precaritization, it becomes ever more crucial to pay attention to positionality, to the way that actors make sense of the world around them, including their place in it, and the way that actors engage in performative productions of power relations and the social space of the border in gendered terms.

The practices and discourses of humanitarian intervention also play a constitutive role; all actors involved in this industry—both locally and from abroad—iteratively produce what Walters (2011) calls the "humanitarian border": the "topological constellation" of regulations, discourse, networks, and practices situated in particular zones of humanitarian operation (Kallio et al. 2019, 1260). With this in mind, it is important to consider how Northern, border-based, or Thai NGOs engage with the kinds of structural violence this book discusses, including labor exploitation, migrant social exclusion, and xenophobic discourse, as well as with local and transnational movements for political transformation.[6] How do they reproduce or challenge discourses of biopolitical self-regulation and dominant notions of femininity, masculinity, and sexuality? And how is this part of the iterative production and reproduction of the borderscape?

Thinking about borders performatively, including a focus on the practices of enacting and enforcing borders, and the experiences of those on borders as materialized and rematerialized iteratively through discourse and encounters is characteristic of what Nira Yuval-Davis and colleagues (2019) refer to as "bordering." As they write, "Borderings are . . . practices that are situated and constituted in the specificity of political negotiations as well as in the everyday life performances of these negotiations, being shifted and contested across individuals and groupings as well as in the constructions of individual subjectivities" (24). They describe the notion of "everyday bordering" as the technologies of maintaining and reproducing social hierarchies and notions of sovereignty in an era defined by neoliberal capitalism, biopolitics, and governmentality. "Any place has become a borderland," they write (17), where subjects encounter othering through a politics of exclusion, including in schools, hospitals, and places of work and worship. Bound up in the work of bordering are also the myriad ways that subjects articulate belonging, sometimes in

---

6. Such examples of structural violence illustrate the ways in which migrants in Thailand experience harm as a consequence of social structures designed to maintain a flexible and low-wage workforce. Thinking here about how policy (both in design and implementation), public attitude, and labor conditions intersect in migrants' lives reinforces the sense in which the notion of "structural violence" refers to state institutions that exclude or discriminate as well as the ways in which unequal relations come to be normalized in a society as status quo (Bourdieu 1999).

direct opposition to the everyday reproduction of exclusionary discourses or those that naturalize migrant precarity. In the zone of exclusion, the kinds of discourses and practices that migrants enact for themselves, the networks they rely on, and the ways they see and use border space to survive, practice mobility, and produce notions of "order" and "humanitarianism" are all important sites for the emergence of alternatives to the dominant framings of migrant bodies and experiences, and to alternative notions of the social space itself.

Such potentially resistive moments demand a closer look when thinking about how borderscapes shift and contain a multiplicity of contested meanings. To the extent that space and its social meanings are performatively constituted, there are, as Valentine (2002, 154–55) writes, "always possibilities that disruptions or slippages may occur in their production . . . with the consequence that powerful discourses are not replicated but are changed or done differently." Ruptures or fissures in dominant social orders and ways of seeing are inherently part of the performative production of space, corresponding to a multiplicity and heterogeneity of "collective and connective assemblages" of relations and forces that intersect in space and time (Dewsbury 2000, 476). The specific ways in which Burmese activists and service providers navigate the structural and interpersonal violence around them can lead to modes of social organization that are outside the dominant regimes of order structured by the state, Northern humanitarian NGOs, or border-based industries. These forms can take on resistive qualities, or be embedded in social networks built around an idea of resisting oppressive forces, but they can also, as this book shows, structure reality and meaning around ideas and practices that still constrain migrant identities in certain ways, even while opening up certain possibilities. That is, even as some migrants in this context organize to oppose their precarity and to restore and rethread some of the social fabric torn through displacement, their discourse may reify in its own way gender and gendered ideas of migration and survival in exile. Rather than thinking of such disruptions as occurring outside the production of social orders like border security and low-wage production regimes, Tsing (2005) reminds us that the machinery of global interconnection requires such moments of "friction" to inhere and materialize in space.

Border Humanitarians brings together the threads of geographic theorizing on bordering and borderscapes and scholarship on performativity, political subjectivity, and positionality in relation to gender and gender violence in contexts of dispossession in the deployment of the idea of gendered border positionalities. To do this, I expand the conceptual potential of the idea of "bordering" within the context of displacement and forced migration to think beyond the moments where the production of borders is explicit. While Yuval-Davis and colleagues (2019) provide dozens of examples of bordering, each of these is limited to practices that directly enact borders, whether physical or social, including interactions between security officials and migrants in border zones or the impacts of changes to visa rules on students from newcomer backgrounds pursuing their education. The authors do not trace the practice of bordering to aspects of everyday life for those whom the state identifies as other, alien, or illegal. And yet, as *Border Humanitarians* shows, bordering shows up everywhere. As Michel Agier (2016, 7) writes, "The border is a place, a situation or a moment that ritualizes the relationship to the other." Such a definition includes what Ann Stoler (2016, 120–21) calls "interior frontiers" that "stretch obliquely across and within" space, privileging particular hierarchies, tools of exclusion, and geographies while subverting others, often in unspoken ways.

Border positionalities in this book, then, has to do with how the border infiltrates everyday life for undocumented Burmese migrants, and how migrant discourse about their experiences and circumstances is in its own right a means of bordering, even when that discourse does not mention the topics of exclusion, refuge, precarity, or legal status, even when that discourse is about managing relationships or about how one navigates the space around them. This reflects what Lems (2020, 117) calls a "phenomenology of exclusion"—that is, an approach to border work as "a lived social phenomenon that cannot be understood detached from the habitual ways people are oriented toward the world." In a population for whom bordering has meant such pervasive social and political exclusion, and where precarity is so structured—both spatially and through the practices of border enforcement and exclusion—resolving social conflict (gender violence in the case of this book) is *itself* a product of the border and bordering, and it is *itself* a bordering process because it performatively reproduces the positionality of migrants vis-à-vis the state, humanitarian actors, employers, and other migrants. Thinking this way can deepen our understanding of how borders—including nation-state borders and those linked to social hierarchies of race, ethnicity, class, gender, and ability, among others—are mutually constitutive as social spaces.

Labor Camps and Other Sites of (Im)mobility amid Multiple "Frontiers"

When I began working in Mae Sot and elsewhere in these borderlands in 2008, I quickly noted a "frontier" discourse that was pervasive, especially in the humanitarian sectors and among the Global North aid workers and self-styled human rights advocates who enmesh themselves in the cluster of secular and faith-based organizations there (see Thornton 2006 for a good example of this narrative). Attention in this sector was on the alleviation of suffering and liberation for internally displaced persons in southeastern Myanmar and encamped refugees in Thailand, as well as those fleeing political persecution by the Burmese government. This focus was part of what Oh (2018) has described as the norms, codes, and ideologies of a moral economy circulating in these borderlands. In this space, gendered and racialized neocolonial narratives of masculine saviorism encounter and overlap with the liberal values of transnational human rights and the principles of humanitarian intervention (Stoler 2002; Horstmann 2018). But these narratives tend to conflate what are, in fact, multiple humanitarianisms that adhere to different logics of aid and action in this borderscape. Part of the goal of this book is to disrupt this trend by amplifying the voices of migrant activists and to surface the heterogeneity of humanitarian and other logics that intersect in this space as technologies of governance.[7] While the aid work associated with this frontier discourse rightly amplifies the experiences of predominately Karen, Shan, Kachin, and Karenni communities who have endured war, militarism,

7. As I discuss in chapters 2 and 6, an analysis of humanitarian discourse sheds light on how the growth of forced migrant-led and ethnic armed civil society on the border intersects with the agendas of Global North donor agencies, including the one that funded the project on which this book is partly based.

and displacement for more than seven decades, these narratives are also part of a humanitarian border (Walters 2011) that renders certain Burmese people more legible than others and in particular ways over others.

Such logics, which underlay the cleanup activity described at the start of this chapter, can often overlook or apply a narrow lens to the precarious conditions of the tens of thousands of Burmese migrants who are outside the refugee camps and who labor in garment factories, industrial farmlands, construction, the domestic sector, hospitality, and other livelihood activities. One manifestation of this is the tendency for scholarship and policy research to analytically divide the population of Burmese displaced in Thailand into two categories: refugees or displaced persons, on the one hand (primarily residents of nine camps along the Thai side of the border), and those whose mobility the state and other actors have characterized in economic terms and who live in Thailand's rural and urban areas, on the other hand (Brees 2009; Grundy-Warr and Wong Siew Yin 2002; Saltsman 2014).[8] The category of "refugee" typically corresponds to rural upland populations of southeastern Myanmar displaced by conflict, as well as those fleeing state persecution, often from more urban areas (Sciortino and Sureephorn 2009; Lang 2002). Thai law, and consequently the UN High Commissioner for Refugees (UNHCR), only regard those in nine designated camps as refugees or as refugees pending status determination. Analysts, donor agencies, and representatives of the Thai government use the category of "economic or labor migrant" to refer to those Burmese people who have moved to Thailand over the last thirty years in search of opportunity (Nobpaon and Hayami 2013). This distinction effectively structures an idea of refugee subjectivity as fixed to the physical space of the camps and imposes a restrictive binary onto the Burmese

8. Making comparisons between migrants and camp-based refugees has become increasingly prevalent in the literature on forced migration, as scholars articulate the importance of urban spaces in terms of protection, economic opportunity, access to social networks, and new ways of articulating the relationship between forced migrants, the state, the host population, and the growing numbers of urban poor (Jacobsen 2005; Agier 2002; Malkki 1995).

population outside the camps: they are either displaced persons in need of aid or members of a labor force in pursuit of opportunity.

Rejecting the common differentiation of "encamped refugees" and urban/rural migrants into opposed ideal-type categories,[9] *Border Humanitarians* recognizes the fluidity of mobility between camp and out-of-camp spaces and between cross-border and border-based economic, social, and political networks. I use "migrant" as an umbrella term in this book rather than dividing the population up by legal-political categories. Interested in the ways that migrants and the borderlands reflect multiple frontiers, including those that relate to humanitarianism and those that pertain to the logic of capital accumulation, the book centers on the lived experiences of migrants living in urban neighborhoods, informal settlements, and labor camps—as opposed to refugee camps.

The use of the term "frontier" in this book's subtitle, then, evokes the many meanings that overlap in migrants' everyday experiences of life and violence. Broadly speaking, I approach the notion of "frontiers" as spaces around which discourses of center, periphery, change, order, and expansion arise (e.g., Mezzadra and Neilson 2013). These spaces also embody the "imperial effects" of remnant colonial logic and contemporary state imaginaries of order and power (Stoler 2016). This includes the many internal frontiers defined by "enclosure and containment" (Stoler 2016, 121)—for example, within work sites, urban neighborhoods, and in terms of lines of differentiation related to notions of ethnicity, religion, and gender. Thinking about the Thai side of the border, Philip Hirsch (2009) outlines three important dimensions of frontier development: agricultural expansion and the moving periphery of space that is considered wild or forested, a moving peri-urban frontier dividing countryside and urban space, and frontiers of the nation-state. Each of these relates to concepts of the

9. My own fieldwork does not support such a rigid distinction, and numerous studies (e.g., Caouette and Pack 2002; Green et al. 2008; Saltsman 2011) provide empirical data to argue that the distinction between refugees and migrants in Thailand is not grounded in reality but primarily in the policies of the UN High Commissioner for Refugees, the Thai government, and many donor agencies.

geo-body, power, and national identity; frontiers in Thailand have often been conceived, forged, and expanded to imbricate with social hierarchies and spatial inequalities. The border region where this book is set reflects all three of these dimensions as well as their enactment on migrant bodies.

Migrant Settlements in the Variegated Borderscape

Border Humanitarians focuses on migrants living and working in the city of Mae Sot and scattered labor camps in the agricultural district to the south in Phob Phra. I include four different settlements. In Mae Sot, I look at the experiences and discourses of migrants living in a settled urban neighborhood, Htone Taung, and the peripheral informal settlement Kyuwe Kyan. In Phob Phra, I included the village of Romklao Sahamit, an agricultural center, and a nearby labor camp that migrants refer to as Pyaung Gyi Win, or "Baldy's land," a nickname for the landowner. The identification of these four sites emerged out of the collaborative research on which much of this book is based.[10]

The city of Mae Sot, in the district of the same name, lies about 4 kilometers from the Thailand-Myanmar boundary and is the largest city in Tak Province and on the border. It is a medium-sized city of approximately 106,000 residents, though this number belies the more than 100,000 migrants living and working without legal status in and around Mae Sot (National Statistics Office–Thailand 2014). Factories and their dormitories dot the urban landscape. Mae Sot has developed along border-town patterns, with growth oriented toward transportation routes, a trend that has drastically increased since the Royal Thai Government hastened Mae Sot's designation as a Special Economic Zone in 2015, a node on routes linking Thailand, Myanmar, southern China, and India (BOI 2018). Mirroring other urban centers in Thailand—and to some extent Southeast Asia—Mae Sot's landscape reflects the growth of urban settlement patterns around and adjacent to peri-urban desakota (*chaan-meuang*) areas

---

10. In addition to planning an assessment in a diversity of locales to be demographically representative of this part of the borderlands, co-researchers and their organizations assessed migrant settlements where they had some relationship with community members but wished to build a stronger network for their GBV response work.

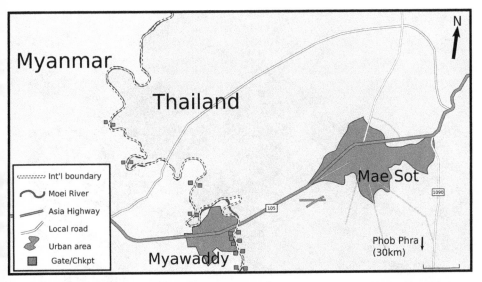

Map 2. Mae Sot and Myawaddy, two neighboring border towns. Source: Adam Saltsman.

where rural agricultural or non-agricultural activities take place (Sutatip and Cirella 2020; Hirsch 2009; McGee 1991).[11]

Htone Taung, one of the sites co-researchers visited for the GBV assessment, and where I conducted fieldwork for this book, is an urban space on the peri-urban fringe with approximately 2,500–4,000 Burmese residents.[12] Situated behind Mae Sot General Hospital, this dense urban neighborhood consists of several blocks, some of which are further divided into communities, like Ya Mar Kin, Medina, and Wat Luang, colloquial names that mostly refer to landmarks such as factories, temples, and mosques. There is a wide diversity of housing in this section, including

11. McGee (1991) refers to "desakota" as space that involves a mix of agricultural and nonagricultural economic activity and that links to one or more urban areas. In the case of Mae Sot, one finds this kind of land use deployed between Mae Sot and its surrounding subdistricts and other districts of Tak Province.

12. This is based on informal estimates from migrant-led, Thai, and Global North NGOs and counts Burmese nationals as opposed to residents who have Thai nationality but Burmese heritage.

2. Htone Taung neighborhood townhouses. Mae Sot, Tak Province, Thailand, July 2017. Source: Adam Saltsman

two-story concrete structures and single-floor row houses divided into two or three rooms. There are also clusters of houses made from found materials, thatch, zinc, and bamboo.

The streets are narrow here and alternate between organized blocks and winding alleys. Although the many blocks have no walls or gates to enclose the neighborhood, there are only three roads to get into or out of Htone Tuang, giving the place a bounded feel with a distinct sense of inside and outside. The back of the community abuts a rice paddy and forms part of the expanding outer edge of Mae Sot town. The fact that one can step out from the last alley of Htone Taung into fields is a reminder that this neighborhood is on the periphery, though the heart of it feels urban. This duality evokes the "edgy" feel that Harms (2011) attributed to peri-urban spaces in Vietnam; such zones demand analysis not just as urban-rural divides but as spaces "thick" with relations, practice, and discourse.

3. Mae Sot's peri-urban edge. Mae Sot, Tak Province, Thailand, February 2014. Source: Adam Saltsman.

Htone Tuang is one of the most diverse neighborhoods in Mae Sot, with many different ethnic and religious groups from Myanmar living there. In some areas the Burmese migrant population shares space with Thai residents. The smaller community within the neighborhood known as Medina is primarily Muslim; it has a mosque and an imam and is connected to the Muslim council of Mae Sot, a Thai organization. There are also several migrant learning centers and unregistered migrant-led organizations. These institutions give the neighborhood a feeling of vibrancy as an organized but varied set of spaces and peoples.

In contrast to the dense urban scene of Htone Taung, Kyuwe Kyan, destroyed in 2014 and 2016, is an informal settlement in the Ruam Reeng neighborhood consisting of approximately eighty-six houses behind a buffalo stable on the southeastern edge of Mae Sot, though this number

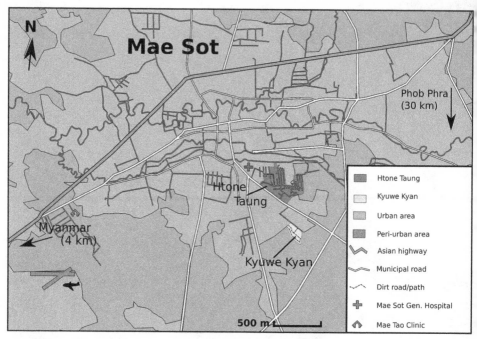

Map 3. Mae Sot's urban area. Source: Adam Saltsman.

fluctuated. Although Kyuwe Kyan is on the outskirts of the city's substantial Muslim quarter, it is around the corner from the Darul Ulum mosque. Facing the neighborhood to the north were private homes and factories divided by streets and alleys that eventually wound their way to the heart of the city. One of these houses was a large two-story villa belonging to a junior police officer. Its high-walled perimeter, which blocks the officer's family from Kyuwe Kyan and the latter's residents from accessing the property, is symbolic of Mae Sot's relationship with this informal settlement.

Everything about Kyuwe Kyan defines it as peripheral in relation to the space and people of Mae Sot. Geographically, two sides of the settlement border wetlands, rice paddies, and cornfields, which extend to outlying villages and eventually the highway. In contrast to the organized concrete structures of Mae Sot, Kyuwe Kyan has less permanent construction. Unlike Htone Taung, which is tapped into Mae Sot's power and water grid, Kyuwe Kyan has no running water and gets its electricity from a spliced wire hooked up to the landlord's nearby house. Whereas Htone Taung supports a more recognized segment of Mae Sot's Burmese population, many of whom work in factories, Kyuwe Kyan residents tend to work in sectors that are invisible to most of the town; their livelihood practices are waste picking, recycling, and sorting, rendering them part of the city's informal economy (Campbell 2018b). Muslim residents of Kyuwe Kyan, whose skin is generally darker, and who are generally poorer than other residents of Mae Sot, including the Burmese population, were subject to racialized hierarchies that defined them as "alien" among a broader population of "alien others."

All these factors labeled Kyuwe Kyan an undesirable place, a "slum" on the edge of town regarded suspiciously by those who are aware of it. Authorities considered its estimated four hundred mostly undocumented residents as inherently prone to crime and drug addiction, although the owner of the property on which the settlement sat is a middle-class Thai man who raises and sells buffalo and cattle, and who has been renting out the space to Burmese Muslim migrants for more than fifteen years. These Burmese Muslim migrants were a minority within Mae Sot's minority, a factor that, as subsequent chapters show, resulted in particular types of discourse, intervention, and discipline.

As I discuss at the end of this book, Kyuwe Kyan no longer exists. In 2014–15, local authorities ordered its removal to demonstrate zero tolerance for drug trafficking and as part of the city's transformation into a regional cross-border transport hub. This trajectory makes it all the more important to write about spaces like Kyuwe Kyan, to challenge the narrative of spatial growth and the progress of Mae Sot as a border town and Special Economic Zone with a reminder of the kinds of erasure that are often involved in frontier expansion (Comaroff 2007).

Heading south from Mae Sot along Provincial Highway 1090, one quickly leaves behind the urban and peri-urban landscape for the foothills of the Dawna Range, which stretch up and down this part of the Thai-Burmese border. Situated in a rolling landscape of fields punctuated with forest, Phob Phra district is an example of Thailand's upland industrialized agricultural sector, a source of cooler-weather, higher-elevation products as well as cut flowers.[13] As is the case with neighborhoods and informal settlements in Mae Sot, there are multiple names for a given place here, depending on who you ask. This is a product of Phob Phra's linguistic and ethnic diversity; its places have varied significance for different actors. Working with a humanitarian NGO, I became familiar first with Phob Phra locales in the language of program catchment areas, which sometimes produced a notion of space in relation to transport routes and logistics, like highway markers measuring distances from Mae Sot.

Not far from the 42-kilometer marker on Highway 1090, one finds a collection of labor camps adjacent to one another. One site is a compound with high walls and dozens of migrant shelters set apart from the landlord's house. While humanitarian organizations maintain a level of direct access to migrant settlements, many of the places migrants live and work lie behind high walls, in private enclosures controlled by landlords and employers.

The place next to it consists of rows of thatch, corrugated-zinc, and bamboo huts on land cut out of a cornfield, giving the impression of a temporary labor camp, one that exists today and can be erased tomorrow. Indeed, a fire swept through this part of the settlement in 2012, burning down an NGO's health post and several houses.

Although these settlements have multiple monikers, in this book I refer to them as Pyaung Gyi Win/Rim Nam.[14] Nearby the labor camp are Hmong households. The Hmong are an ethnic minority group in

---

13. Although much research has been done on migration and labor issues in Mae Sot (see, for example, Arnold and Hewison 2005; Aung 2010; Campbell 2018a; Pearson and Kusakabe 2012; Pollock and Aung 2010; Saltsman 2014), few studies mention Phob Phra, despite it's central role in the historical production of the borderlands.

14. NGOs refer to the whole area as Kilometer 42, while others call the labor camp in the cornfields Rim Nam or Kor Mor See-Sib See (KM44) and the compound Pyaung Gyi Win ("Baldy's land"). The owner of Pyaung Gyi Win—"Baldy," as it were—lives in the cluster of houses near the Kilometer 42 marker, while the labor camp adjacent to the compound has an owner that lives in a nearby village.

4. Walled in labor camp in Pyaung Gyi Win. Phob Phra district, Tak Province, Thailand, July 2013. Source: Adam Saltsman.

5. Migrant housing in Rim Nam. Phob Phra district, Tak Province, Thailand, January 2014. Source: Adam Saltsman.

Thailand that moved into this particular area from other highland areas of the country during the twentieth century.

These settlements are close to the highway, yet they feel isolated because they are on employers' properties and are not part of any town or village. When migrant workers need to go to a market or a facility such as a school or health clinic, they must first traverse others' land and then walk at least 1 kilometer on a dirt road to the highway. There is limited sanitation and no running water here. In the labor camp in the cornfields, there is limited electricity; only a few houses have small wires that lead off from the farm through the roof. In front of each house is a small plot for gardening and a wooden frame on which to hang equipment or clothing to dry. Among the 2,000–2,500 migrants who live in these settlements, some reside only for a season, while others have lived here intermittently for more than twenty years. There are religious and ethnic differences in

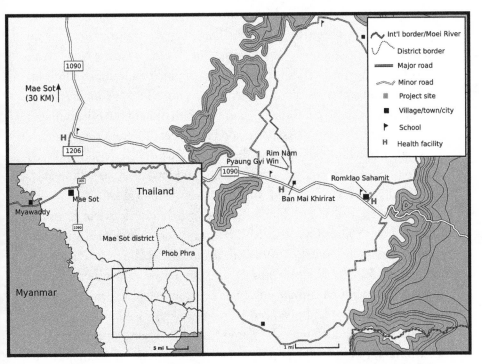

Map 4. Phob Phra communities Romklao Sahamit, Pyaung Gyi Win, and Rim Nam. Source: Adam Saltsman.

these settlements, with many residents identifying as Christian or Buddhist, and ethnically as Bamar and Karen.

Six kilometers down the road from these labor camps is a village officially named Romklao Sahamit (lit. "under the protection of the king"). The name communicates something of this place's involvement in the Thai government's efforts to secure the borderlands in the late twentieth century. Colloquially, residents refer to this village as KM48 or just 48 (Thai *See-sib bet*; Burmese *leh sey shit*). As the name indicates, the village is 48 kilometers from Mae Sot. Its diverse population stems from Thailand's anticommunist counterinsurgency campaigns in the 1970s and 1980s (the former head of the village had been a militia commander with one of Thailand's paramilitary groups). Romklao Sahamit represents the many layers of social dislocation and violence that give Phob Phra the topographical and demographic contours it has today. Although the village is only a few kilometers from the border with Myanmar, there is no official border crossing here; the international boundary is the Moei River and is minimally enforced in Phob Phra. Romklao Sahamit is a hub for all the agricultural trade along a 15-kilometer stretch of the highway. It is larger and has a more centralized character than most of the other villages along the road. Street blocks are divided by fifteen different *soi*, or alleys, the smaller of which are dirt and the larger of which are paved and pass by a small market, a handful of restaurants, and rows of shops selling farm equipment, all of which attract workers and employers alike.

Organized as it is into blocks, Romklao Sahamit does not have the same feel as Pyaung Gyi Win/Rim Nam just down the road. It is less isolated and more crowded; there are a number of different enclosures and a high diversity of ethnic groups and languages spoken here. Closer to the border with Myanmar one finds predominately Karen communities, both those that had been settled for decades as well as those whose residents were affiliated with the Karen National Union's struggle for self-determination. Besides the population of migrant workers, the majority of residents in Romklao Sahamit come from immigrant backgrounds and have permanent status as ethnic minorities in Thailand. The 1,500–2,000 Burmese migrants here typically live with property owners in their enclosures, sometimes working for those landlords as farmhands or domestic workers, or else renting the space from landlords so they can travel to nearby farms to do agricultural work.[15] As a result of this layout, one cannot talk about a single community of migrant workers here. Migrants' situations vary greatly depending on their relationship with their landlord or employer, the size of their compound, the number of workers living together, and the housing conditions within enclosures.

Together, these four settlements in Mae Sot and Phob Phra illustrate the social diversity of migrant labor and life in the Thai-Burmese borderlands. They also provide a lens for thinking about the ways in which the

15. These estimates are based on results of NGO and Thai public-health surveys in the mid-2010s.

physical and social space, layered through topographical as well as social, economic, and political change, is intertwined with migrants' navigation of everyday life and efforts to effect a sense of social order. The performative reproduction of borders, precarity, order, and governance is embedded in this landscape and contingent on the histories of empire and the imaginaries of global connectivity that have played a role in shaping it.

Outline of the Book

Chapter 2 provides a conceptual and historical framework for thinking about the relationship between space and social relations in the Thai-Burmese borderscape. The chapter locates migrant experiences within a frontier genealogy that considers the ways that mobilities, including migration patterns and the flows of capital, and state and regional logics of development have intersected over time to produce physical and social spaces. Through this genealogy, borders emerge as sites for the production of racial or ethnic gendered hierarchies affixed to territory and conceptions of nation-space. In particular, I look at the ways in which colonial and postcolonial trajectories of security and control and the movement of people and capital have been mutually constitutive. I show as well that the production of a spatially determined and precarious labor pool is contingent on these trajectories and the everyday bordering practices of local state officials and employers. This focus allows me to demonstrate that the violence of the border, migrants' responses, and the gendered positionalities that emerge in this space are related to not only the more recent dynamics of advanced capitalism but also to the role of the borderlands in the state imaginaries of Thai and Burmese nationhood. The borderscape, as a space of periphery, exploitation, political possibility, and also refuge, exerts its own kind of force on subjects in terms of how they see themselves and the world around them.

Chapter 3 examines migrant voices, considering some of the ways the social space around migrants materializes as structural and interpersonal violence in Mae Sot and Phob Phra. This includes the ways that precarity is performatively reproduced in gendered terms through migrants' encounters in the workplace and at home. Migrants are constantly reminded that they are insecure in Thailand, that their lives have less value, and that their bodies are susceptible to violation and abuse. As I illustrate, these encounters include moments when families experience violence and conflict, which furthers certain notions of gender identity and disregards or subverts others. I look at how migrants attempt to make sense of the sexual and gender violence around them, and I consider in particular a pattern in their narratives of relying on certain dominant interpretations of gender identity as both an explanatory tool and a mechanism of discipline to repair a torn social fabric. I underscore that in these processes of narrating the constraints of life in Thailand, the trend of relying on conservative notions of home and culture may prove useful in fostering a certain solidarity, at the same time that it reifies a narrow view of gender identity that excludes the lived reality of many men and women. Actors use interpretations of femininity and masculinity to police as well as contest social practice and social order. I see these dynamics as a manifestation of how gender can be a generative force as a set of discourses, a way of grasping and interpreting reality, and an ideological platform on which to try to foster a sense of social organization and order. This analysis of gender deepens our understanding of social reproduction among men and women on the move in a precarious environment—that is, how they are embedded within the practices and discourses of reproducing the relations of border capitalism. Gender as a trope becomes a means for the displacement of the injustices migrants face from the relations of capital to their own bodies and families. Gendered positionalities are important because they embody the struggle over subjecthood in a space of dispossession, and because they are ultimately part of the social reproduction of the conditions of precarious labor in the Thai-Burmese borderscape, as well as alternatives to this precarity.

By taking a more reflexive turn, chapter 4 explores some of the ways that humanitarian research itself is implicated in the production and circulation of particular gendered discourses related to mobility, migration, and displacement. I explore questions of positionality and knowledge construction among my group of co-researchers during our collaborative assessment of GBV on the border, reflecting on their own stories as well as on the social impact of working together. The chapter analyzes the subtle politics of participatory research in humanitarian contexts among Global

North researchers and border-based migrant activists and direct-service providers. As a case study, I consider how our collaboration sheds light on what it is like to work under the explicit pressure that Global North NGOs impose on border-based partners to professionalize and meet international humanitarian and human-rights standards. In this context, NGOs translate the everyday lived experience of migrants and their struggles to deal with gender and sexual violence into the technocratic language of program management. This involves the mediation of multiple tensions, including donor demands and the assumptions circulating between actors from a variety of backgrounds with different hierarchies of privilege. The chapter shows how knowledge rooted in experience is itself insecure in a discursive space fraught with conflicting power-laden agendas. But also at risk are analyses of GBV that deviate from "global" definitions and that incorporate a critique of the broader structural violence associated with the injustices of exploitative labor of global supply-chain production. Amid these tensions, and by looking at how we co-created particular kinds of knowledge about migrants in the borderscape, I show that our collaborative research process itself was a space for reproducing and contesting gendered border positionalities, both within the research team and among the broader migrant population, about whom we were generating data.

Chapter 5 looks at how the precarious living conditions of migrants in labor camps on the border intersect with humanitarian action and migrants' own social and political translocal networks to produce mutual aid and parallel systems of governance and security. The chapter focuses on the mechanisms that migrants in different parts of the border rely on to respond to sexual violence and resolve intimate-partner violence. Employers, state actors, humanitarian NGO staff, and representatives of armed political organizations coalesce in Mae Sot and surrounding areas to impose a variety of orders that are outside their official capacities and that intersect with migrants' own tactics to maintain their security. In some ways, these order-making mechanisms are unique products of the border, where sovereignty is fragmented by the multitude of disparate technologies of governance that transgress official boundaries. I find that amid conflict-resolution practices, discourses related to femininity and masculinity—as well as to ethnicity, culture, and religion—are intimately connected to ideas about insecurity and order for the migrant population. While conflicting ideas about gender are often bound up in conflict-resolution practices in response to gender violence, this chapter shows that for migrants who are socially and politically excluded from the state and its juridical system, the gendered border positionalities of mediators and other situated authorities take on heightened significance. Mediators' (and other authority figures') notions of how to survive and manage displacement, which are often rooted in ideas of femininity and masculinity, have material consequences in migrants' lives. The gendered discourses of order-making and conflict resolution among migrants on the border frame masculinity and femininity in terms that translate to notions of ethical and productive labor, moral codes that are themselves implicated in the reproduction of certain gendered and ethnic hierarchies.

Circulating amid the assemblages of resistive, disciplinary, and order-making forces on the border are the discourses of humanitarian agencies—both border-based and Global North NGOs—regarding women's empowerment. Chapter 6 asks how the language of empowerment linked to women's rights operates in migrant communities, and what this means for the possibility of political change. I center varied interpretations of gender justice and empowerment among the migrant activists and service providers with whom I have spoken over the years. Situating the global movements related to gender justice and the practices of the humanitarian industry within the context of capital accumulation, the chapter reveals the tendencies for such forms of intervention to reproduce the neoliberal emphasis on individualized bio-welfare, self-care, and self-protection. Racialized overtones about "Third World women" that invoke neocolonial hierarchies are a key feature of global discourses about women's rights. I analyze local activists' notions about what is needed to achieve a level of gender justice for Burmese women on the border and in Myanmar, comparing their discourse regarding social change with migrants' own comments about how they interpret humanitarian efforts to empower women and advocate for equality. With this focus, I ask how border humanitarians navigate the logic and framing of Global North agencies' ideas, especially ideas of empowerment and the prevention of GBV. This approach expands the conversation regarding "gendered border positionalities" by underscoring the contested nature of divergent interpretations of gender and gender violence, and the varying discourses around feminist struggle. This chapter also argues that it is crucial to think about positionality in precarious border spaces in relation to the political and social history of Burmese women's rights activists and other migrants prior to and beyond their work at the border. That is, gendered border positionalities are both generative of subjecthood and contingent on various life experiences, memories, and perceptions. The work of subjectivation here is full of ambivalence and struggle.

I conclude with the story of Kyuwe Kyan's destruction, thus centering the question of what such a violent act of erasure—one that is replicated innumerably upon migrant settlements everywhere—means for the social ties that migrants formed amid their dispossession, for the work of NGOs with limited views of empowerment, for the research project on which this book is based, and for the ways in which gender is a productive force in helping to resist insecurity and navigate displacement. I highlight that in such contexts, it is imperative for researchers not to approach the field with a narrowed lens that unwittingly reproduces migrant precarity. Instead, witnessing these acts of erasure can perhaps drive us toward more engaged forms of collaboration and shared struggle in which we take an honest look at positionality and use our reflexive lens to better "think from the border" and co-create knowledges that are rooted in migrants' own search for dignity and social justice.

2

Border as Other

Reading through news coverage of Thailand's borderlands and migrant-labor regime, one can often encounter what might seem like a contradiction. Consider these two examples:

> Mae Sot district in Thailand's northern Tak Province has been chosen as a pilot project for the creation of a special economic zone . . . Due to its unique position as a major gateway between Thailand and Myanmar, especially for migrant workers, businesses in Mae Sot have long wanted the Thai government to establish a special economic zone here, in order to boost manufacturing activities as well as cross-border trade. (Panu Wongcha-um 2014).

> Thai Prime Minister Prayut Chan-O-Cha on Monday blamed a coronavirus outbreak linked to the kingdom's largest seafood market on low-paid migrant workers employed in the country's lucrative shrimp industry . . . He accused [them] of illegally crossing the porous Myanmar-Thailand border. "They snuck out and came back in," he said. The market and its vicinity have been on lockdown since Saturday, with the thousands living there barred from leaving. On Monday the market was ringed by barbed wire, and authorities distributed food to workers quarantined inside (AFP 2020).

Taken together, these excerpts reflect an apparent tension in the relationship between the social, economic, and political institutions of the Thai state and a constructed representation of the Burmese migrant body of labor there. While the first celebrates a Burmese migrant workforce as foundational to the border-based manufacturing economy and cross-border trade, the second positions Burmese migrants as a threat to Thai society and in need of draconian containment. The quotes are not contradictory but rather reflect a particular historically produced duality that identifies such labor as a resource, but one that, due to its "alien" nature or alterity, needs to be relegated to the borderlands (Decha 2015). Thailand's policies toward its migrant workforce over the last three decades have cumulatively produced geographically determined labor precarity. As the general-turned-prime-minister Prayuth Chan-Ocha explained less than a month after seizing control of Thailand,[1] the government's goal is not to rid the country of migrant labor but to establish policies so that migrants remain in border provinces. This perspective, alongside his more recent words blaming Burmese migrants for the spread of COVID and the harsh response of local authorities, speaks to the overlap between geography, state violence, and racialized narratives that have long circulated in Thailand about Burmese within Thai territory and that are embedded in the state's imaginaries for economic power and global connectedness (Harkins and Ali 2017).

These kinds of practices, policies, and discourses suggest that in order to better understand the politics of order and insecurity in the Thai-Burmese borderlands, we need to pay attention to the broader patterns and trends that construct the idea of "frontier" in particular local and global imaginaries. This means piecing together a frontier genealogy to think about the forces that have coalesced (and continue to coalesce) in that space and beyond to produce a physical and social landscape of precarity for Burmese migrants there, as well as elsewhere in Thailand. Such

---

1. The May 22, 2014 coup d'état in Thailand was the culmination of months of political tension between the Pheu Thai party that held power in the government at that time, their allies the United Front for Democracy against Dictatorship (UDD), and the People's Democratic Reform Committee (PDRC). But beyond this specific event, the coup was only the most recent iteration of more than a decade of unrest and political conflict between multiple factions divided along social class, center/periphery, pro-/anti-monarchy, and geographic lines. Additional incidents in the last decade include a coup in 2006, which ousted Prime Minister Thaksin Shinawatra, and the government's suppression of mass protests in 2010 with military force, resulting in more than ninety deaths. For a detailed account of Thailand's political conflict from 1994 to 2014, see the special issue of *Current Anthropology* online, "The Wheel of Crisis in Thailand," 2014, edited by Ben Tausig, Claudio Sopranzetti, Felicity Aulino, and Eli Elinoff, http://www.culanth .org/fieldsights/582-the-wheel-of-crisis-in-thailand.

inquiry is essential to understanding the kinds of assemblages bound up in everyday bordering, including border enforcement, humanitarian programming, precarious labor regimes, and the resolution of social conflict and gender violence. Industrial production and peri-urban informal settlements, Thailand's migration policies, modes of social organization in the borderscape, the gendered discourses and practices migrants navigate, and the emergent political subjectivities of migrant activists and service providers reflect the external and internal "frontiers" of colonial pasts and present. As Ann Stoler writes (2016, 369), "Modernity and capitalism can account only partly for the left aside; it cannot account for where people are left, what they are left with, and what means they have to deal with what remains."

Stoler's work on "imperial durabilities" provides a helpful lens here, as she writes about "duress," the hardened and durable—if not always visible—ways in which colonial histories are implicated in the production of the present. These durable effects are full of generative possibility and they inform the differentiated exposure of certain segments of populations to harm. Her analysis includes consideration of how "empire's ruins contour and carve through the psychic and material space in which people live, and what compounded layers of imperial debris do to them" (339). An important focus, then, is on how the logic, networks, and relationships that took shape as a product of colonialism continue to inform the political, social, and economic reality of places like borderlands.

The particular outline of the borderscape not only resembles the living vestiges of empire but has also been wrought into being through the agency of those dispossessed by the contestation over and settling of frontiers. The infrastructure of border enforcement, cross-border trade and industry, and migrants' everyday lived experiences of violence and order reflect the spaces where agency and the frontier logics of states and private enterprise have collided and continue to overlap in ways that produce new arrangements and assemblages, a form of what Anna Tsing (2005) calls "friction." This chapter, then, builds on the idea of "frontier genealogy" by focusing on both agency (especially mobility) and the production of frontiers (and margins), considering a partial assortment of traces and effects from across multiple temporalities and spaces that intersect in the Thai-Burmese borderlands. Both agency and frontiers, I suggest, are embedded in contemporary spatial fixes and state and market imaginaries of regional and global connectivity that center the borderlands as sites of economic promise and that exert pressure on migrants to perform labor in particular ways and under particular conditions.[2]

Refugee and Capital Mobility

The movement of people and goods across the Thai-Burmese borderlands has figured significantly in the state and colonial production of the "frontier." The mobility of Burmese who perform wage and day labor or seek refuge along the border can constitute moments of rupture, multiplicity, and heterogeneity in space, confounding logics of security and capital's desire for exploitable surplus labor. Yet even when they disrupt or expose contradictions, mobilities are nevertheless integral to the production of capitalist relations. As Tsing (2005, 6) writes, "Friction makes global connection powerful and effective" at the same time that it "gets in the way . . . causing everyday malfunctions as well as unexpected cataclysms."[3] Thinking this way, one can track the contemporary Thai-Burmese borderscape in Mae

2. David Harvey (2006) uses the term "spatial fix" to refer to state strategies to recover from the crisis of capital overaccumulation, especially those strategies that seek to expand capital to sites of lower-cost or lower-regulated production. Glassman (2007, 349) provides a helpful example of the "spatial fix" concept in Thailand, noting that "processes of recovery are not merely economic or technical, but are centered in political and social struggles" within particular geographies. The relocation of manufacturing investment and infrastructure away from the Bangkok metropolitan region and toward more outlying areas (e.g., garment production to the Thai-Burmese borderlands) reflects, in part, a spatial fix to the economic crisis of the late 1990s and includes assumptions about a flexible low-wage workforce in peripheral parts of the country—for example, Burmese migrant workers.

3. In recent years, scholars have tended to describe movement, displacement, and refuge in these borderlands through the concept of "friction," pointing to either the terrain or the border itself as topological or cartographic mechanisms by which Burmese attempting to move or find safety are able to avoid detection and containment by the Burmese or Thai security regimes (Scott 2009; Aung 2014). These accounts focus on the trajectories of those on the move but primarily from the perspective of resistance or escape.

Sot, including the fractured social order and labor precarity that migrants encounter in urban neighborhoods and agricultural labor camps back to the people that, over the last several centuries, have traversed and made use of this space. Here, some aspects of border-based humanitarianism stem from the long history of using the border as a space of refuge, exile, and activism, taking into account the shifting relations between upland communities and lowland polities.

Trade Routes and Zones of Refuge

Mae Sot lies in a broad river valley amid the mountains of the Dawna Range, Shan Highlands, and the Tenasserim Hills, which run longitudinally, forming a natural barrier between the lowland Irrawaddy River basin of Myanmar and the Chao Phraya River basin of Thailand (Gupta 2005).

The mountains are part of a massif that extends through what is now mainland Southeast Asia and Yunnan China and that is historically the geographic divider between highland communities and lowland polities, long before the current 1,300-mile boundary divided the national territories of Thailand and Myanmar. The highlands and their inhabitants have played a central role in the lowland polities' accounts of nation-building: the highlands are portrayed as the undefined edge of lowland kingdoms, as a wild periphery, and as a space and people that were neither Thai nor Burmese but that merited incorporation into the kingdom's sphere of allegiance and influence (Thongchai 1994). Rather than being completely distinct groups, upland and lowland territories were interlocked in economic and political relationships, what Leach (1960, 50) called "zones of mutual interest," with the latter making claims on the former for resources and manpower (see also Leach 1954; Thongchai 1994; Keyes 1979).

At least since the fourteenth century, the territory of present-day Mae Sot and surrounding areas provided a natural mountain pass in proximity to riverine transport routes and was an important point of transit for trade and military campaigns (Anurak 1998).[4] From an early-twentieth-century

---

4. This includes attacks launched by the Burmese kingdom against the kingdom of Ayutthaya in the seventeenth and eighteenth centuries, campaigns that Thai politicians

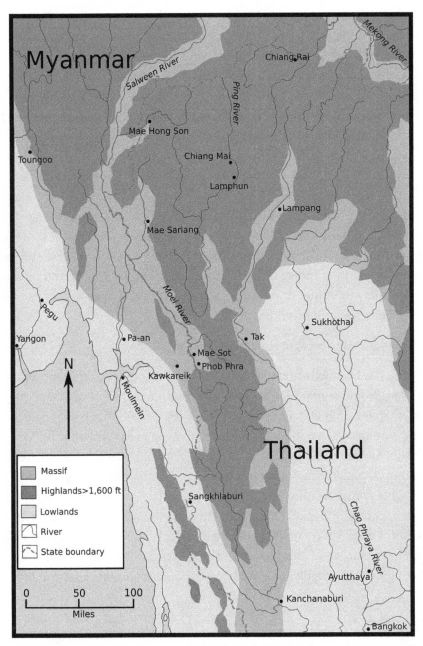

Map 5: Thailand-Myanmar borderlands and the Southeast Asian massif.
Source: Adam Saltsman, adapted from Keyes et al. ©1979. Reproduced by
permission of Taylor and Francis Group, LLC, a division of Informa plc.

account, Chinese caravans passed through the town en route from Yunnan to Burma, with Indian lenders managing currency exchanges (the British Indian rupee being the dominant currency). The dominant population was Bamar and Shan (not Thai), and the town had a large multiethnic Muslim community (Lunet 2001; Wahyu 2018). Mae Sot was a space of access, transit, and confluence for both upland communities and lowland kingdoms, but it was on the periphery of both Burmese and Thai lowland polities and surrounded by more remote terrain.

James Scott (2009, 24) argues in his oft-cited *The Art of Not Being Governed* that the Southeast Asian massif is "one of the most extensive and oldest zones of refuge," as both lowland and highland communities fled the threat of bondage and conscription by lowland polities. Scott sees the highlands of mainland Southeast Asia as a site for mobility and for settlement beyond the sphere of lowland influence and control; its mountains and valleys are difficult or impossible for lowland armies to navigate—a fortuitous "friction of terrain" (43).

Borderlands as Spaces of Refuge and Transit

In the late twentieth- and early twenty-first centuries, its geographical positioning would render Mae Sot a hub for continued mobility: a transit space for migrant labor and a refuge for those fleeing the Burmese government, the Tatmadaw (its military), and its decades-long civil war with the Karen National Union (KNU) and other ethnic groups fighting for autonomy (Lang 2002). During these decades of conflict, the Burmese government sought to crush rebellion by waging a total war against the highland populations, committing atrocities and destroying thousands of villages (Karen Human Rights Group 2009; Maung Aung Myo 2009; Smith 1991). This led to displacement on a massive scale, with more than half a million people uprooted internally, and hundreds of thousands seeking refuge in India,

---

have often invoked to frame Burmese labor migration to Thailand as an invasion (Harkins and Ali 2017). Contemporary highway routes, including those that are integral to regional plans for trade and connectivity, follow the same natural mountain pass through Mae Sot, linking Thailand to the Andaman Sea.

China, Bangladesh, Thailand, and elsewhere (The Border Consortium 2012). In the mid-1980s, as fighting produced intensified displacement, a growing number of Karen peasants found temporary or long-term shelter on the Thai side of the border, continuing the practice of using the highlands as a place of refuge. This greatly intensified in 1995, when the capital of the autonomous KNU in Manerplaw fell to the Burmese military. Not only did thousands more Karen refugees relocate en masse to Thailand, but Mae Sot and other areas up and down the border increasingly became sites for Karen political activity in exile (Lang 2002). It was during this period that a scattering of informal settlements along the 1,200-kilometer border coalesced into formalized camps, nine of which remain in operation today and are inhabited predominately by Karen refugees as well as by Karenni in the north of Mae Hong Son Province.[5]

The possibility of refuge and political engagement in exile is, in part, what attracted many thousands of Burmese urban residents fleeing their governments' crackdown against students and democracy activists in 1988 and 1989 and during the post-1990 election repression (Fink 2009). As an increasingly well-trafficked hub with infrastructure to support Burmese mobility (including Burmese-language commerce, licit and illicit cross-border transport, and a network of brokers and smugglers), Mae Sot emerged as an ideal stop for several million migrants seeking opportunity in Thailand and fleeing economic dispossession in Myanmar (Smith 2007; Matthews 2006). Arriving at the Thai-Burmese boundary, these migrants have tended to find lax immigration and border enforcement as well as more than two-dozen piers and gates to the north and south of Mae Sot that could be used to easily (and cheaply) cross the unregulated border into Thailand.[6] By the end of the twentieth century, Mae Sot was a hub

5. Some of the contemporary camps were not set up initially but established later as sites to concentrate refugees instead of leaving them in more numerous and smaller sites.

6. This is not to say that migrants find a welcoming environment in Mae Sot. Instead of cracking down on unauthorized border crossing at the Moei River, Mae Sot police and other Thai security officials tend to stop migrants at checkpoints close to the border, throughout town, and on routes leaving Mae Sot. Human-rights organizations have documented the many forms of abuse that migrants encounter at these checkpoints,

6. Ferry crossing at Moei River north of Mae Sot. Tha Sai Luad subdistrict, Tak Province, Thailand, February 2014. Source: Adam Saltsman.

for migration, the prime headquarters for forces opposed to the Myanmar government, and central in narratives of resistance.

Alongside the KNU's political and civil-society institutions, pro-democracy activists relied on Mae Sot as a safe corridor from which they could engage in advocacy and regroup beyond the reach of the Tatmadaw, many joining the armed struggles of different ethno-nationalist insurgents, and others staying to start Mae Sot's budding yet unregistered civil-society industry.

---

most frequently extortion, but forms of assault, including sexual violence, have also been reported (Human Rights Watch 2012; Meyer et al. 2019).

Frontier Sovereignties and Emergent Humanitarianisms

Amid loss and displacement, the Burmese civil wars have engendered a number of nationalisms and fragmented sovereignties that have, in turn, multiplied and shifted over time and in relation to local, regional, and global politics. There continue to be a growing number of armed groups that exert control over people and territory and that sometimes fight alongside the Burmese government. For people living under insurgent control or in mixed-control areas, life is extremely complicated, as they are "under the authority of multiple 'states' or 'state-like' authorities that extort resources from citizens, both mediate and cause conflict, and provide some services for residents and commercial interests" (Callahan 2007, xiii; see also South 2008; Brenner 2019). The emergence of such networks has influenced the kinds of "everyday justice" deployed in conflict zones as well as on the Thai side of the border in migrant communities (McConnachie 2020). In these places, the Burmese borderlands' economic landscape has developed as a web of interconnected networks engaged in the production and trafficking of drugs, and struggles over the control of natural resources, trade, and transport routes (Smith 2007).

These networks are also instrumental in the mobilization of humanitarian aid for displaced Burmese, including Karen and other ethnic minority groups. Alongside pro-democracy activists who fled to Mae Sot, ethno-nationalist organizations and networks represent varieties of the border-based humanitarianism that emerged out of the mobilities and resistance political projects described in this chapter (Sharples 2020). Burmese activists and service providers established health centers and clinics, schools, orphanages, shelters, labor associations, and human-rights groups in Mae Sot to aid displaced Burmese and to facilitate pro-democracy—or anti-military government—organizing (Arnold 2013). Political groups like the KNU, the Karenni National People's Party, and the New Mon State Party (and their armies) built up complex political and social systems up and down the border, which included departments for relief, development, health, and education (Jolliffe 2014; South 2011). These entities continue to provide aid to displaced populations in southeastern Myanmar as well as to encamped refugees in Thailand, though Northern NGOs and UN agencies regard this form of humanitarianism with suspicion and are critical of its lack of neutrality (South 2011).

Although these forms of humanitarian action were *of* the borderlands and forged out of dispossession, they were, from the early days, also part of broader networks of activism, aid, and funding. For example, pro-democracy activists attracted funding from Global North philanthropists and liberal governments while aid linked to the KNU, which is defined by its predominately Baptist affiliation, was largely faith-based through the 1980s and into the 1990s (Barron 2004). This serves as a reminder that the line between social forms rooted in mobility, autonomy, and forced migrant agency, on the one hand, and those derived from "imperial durabilities" (Stoler 2016) on the other hand, is often, if not always, blurred. After all, as Horstmann (2011) points out, faith-based aid to Karen and Karenni camps and internally displaced persons took shape in the manner of Christian webs of connection with roots in American and British missionary work. The line is similarly blurry when thinking about cross-border trade, which is a product of borderland conflict, mobilities, and semi-autonomy, but is also interconnected with global and regional flows of capital.

Turning Conflict into Profit

Like human mobilities in the borderscape, cross-border trade tells part of the story of this frontier space, situating it as a zone of unregulated or semi-regulated economic activities on the peripheries of the state, a designation that would render Mae Sot and surrounding areas an attractive place for flexible capital investment in the late twentieth and early twenty-first centuries. Building on its trade-route history and with multiple armed groups looking to fund their operations, Mae Sot was a focal point for a black market, especially during and after the government in Burma shut down border trade in the early 1960s. Historical accounts describe dozens of trade posts from which basic household goods moved to Myanmar (Mya Maung 1991). Going the other direction, smugglers brought gems, hardwood, opium and other drugs, and more into Thailand through Mae Sot district's many river "gates" (Takamuri and Mouri 1984). While the KNU initially controlled these gates, as it lost territory to the Tatmadaw in the mid-1990s, control over this trade was mixed but largely ended up under the authority of the Democratic Karen Buddhist Army (DKBA) (a breakaway faction of the overtly Christian KNU), which was subsequently folded under the Tatmadaw's proxy Border Guard Force (BGF) in 2010. Since the late 1980s, and especially after the Burmese government signed ceasefires with a number of ethnic armed organizations in the 2010s, the once-illicit networks for logging and mining remain intact and were rebranded as "liberalization" as they attracted the interest of multimillion-dollar foreign direct investment from firms no longer restricted by sanctions (Fujimatsu and Moodie 2015).[7]

Rather than suggesting an end to illicit trafficking, the window of democratization and liberalization in Myanmar has translated to space for armed groups to further capitalize on the borderlands as a somewhat mixed space of extraction and trade where it is hard to discern the legal from the illegal. This includes nearly a dozen casinos opened on the Burmese side of the Moei River despite the fact that gambling was illegal there until 2019. The BGF has maintained control over these casinos, reaping profits from the largely Thai and Chinese patrons, including those who cross from Thailand illegally in ferries (Nitta 2018). The BGF, which is a proxy force for the Tatmadaw, has also partnered with the Chinese investment firm Yatai International Holdings Group for a multibillion-dollar, semi-legal plan to transform the village of Shwe Koko in Karen State, close to the Thai border, into a "Smart City" and trade hub with an international airport, luxury hotels, and casinos (Han 2019).

The tension between the border's designation as external and semiautonomous and the desire for the Thai state to incorporate, regulate, and make this space useful has resulted in Mae Sot's growth as a hub for capital and migration. Black-market brokers in the 1980s and multinational capital investment in the 1990s flocked to Mae Sot. By the mid-2000s,

---

7. Cross-border trade has weathered numerous disruptions, including multiple iterations of armed conflict and the COVID-19 pandemic that precipitated a total shutdown of border trade. See for example Han and Kean 2020. The complete breakdown of these ceasefires after the military coup in February 2021 has disrupted trade networks and investments, though it is likely that formal and black-market trade will continue in one form or another under the armed group that holds control of the Burmese side of the border (Bangkok Post 2021).

goods passing through this city represented 14 percent of Myanmar's *official* border trade, which accounted, in 2007, for about 13 percent of all of Myanmar's imports and exports (Kudo 2013).[8] In 2019 Tak's Chamber of Commerce recorded 80 billion baht (US $2.3 billion) of cross-border trade (The Nation 2020). During the 1990s, improved relations between Thailand and Myanmar also led to a series of new economic initiatives centered around this vibrant cross-border activity, including Thai investments in Burmese contract farming and logging initiatives, hydropower, and mining—only some of which was legal (see, for example, Felbab-Brown 2013).[9] A budding garment industry in Mae Sot was another source of investment, tailored according to gendered assumptions to capitalize on the thousands of Burmese women and men entering Thailand through this town (Chuthatip 2006). Such investments tell us that the notion of borderland as peripheral frontier is increasingly attractive for border capitalism. But the movement of people and capital have also been embedded in Thai-state anxieties about its sovereignty, its frontiers, and the boundaries of membership in an evolving sense of national identity.

Securing Frontiers

Such anxieties can perhaps be explained by Thailand's complicated colonial history, which in turn provides a road map for thinking about some of the ways imperial durabilities link to today's border regime. Though it was not formally colonized by European powers, under pressure, Siam negotiated away large swaths of its territory to Britain (much of what is now Shan State in Myanmar) and France (part of what is now northwest

---

8. Kudo (2013, 190) compared Burmese and Thai statistics from FY 2006 and found significant discrepancies regarding the value of imports and exports between Mae Sot and Myawaddy. According to Myanmar, there were US $61 million in exports to Mae Sot and US $95.1 million in imports from that port. However, according to Thailand, the former was only US $34.2 million and the latter was US $289 million. The enormous discrepancy may be indicative of the double flow of legal and illegal goods and a lack of agreement between the two countries about which goods show up in official records and which do not.

9. This coincided with the formal renewal of official border trade between Myawaddy in Myanmar and Mae Sot in Thailand in 1998 (see Lintner 2013).

Cambodia), oriented its economy to facilitate colonial extraction, and has its own history of expanding from its lowland centers and annexing peoples and territories to produce what we now consider Thailand (Raquiza 2012; Glassman 2010; Saratsawadi 1996).[10]

Here again, Stoler's approach to "durabilities" serves as a useful lens in that she links colonialist concern regarding differentiation and containment to the logic of contemporary states and their political discourses of security and insecurity that proliferate in late capitalism. Security, writes Stoler (2016, 231), was "a feature of imperial governance" deployed widely to justify imperial military occupation, the legal codification of race categories, "treatises on colonial household management," and the work of rendering legible membership in "categories of persons against which society had to be defended." Today, the rationale of "security" provides cover for state practices of carcerality and the containment of mobility as well as other practices that violate the state's own liberal moral codes. It is not hard to see that such moves are possible only because of the logic of differentiation that has drawn visible and invisible boundaries around populations and territories, rendering some spaces marginal and some lives surplus and thus less valuable.

Constructing the Ethnic Other in Space

Anxieties over the periphery in Thailand link to the state's historical project of forging an idea of national identity by demarcating who was outside the boundaries of Thai-ness. A dominant system in Siam for classification consisted of dividing people into an inclusive Tai and an other, or *kha*,

---

10. Tamara Loos (2006) notes that Thailand—then Siam—resembled both a colonized territory and an imperial power. While the polity lost territory to European colonial empires, Siam also adopted the modernistic logic of these empires and applied it culturally and through the development of its jurisprudence to populations considered external to the emerging notion of "Thai-ness," including the large Muslim minority in the south. As well, in 1885 Siam signed the Bowring Treaty, giving Britons exceptional levels of legal immunity and trade rights throughout Thailand. Herzfeld (2002) uses the term "cryptocolonialism" to refer to Thailand, in that it was a buffer state between imperial powers that managed to stay independent by sacrificing territorial and economic independence.

which corresponded roughly to the spatial categories of *muang* ("town") and *pa* ("forest") (Turton 2000). These political-spatial categories referred to the territory and people associated with sovereignty, on the one hand, and those who were beyond the pale, alien, and less civilized, on the other. Taking these terms together, center (*muang*) and periphery (*pa*) make up the state in the sense that the center desires the population and the resources of the highlands/mountain/forest/periphery. The deployment of these terms by lowland scholars and other authority figures constituted a technology of power—that is, a means to reproduce social order and social hierarchy via the discourse and everyday practices of social, cultural, economic, or political institutions. Muang and Pa offered analytical categories of identity for diverse groups based on social hierarchy and geographic location in a way that conformed easily to colonial projects of racialization in the region during the nineteenth century (Keyes 2002).[11]

A second technology for exerting social and political control over the nation of Siam during the late nineteenth and early twentieth centuries lies in the efforts made by the government to "know" and classify the diverse groups of people living within Thai territory. Pinkaew (2003) writes that "as *pa* (forest), the non-Tai entity, has been gradually incorporated into a new spatial organization . . . the uncivilized *khon pa* (wild people), the non-Thai ethnic category, has become a salient object of interrogation" (26–27). As part of this project, one finds a proliferation of Thai ethnographies at the end of the nineteenth and beginning of the twentieth centuries, creating and shaping ethnicity through the practice of making people "legible," a process that was echoed in neighboring colonial territories as well (Edwards 2007; Thongchai 2000a). Underlying this ethnogeographic project was Thai interest in defining themselves as superior to other ethnic groups and thus civilized (*siwilai*), alongside the other modern nations exerting their imperial authority in the region (Thongchai 2000b). The work of classifying what Thongchai (2000a, 41) refers to as

---

11. This production of hierarchized difference along ethnic lines also reflects what Quijano (2000) refers to as coloniality—that is, racialized hierarchies that justify colonial forms of conquest but that also endure beyond the colonial era.

the "others within," adopted European racial/ethnic hierarchies, colonial ideas of civilized and primitive peoples, and spatial concepts of center and periphery (see also Renard 2006). In this sense, the peoples inhabiting the borderlands are both included within the Thai national consciousness and kept at a distance, serving as a contrast to highlight the modernity of Siam, and of Bangkok in particular.

Colonial Boundary-Making

During the late nineteenth and early twentieth centuries, at the height of colonial expansion in Southeast Asia, Siam solidified both geographic and social ideas of "center" and "periphery" through the formal demarcation of its nation-state boundaries, the establishment of an administrative system for governing units of territory, and the classification of its peoples. Under the strain of remaining independent and out of competing economic interests for the vast teak forests of the highlands, Siam negotiated the Thailand-Myanmar boundary with Britain, which had pushed the boundaries of British India to the eastern edge of what is now Myanmar (Thongchai 1994). The boundary divided the space of highland groups like the Karen into Thai and British colonial (and then Burmese) territories, complicating the former's social and economic system on some level (Thongchai 1994). Along with widespread changes to state administration,[12] the kingdom established border towns and military outposts and forced highland inhabitants to swear allegiance to the Thai king, all part of the state's effort to manage the teak trade and exert control over the edges of its newly demarcated territory (Pinkaew 2003; Thongchai 1994; Vandergeest and Peluso 1995).[13] The conflation of state power, resource extraction, and

12. Bangkok issued multiple administrative reforms during this period in an effort to adapt its means of exerting control over people, space, and things to current imperatives; they established new political ministries, divided territory into Western units of governance, surveyed national territory, and rendered all untitled land the property of the government (Bunnag 1977; Vandergeest and Peluso 1995).

13. For example, in one historical account of the current Mae Sot area, the newly appointed governor of the area only made an appearance "during the dry season to oversee the logging activities which only took place during that time of year" (Pitch 2007, 391).

profit resulted in particular assemblages of state power and infrastructural developments along the border. These assemblages would continue to exert a force on the borderlands and its inhabitants into the second half of the twentieth century as the Thai government began to see its peripheries through a Cold War lens.

Geopolitics and Creative Destruction on the Frontier

Embracing a nationalistic notion of state boundaries that conflated territory and ethnic/racial identity, Thai state and society increasingly identified non-Tai peoples of the highlands as alien and non-citizen.[14] Concerned about a growing communist threat within its borders, the Thai government targeted some ethnic minority highland communities, viewing their populations as illegal, their perceived lack of assimilation as a sign of disloyalty, and their involvement in swidden agriculture and opium cultivation as unlawful (Pinkaew 2003; Renard 2000). The Thai government considered other groups that were explicitly anticommunist as proxy allies in their struggle, including the KNU and its armed branch, the Karen National Liberation Army, and the Kuomintang Chinese soldiers and Shan militants whose expansive opium production and trade networks the government agreed to ignore because they battled communists in Thailand and in Burma (Cooper 1979; Lintner 1999).

The Thai government's view of upland autonomy through the lens of anticommunist struggle helps explain their militarized response to certain ethnic-minority expressions of autonomy in the border region in the 1960s and 1970s. Throughout the 1970s and early 1980s, the Thai government waged war on their own highlands in an attempt to stamp out rebellion, at the same time that their repressive tactics motivated increasing numbers of peasants, students, and ethnic minority groups to join the insurgency (Marks 1994).[15] Journalists covering the conflict in the mid-1970s saw

14. This was the case even with the Thai Nationality Act of 1913. All those within Thai territory had access to citizenship, though it was considered in terms of lineage from Thai parents.

15. Also fueling rebellion was the police and paramilitary crackdown on student protesters at Thammasat University on October 6, 1976 and the subsequent coup and

analogies to what was taking place in Vietnam: napalm dropped indiscriminately in forest areas and "wanton killing and damage inflicted on the rural people in the remote areas where the heaviest fighting takes place" (Economic & Political Weekly 1976, 1,823).

Simultaneous to its tactic of military might, the Thai government also engaged in a substantial campaign to "develop" highland areas and extend the "border of Thainess" (Thongchai 1994). The Thai state established multiple paramilitary organizations to combat the communist threat and it engaged a newly founded Hill Tribe Division of the Public Welfare Department of the Ministry of the Interior to "resettle" upland communities to lowland/foothill areas and encourage their participation in industrial agriculture practices. The Thai state reconfigured the system of landholding and forestry through policy changes and enforcement during this time, which, together with "resettlement and development" and a military presence, displaced approximately five-to-six thousand people (Tapp 1989; Walker and Farrelly 2008) and furthered a discourse of ethnic minorities as unlawfully living in spaces that needed to be regulated.[16]

Meanwhile, using the language of humanitarian necessity, the United States Agency for International Development (USAID) poured tens of millions of dollars into "Accelerated Rural Development" programs that sought to improve the production capacity of rural communities, build

---

takeover by the military. Though the military asserted the need to be in power to combat the widespread communist insurgency, its takeover appeared only to galvanize widespread support for the uprising.

16. Under the Reservation and Protection of Forests Act of 1938, which prohibited grazing animals or clearing land in reserved spaces, in the 1950s and 1960s, the Thai government began designating large swaths of territory as protected areas, even when sections of these areas were in use or inhabited. Through this process, over 40 percent of Thailand was considered "protected" by 1985 (Vandergeest and Peluso 1995). Other initiatives in the second half of the twentieth century marked certain areas as national parks and protected watersheds. At the same time, in the 1950s the government instituted reforms to the landholding system such that property owners had to register their land within 180 days or it would be considered uninhabited and thus the state's (Vandergeest and Peluso 1995). The policy was based on fixed property lines, which did not support the shifting agriculture of many highland communities.

roads connecting rural to urban areas, better extend government authority to the village level, "promote the growth of democracy," and provide vocational training (Vichit 1966; see also McNabb 1983). Such infrastructural programs were often ways to extend state access to previously semi-autonomous areas of the highlands and reshape the social, ethnic, and political structure of those spaces. For example, to the south of Mae Sot, the mountainous district of Umphang emerged as a communist stronghold in the 1970s because the area was heavily forested, remote, and largely controlled by Thai Karen communities and not by the state government, making it an ideal place for dissidents and students-turned-insurgents to hide (Pinkaew 2003; Pitch 2007). To suppress rebellious Karen and Hmong villages in this area, the government initiated infrastructure and social-relocation projects aimed at pacifying the people. This included the construction of a road in 1973 and the establishment of several towns and settlements with schools and police stations over the following years, including the two Phob Phra sites where research was conducted for this book.

Using one ethnic minority group to pacify or displace others, the Thai army requested support from the anticommunist KNU and its military, the Karen National Liberation Army (KNLA), which controlled the territory on the Myanmar side of the border, to help guard the road builders and to patrol the surrounding hills (Pitch 2007). The army also sent in a paramilitary group known as Krathing Daeng (red gaurs) made up of highland migrants from Burma (including Akha, Lahu, Lisu, and Yao peoples) and Kuomintang soldiers from China to guard the civilian road crews (Schmid and Jongman 2005). To express gratitude for the frontline fighting of the KNLA and the Krathing Daeng, King Bumiphol of Thailand granted them the right to settle in the area close to the 48-kilometer marker and, according to one veteran still living in the area, "cultivate all the land we could see." Today there are a number of Karen villages in this part of Phob Phra that remain closely affiliated with the KNU across the border. We revisit this social and political dynamic in chapter 5. The area settled by the Krathing Daeng became an official village in 1977. The Thai government named this nationalist, anticommunist settlement Romklao Sahamit (lit. "under the protection of the king")—a pocket of loyal subjects implanted on land that used to belong to rebellious Hmong opium farmers.[17]

Complementing practices of dislocation and relocation, the government incentivized lowland farmers to expand their cash-crop production into highland areas, engaging in what Hirsch (2009: 125) calls "frontier-taming." Hirsch describes this project as a continuation of the "state's civilizing mission" of its peripheries, but also notes that the settling of the highlands also had to do with "global market demand for commercial rice and other crops" including sugar, pineapples, cut flowers, and even prawn farms (Hirsch 1992). This includes Phob Phra, which, with the construction of the road, the establishment of outpost towns, and the ongoing control of certain areas by the KNU, developed as a site for both Karen resistance and intensive resource extraction. With the arrival of capital-intensive agribusiness in this fertile highland territory, the two-lane highway increasingly wound through massive plantations with thousands of acres of roses, corn, cabbage, palm sugar, and other crops. Today these are interspersed with smaller Hmong and Karen farming communities. The state had both further excluded its highland communities and laid the groundwork to transform the space into a site of labor-intensive production, a pattern found on "resource frontiers" throughout the Global South (Tsing 2005).

Securitizing Karen Encampment

Alliances forged or strengthened through Thailand's counterinsurgency and frontier-taming work shaped the state's early responses to ethnic minority communities' crossing the border to seek refuge. For example, seeing the Karen refugees of the late 1970s and early 1980s as affiliated with their KNU allies, the Thai government initially allowed these refugees to settle small border-based villages, or to integrate into existing Karen communities in places like Umphang or Phob Phra in Tak Province and

17. King Bumiphol played a major role in the military and government project of using the royal name to construct a sense of unity in a fractured country.

in Mae Hong Son Province, as long as their stay was temporary and as long as the situation avoided large-scale international attention (Barron 2004). (At the time, the Thai government was engaged in a large-scale international humanitarian response with displaced Cambodians in the northeast provinces.)

However, when fighting intensified close to the border, and with the influx of so many more refugees, the Thai government grew increasingly anxious about its role as host to this displaced population (Hyndman 2002). The Thai government's growing anxiety about them played on historical conceptions of Karen and other upland communities as external or peripheral (Pinkaew 2003). As well, by the late 1990s Thailand was less concerned about the KNU and more interested in pursuing economic partnership with the Burmese government and its proxy forces that had largely taken over border trade (Hyndman 2002). In 1998 the Thai government formally invited a collection of NGOs and UN agencies to provide assistance as they converted the dozens of scattered refugee settlements into camps designated as "temporary shelters" to house those fleeing war and militarism in Burma (Bowles 1998; Lang 2002). There are currently nine camps along more than 1,300 miles of borderland with 77,000 refugee inhabitants (down from a high of close to 150,000 in the early 2000s; see The Border Consortium 2021). Though these sites have now existed for more than twenty years, the Thai government's official position that they are short term has impacted refugees' quality of life in numerous ways.[18] And while scholars have argued that these predominately Karen camps have provided a kind of demos for the exiled KNU (and the Mon and Karenni political establishment in the southern and northernmost camps, respectively) (Horstmann 2014; South 2008), these are sites of carceral care produced and maintained out of the Thai government's discourse around national security (Vitit 2007).

18. There is a substantial body of research documenting the effects of "extended exile" in Thailand's refugee camps. This includes malnutrition and stunted growth (Panrawee et al. 2019), depression and other mental health problems (Kaiser et al. 2020), lack of access to education (Oh 2010), and a variety of human rights violations (Human Rights Watch 2012).

Layered onto this landscape of paranoia and anxiety are the kinds of humanitarian actions the Thai government invoked but which the Global North funded, staffed, and designed following its own imperial logic of compassion, care, and pity (Fassin 2012). The variety of well-documented practices include the management of population counts to allocate dwindling quantities of food (for examples from other contexts, see Hyndman 2000). Humanitarianism's imperial origins and its Cold War manifestations helped shape this borderscape too, and continue to underlie contemporary Global North interventions among refugee-camp populations and elsewhere along the border. These interventions are intertwined with the border-based humanitarianism described earlier. Both constitute sets of relations and discourses that are part of the assemblage of power impacting the opportunities and constraints in migrants' everyday lives. As subsequent chapters elucidate in more detail, these interventions include the influx of tens of millions of dollars in aid money into Mae Sot and other points on the border, the division of the borderscape into program catchment areas that are legible to Global North donor agencies and technical experts, zones of KNU influence, and the circulation of both KNU-oriented and "international" project-related discourse aimed at addressing social problems like gender violence among the displaced.

Migrant Labor Policies

A similar discourse of security permeates the Thai government's efforts to establish sets of laws and policies governing the out-of-camp migrant labor population. While regional policy opened up avenues for formal labor recruitment systems, the high cost and long wait period means only a small percentage of the three-to-four million migrants currently in Thailand arrived legally. The vast majority cross from neighboring countries, especially Myanmar, and either work without authorization or, once in Thailand, navigate a complex process to receive temporary and partial permission to work. Thailand outlaws all unauthorized migration but gives the Cabinet and the Ministry of Foreign Affairs discretion to temporarily stay deportations through specific resolutions. Laws for migrant employment make it clear that the consequences for migrants without a work permit are severe; various iterations of alien employment acts and royal decrees criminalize and restrict the rights of migrants.[19]

In addition to these laws, the discretionary nature with which the Thai government determines and changes migrant regularization schemes produces immense uncertainty for the vast majority of migrants entering Thailand. Where migrants can legally work and in what sectors has changed more than a dozen times in the last three decades.[20] Most resolutions have excluded from registration schemes domestic and seasonal agricultural workers as well as those working in fisheries, which collectively account for a significant portion of the migrant labor force. Migrant workers in these industries also find fewer protections under Thai labor law, and migrants are prevented from officially forming unions. A Cabinet resolution in March 1992 specified that unauthorized Burmese migrants may be granted temporary permission to remain and work in Thailand for one year only in four border provinces and for their employer at that time; by 1995 the Cabinet had widened the list to nine provinces. A 1996 Cabinet resolution expanded the list of approved provinces to forty-three and granted migrants from Myanmar, Cambodia, and Laos temporary permission to work in Thailand. This was designed as an amnesty whereby employers had to bring their "illegal" workers to the immigration office, "bail" them out, and get them registered.

Subsequent resolutions in early 2000 eliminated geographic restrictions, but migrants' legal status was still tied to their employers, limiting their mobility significantly. And migrant workers were permitted to change jobs and get new work permits only if their employer died, terminated their contract, committed abuse, violated labor laws, or consented to their departure, criteria that left little agency for migrants themselves. Moreover, with laws that rendered migrant legality partial at best and that

19. This includes the possibility of imprisonment for up to five years and penalties up to 100,000 baht. Authorities can conduct raids to look for undocumented migrants without any warrants, and migrant workers are required to contribute to a fund from which authorities cover the cost of deportations.

20. For a more detailed account of these policies and resolutions see Kritaya 2007; Kritaya 2010; and Kritaya and Kulapa 2008.

tie this partial legality to particular jobs, migrants were faced with a choice between two kinds of insecurity: register with a local employer immediately upon arrival—that is, in a border locale where the wages are lower and labor conditions often worse—or risk the consequences of traveling unlawfully to more central parts of the country in search of work permits with higher-paying employment. While these laws may have helped maintain a low-wage labor force in the borderlands, Campbell (2018a) documented that they also pushed even those migrants intent on regularizing their status to rely on brokers and human smuggling networks to move them safely throughout the country, and engendered a migrant registration system that in practice depended on partnership with illicit (or semi-legal) enterprises. Smugglers and brokers have often charged exorbitant rates to provide migrants with fake work permits and for illegal passage to other parts of Thailand, which can come with grave risks (Gjerdingen 2009).

In 2009, in response to the fear that there were millions of undocumented foreigners throughout Thailand—a fear that struck at the heart of Thai national identity—the state established a program requiring migrants that had entered the country unlawfully but had work permits to undergo a process of "nationality verification." Those without official identification received temporary passports that they would use to renew their work permits. As these passports permitted lawful travel throughout the country, increasing numbers of migrants moved to inner parts of Thailand in search of higher-paying and safer work, much to the consternation of employers in places like Mae Sot. In response, many employers in these places refused to issue work permits to workers, or illegally held on to their workers' identification and work permits to prevent an exodus. In 2012 the Tak provincial government initiated a policy of blocking migrants from leaving Mae Sot, even if they had official passports and promises of employment elsewhere in Thailand (Lawi 2012). Such practices illustrate the conflict between the central government's preoccupation with security and the provincial government's concern with maintaining a border-based low-wage migrant labor force. They also highlight how much state effort goes into producing and maintaining this pool of low-wage and flexible labor.

The state has continued in recent years to issue new resolutions and decrees that amount to registration deadlines and threats of mass deportation. The almost cyclical nature of these policies and their convoluted bureaucratic processes, the media and politician-driven xenophobia, and the fear of violent raids has the cumulative impact of continuing migrant precarity. Analysts have often interpreted the state's harsh policies toward unauthorized migrant labor and industry's demand for low-wage labor as two contradictory forces; they point to the complaints lodged by employer associations in the wake of government crackdowns on unauthorized migration (Harkins and Ali 2017; Tunon and Baruah 2012). However, I have shown here that—whether deliberate or not—the state's regulation of migrant labor, its enforcement of such policies, and the reactions of employers are all key elements that ultimately work together to reproduce precarious living and employment conditions for migrants in Thailand. This includes a renewed emphasis on the geographic containment of migrant labor to the borderlands. The material conditions of migrant labor and the state's concerns for security accompany the Thai government's efforts to achieve the Association of Southeast Asian Nations (ASEAN) Economic Community's roadmap to regional integration. Thailand's imaginary of regional connectivity cannot be divorced from the realities of migrant mobilities, and they inform the particular constellations of governance that migrants encounter in their everyday lives.

Flexible Capital and Labor in the Borderlands

The confluence of imperial durabilities regarding the frontier, Burmese migrant mobility, and gendered assumptions about feminized surplus labor are embedded in the rise of a garment industry in Mae Sot and efforts by investors and employers to establish a Special Economic Zone (SEZ) there. This is, after all, a space long-identified as a zone of unregulated capital accumulation and trade. Such material conditions enable what Jessop (2012) refers to as "regional imaginaries": ambitions for capital and connectivity that superimpose a vision of nodes of transport and manufacturing operations, and efficient logistics onto the topography. These imagined geographies of potential flows of capital, people, and goods inform governance over the spaces they appropriate, which is why we consider them here (Mezzadra and Neilson 2013). However, even as imaginaries transform the material, they are still virtual roadmaps based on only a partial accounting of actually existing conditions. As we will observe, migrant mobility plays into the way capital and the state see the geography of the borderlands at the same time these mobilities have the potential to disrupt them.

The garment industry has steadily grown in Mae Sot as a result of local, regional, and global factors. The 1997–98 Southeast Asian economic crisis effected a complete reconfiguration of the relationship between industry, labor, and capital in Thailand to transform this localized, predominantly agricultural zone of border trade into an industrial site connected to distant centers of capital (Chuthatip 2006). The crisis itself was a response to more than a decade of market liberalization in Thailand, with an emphasis on transforming the economy to export-oriented manufacturing, foreign direct investment (largely East Asian sources at first, and then European and US firms), and deregulation leading to sizeable private-sector debt (Deyo 2012; Bello 1997; Pasuk and Baker 2008). An estimated two million people lost their jobs in Thailand amid massive shutdowns in the industrial sector, including more than a hundred thousand Thai women working in the garment and textile industries (Mills 1999; Piya 2007: 134).[21] Natenapha (2008) estimates that 25 percent of Thai capital was either liquidated or subordinated to foreign investment acquiring stakes in those firms.

Post-crisis, in a Thai economy marked by further liberalization and less regulation, multinational capital was increasingly mobile in search of low-cost production strategies that could circumvent new labor-protection standards and Thai labor unions (Klein 2007). Through the creative

21. There were certainly many men who lost their jobs as well, in that the crisis hit multiple industries. However, more flexible, low-wage manufacturing industries, which have a disproportionately female workforce, were quicker to close doors and relocate elsewhere. It is often the case in financial crises that flexible industries dematerialize and rematerialize. Women are usually the first to be laid off in such crises, with the assumption that men are the real income earners in their households (Pollard 2012; Pollock and Soe Lin Aung 2010).

destruction that left many hundreds of domestic firms closed or converted into majority-foreign companies, there was an opportunity to assert a new model for production that reflects what Arnold and Pickles (2011) refer to as "dual-space economies." As investors in Thailand and elsewhere sought to drastically reduce the operating costs of the garment industry, they employed a number of initiatives that effectively relegated garment production to "Third World" spaces and practices, in contrast to high-value, more central "First World" sites. As elsewhere, in Thailand this meant the breakup of larger firms with assembly-line systems into a network of subcontractors operating in borderlands and filling orders at a piece rate for multinational companies, all of which lowered production costs (Bello et al. 1998).

This was a new era for the Thai garment industry, which, in order to remain competitive, relocated to Mae Sot, where production costs were cheaper and there was less regulation, less accountability, and lower wages. Local business leaders, and town, district, and provincial authorities, heavily lobbied investors and the central Thai government to make Mae Sot a SEZ in order to incentivize further growth there (Decha 2015). Since stakeholders in Mae Sot have thrived on largely illegal trade in timber, gems, and all the other black-market goods moving between Myanmar and Thailand, this lobbying fit well with long-standing ambitions to transform the town into an unregulated labor-intensive sector. In addition, Thailand's outlying provinces, like Tak, had lower minimum wages than did central provinces like those around Bangkok (Piya 2007). Finally, the population of women migrants invoked gendered ideas around surplus labor and the notion that women can earn less, work at a contract or piece rates, including from home, and are easier to manage and fire (Wright 2006).

With investors receiving exemptions from paying taxes on imports, businesses, machinery, raw materials, and equipment, regional capital eagerly clustered in places like Mae Sot, especially in 2000–2005 (Sai Silp 2007; Chuthatip 2006). In my own inquiries with the Mae Sot branch of the Federation of Thai Industries (FTI) in 2014, 2017, and 2020, representatives told a story of success, eagerly providing statistics to illustrate

7. Migrant workers at an unregistered toy factory near Pyaung Gyi Win. Phob Phra district, Tak Province, Thailand, February 2014. Source: Adam Saltsman.

the growth of their sectors along the border. At a high point in 2016, the FTI noted 398 registered factories in Mae Sot alone, and close to 700 across Tak Province that employed more than 50,000 registered workers— a gross underestimate, as other local government officials have put the figure closer to 350,000 workers, including both regulated and unregulated (Peeradej 2011).

Mae Sot as a Node in the Greater Mekong Subregion

Contemporaneous with its growth, Mae Sot increasingly featured in new regional spatial plans that reimagine the geography of mainland Southeast Asia in economic terms and that recast the role of women and men as surplus labor in global production circuits (Glassman 2010; Arnold and Pickles 2011). That is, since the government of Prime Minister Chatchai Choonhaven committed to transforming the borderlands and "turn[ing]

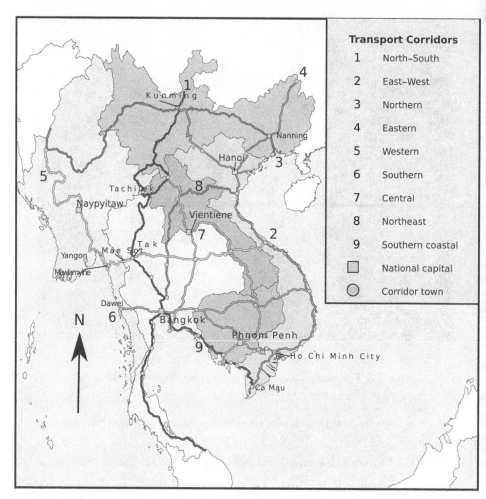

Map 6: Greater Mekong Subregion economic transport corridors. Source: Adam Saltsman.

battlefields into marketplaces," Mae Sot has become increasingly visible as one focal point on the maps of regional governmental bodies, investors, and multinational financial institutions, particularly the ASEAN Economic Community (Piya 2009). These maps convey the notion that Mae Sot plays a significant role in broader regional development, as it represents Thailand's westernmost point on what is known as the East–West Economic Corridor, part of a development plan for the Greater Mekong

Subregion (GMS) (Glassman 2010).[22] This corridor and the broader subregion are constructs of the Asian Development Bank and ASEAN geared toward enhancing economic activities among mainland Southeast Asian countries, strengthening south-south linkages, and enabling greater global competitiveness through transport routes that cut across borders and connect trade zones (Glassman 2010; ADB 2010; ADB 2011). Mae Sot lies squarely on the Asia Highway (which follows the path of the East–West Economic Corridor, as shown in Map 6) and represents a gateway between eastern and western Mekong states and beyond.

Regional development plans have prompted investors, employers, and local government officials in Mae Sot to lobby Bangkok and financial institutions for infrastructural investment and policies that they argue will help realize cross-border connectivity and would also satisfy their needs for particular labor arrangements.

The Tak Special Economic Zone and the Shifting Borderscape

Establishing a Special Economic Zone in the Mae Sot, Mae Ramat, and Phob Phra districts of Tak Province in 2015 was a clear step toward achieving the status of transport node on the East–West Economic Corridor and integration with the ASEAN Economic Community. This development makes formal what were already substantial cross-border arrangements built on the history of the borderlands as a space where particular kinds of economic activity take place. Indeed, the assurance of a surplus of migrant labor features in many brochures aimed at prospective investors in Mae Sot, with Thailand's Board of Investment promising "access to [a] Myanmar labor force, including over 72,000 registered in [the] Tak area" (BOI 2016).[23]

---

22. During its 2011 to 2021 period of political openness, changes in Myanmar that led to the lifting of international sanctions and an influx of foreign investment inspired fear among some Thai employers that they would lose their migrant labor force. Since 2012, the Japanese have been investing in large-scale infrastructural development projects on the Burmese side of the border—what will become production zones with even lower operating costs—in order to take advantage of Thailand's decreased capacity to ensure cheap labor.

23. It is not clear where these numbers come from, as other sources indicate the number of registered migrant workers in the SEZ zone is much lower, closer to 40,000 people.

And yet the reality of migrant mobility and mobile capital reveals that this move for global connectedness is full of contradiction.

Once the Royal Thai Government passed the "Special Economic Zone Policy" in late 2015, the state embarked on an ambitious infrastructure program in ten new SEZs.[24] As of 2017, the Thai government had invested several billion baht for a new cross-border bridge and highway expansions in the Mae Sot area, and with the support of Japanese investors had committed even more money to finalize highway construction through Karen Sate.[25] In recent years, the government opened the second Thai-Myanmar Friendship Bridge and adjacent land ports in the Tha Sai Luad subdistrict, expanded Mae Sot Airport by lengthening the runway and adding terminal space, and improved infrastructure in urban and peri-urban areas, including increasing the capacity of the electrical grid. New big-box commerce stores and hotels have opened up along the highway to the border as well (Gray 2015).

These developments, along with a slate of incentives, are aimed at drawing in Thai and foreign investors. They have precipitated substantial changes to the economic and physical landscape, influencing the lives of Burmese migrants as well as Thai residents, including local officials, landowners, and employers. New roads cut across the informal Kyuwe Kyan settlement. Since 2015 the Thai government has appropriated 3.5 square kilometers in the Tha Sai Luad subdistrict for an industrial park in addition to the dozens of square kilometers transformed into cross-border transportation terminals (BOI 2016). As well, after the official SEZ designation, land prices in Mae Sot and surrounding areas skyrocketed, changing the demographic that could afford to buy or lease land, or would want to (Assawin 2019). These changes amount to a rapid urbanization project layered onto Mae Sot's long history as a site of trade and transit, of refuge and exile.

24. Formalizing the Tak SEZ was a key priority for the military government after it seized power in 2014, though the plan for the SEZ dates back to the early 2000s and the government of Thaksin Shinawatra.

25. Interview with Thai Board of Investment, Office of Tak Special Economic Zone, Mae Sot, July 3, 2017.

Table 1

Factories, capital, and workers in Mae Ramat, Mae Sot, and Phob Phra districts

District	No. Factories			Capital (mil. baht)			No. Workers		
	2013	2016	2019	2013	2016	2019	2013	2016	2019
Mae Ramat	23	24	15	173.0	552.0	583.6	515	485	200
Mae Sot	365	398	295	6,013.0	7,230.0	7,627.7	49,101	45,309	40,857
Phob Phra	26	32	15	125.7	381.3	318.4	306	424	248
Total	414	454	325	6,311.7	8,163.3	8,529.7	49,922	46,218	41,305

Source: Federation of Thai Industries.

It is not hard to imagine the implications of these transformations for the composition of labor in Mae Sot and for the lives of migrants living there or transiting through. In addition to literal displacement, landowners have engaged in speculation, threatening both light manufacturing and the pace of SEZ investment, and prompting new policies to impede rapid buying and selling (Thai News Service 2015; Assawin 2019). As table 1 shows, the number of factories in Mae Sot and the number of registered workers has actually dropped since 2016.

Even recognizing that this table does not represent undocumented workers or unregistered factories, investment figures suggest that the borderlands remain attractive to mobile capital even as production conditions change. As representatives from the SEZ office and the Ministry of Commerce told me in 2017, the community of investors that had largely built up the garment industry in the early 2000s is being eclipsed by a newer group (also Thai and East Asian for the most part) more focused on logistics and transport. Production costs for the garment industry, they agreed, were becoming unreasonable, the cost of registering migrants too expensive, and investment in factories employing migrant labor too risky, given that migrants tend to leave the border area. However, key points were missing in their narrative: wages were officially uniform throughout Thailand now, and migrants have learned to mobilize collective action and have found ways to circumvent local strategies to contain labor at the border. Also missing were the perspectives of border-based employers and others who had hitched their livelihoods to the kinds of labor they had helped render precarious. For many of these actors, according to several that I interviewed over the years, fair wages, registration costs, and migrant mobility translated to an unsustainably low profit margin.

The shifting landscape of labor and investment speaks to what Campbell (2018a, 50) calls a "heterogeneity of interests" in the constitution of a local labor regime, including border-based firms, Bangkok-based government agencies, and regional or global investors. As investors reimagine the borderscape for its regional logistical potential, the local actors that lobbied for Mae Sot's special status in the first place find themselves in a more difficult spot as a consequence of both mobile capital and persistent migrant mobility.[26] The resulting anxiety among local employers and officials—which has manifested in a series of punitive and often illegal labor practices to maintain worker precarity—bears implications for the kinds of constraints and opportunities migrants face as they produce forms of social order in their everyday lives.

Anxieties about decreasing profit margins among border-based employers is just one reminder that the Thai-Burmese border is a space under constant negotiation, produced through iterations of conflicting interests. Employers' and local officials' desire to craft the technologies of governance to enable better control over migrant labor is part of the historical project to tame and reshape this frontier, to render it a resource for a certain kind

26. Local officials, including those from Mae Sot municipality, the Chamber of Commerce, and the Federation of Thai Industries have tied their hopes for SEZ status to the possibility of profit, but also to the resolution of long-standing border-based dilemmas. As Mae Sot's mayor Teardkiat Shinsoranan explained in 2011, cross-border trade and the influx of Burmese migrants benefited the rest of Thailand but represented a burden on the town. He shared with journalists his hope that official SEZ status would help the city by bringing uniformity to border policies, better regulating (and thus capitalizing on) cross-border trade, and perhaps most important, "migrant workers . . . could all be registered and prohibited from leaving the area" (Peeradej 2011). This expectation resonates with the practice of local authorities in Mae Sot who prevent Burmese migrant workers from traveling to central parts of Thailand, even those with authorization to do so, and reveals the geographic anxieties among officials and employers along the border.

of extraction, and to manage the mobility of the marginalized who are outside the boundaries of Thai-ness. We have to keep in mind that the textures of state logics regarding the development of frontier spaces emerge over time through assemblages of power, including via heterogeneous and often conflicting perspectives and interests, but these are always intertwined within broader political and economic systems (Springer 2011). Such logics map onto the gendered assumptions about labor that have become familiar in supply-chain capitalism, on resource frontiers,[27] and in Global North-dominated narratives of humanitarianism. The figure of the Burmese migrant within Thai political consciousness complements global myths about disposable labor, and both discourses collectively naturalize the exploitative treatment migrants face in the borderlands, at the same time that they inform the shape and trajectory of material changes to the borderscape. As we will see in subsequent chapters, humanitarian programming focused on biowelfare and care tend to leave this exploitation unchallenged and consider it beyond the analysis of social problems like gender-based violence.

As this chapter has suggested, it is helpful to think about how the contemporary flow of capital that places Mae Sot at the center of transnational land shipping routes is layered onto the complex history of mobility, marginalization, and security in the region. Spaces considered peripheral are more easily subsumed into new sites for production. Special economic zones that rely on different regimes of regulation, governance, gender relations, and wage scales are likely to profit from employing those who might already be considered "other." That these zones and assemblages are built on the durable foundation of older logics of development and methods of differentiation, containment, and governance have implications for the terrain migrants have to navigate in their everyday lives. Such durabilities inform the contemporary geography of structural violence for migrants as

---

27. In the Thai-Burmese borderlands "resource frontiers" refers to both spatial and human possibilities for extraction, including the migrant workforce and the development of the land as industrial agriculture or sites for speculation.

well as the organizing and agency such migrants can leverage in pursuit of social order, stability, and mobility. As the next chapter will show, gender as both a mode of subjectivation and a discursive tool for making order is an important aspect of this agency, part of how migrants and migrant activists make meaning of and respond to the violence around them.

3

Gender Violence
and Narrative Power

Ko Min Thu and I talked for hours in his office at a border-based women's organization in Mae Sot. Sitting behind his metal desk in the small room, he had an even more commanding presence than usual, tempered by his disarming smile. We had worked together often over the last few years, and we were meeting so I could ask how he became a gender-violence and child-welfare activist. As we talked, I periodically glanced at the dozens of framed photos on the walls depicting Burmese migrant youth engaged in various activities, with captions like "outing activity" or "team-building." On another wall were poster boards with neatly organized photographs of women who had stayed at the organization's shelter; some showed signs of the abuse that had driven them there, suggesting that the photos were taken during the intake process.

Our conversation moved back and forth over recent decades and between Thailand and Myanmar, mirroring the paths of the hundreds of thousands of Burmese migrants living, working, and passing through this border region in search of refuge, stability, and opportunity. Ko Min Thu's own story intersects with Myanmar's long history of human rights violations and the structural violence of precarious labor and undocumented migration in Thailand. At first, he mentioned the suffering and death of Burmese migrants as his primary reason for quitting factory work in Thailand to become a full-time activist-in-exile. "Burmese people in Thailand do not have access to the law," he reflected. "If a Burmese person is killed here, there is no law to protect the victim. If a man abducts a Burmese girl and rapes her, nothing happens."[1]

However, as we spoke, his narrative veered from what I expected would be a focus on a moral imperative to fight for human rights. Upon further reflection, he stressed that he was ultimately moved by what he saw as a lack of social order among migrants, which, he argued, was at the root of such problems. "In the morning when people leave to go to work, the children and a few elders are left alone. When people are away the children rob houses. Drug traffickers used them to bring drugs into the community. Some of them would play in the pond—no adults were watching—and they drowned." Looking around us, he gestured to a woven bamboo mat to illustrate his point: "A mat needs to have an edge, Adam. If it doesn't, what will happen?"

Ko Min Thu's question gave me pause. He invoked images of murder, rape, and children drowning in irrigation ponds, left alone while able-bodied adults worked twelve-to-fifteen-hour shifts for half or less of Thailand's minimum wage. He was not just talking about his vocation for activism. Nor was he referring solely to gender violence or violence against children as a social problem. Ko Min Thu was applying a metonymic function to violence, including gender violence, in order to make a point about the ways in which migrants' social relations had frayed like so many strands of an unraveling mat in an environment defined by precarity. Like many others with whom I spoke, he explicitly and implicitly referred to gender and gender violence to make meaning of migrants' precariousness: alongside murder, acts of sexual violence that are conducted with impunity represent individual and collective insecurity on the most intimate level. The remarks about children stealing and trafficking drugs, and the horrifying image of drowned children translate to neglect, specifically maternal neglect in communities where the expectation of care is placed on women.

---

1. There are Thai laws that deal with such matters to protect sexual assault victims, but Ko Min Thu alluded to the fact that many Burmese in Thailand feel they do not have access to these protections.

These incidents may take place at home or in the community, but Mae Sot worker dormitories and labor camps are sites embedded in and determined by the relations of production, which are defined by greater risk. Redefining the relationship between family, household, and labor is a global phenomenon, write Mezzadra and Neilson (2013, 90), and "a growing number of precarious workers are unable to support a household." Under such circumstances, they continue, "the capacity of labor to reproduce itself becomes uncertain." Seeing labor camps and informal migrant settlements as sites of social reproduction for insecure work, these are where the cultural forms, practices, and social structures of everyday life are reproduced and maintained in ways that enable or contest the dynamics of production in which laboring residents are engaged (e.g. Heynen et al. 2009; Elias 2010; Katz 2004). The gendered overtones in Ko Min Thu's narrative description of violence suggest implications for how men and women in precarious situations think about and strive for order as they reproduce or contest the social structures of family and labor.

How then, are gender and worker precarity mutually constitutive in this border space? That is, in what sense is gender both a tool to make meaning in a context of displacement and insecurity and a site for order-making as migrants navigate the uncertain landscape around them? "When things fall apart," McGuffey (2008, 216) writes, "we learn a lot about structure and agency by observing the ways social actors attempt to put things back together again." From this perspective, analyzing the "communicativity" of gender violence provides an important lens to deepen our understanding of both the precarity of the Mae Sot borderlands and the strategies migrants and migrant-rights activists deploy to respond to many of the social problems there. Moreover, the question of who do actors communicate with bears meaning. It was not lost on me that Ko Min Thu—and the many others who recounted stories of horrific violence in the course of this research—were performatively offering particular narratives about Burmese migrant lives and survival to my co-researchers and me as part of either collaborative NGO research or this book project. Throughout this book, applying a reflexive lens to the question of the communicativity of violence allows for the inclusion of me, my positionality, and the others involved in this project as agents in the borderland's complex and shifting assemblage of power.

While the previous chapter outlined in broad terms the production of precarious spaces and a flexible migrant labor pool to fulfill state and regional imaginaries of a border economic zone, this chapter is concerned with how migrants themselves make meaning of and navigate this space. I weave together migrants' narratives about the violence happening in their communities with activists' own analysis of insecurity, interpersonal and intimate-partner violence, accountability, and social order. By looking at discourse around gender violence in the community and at home as well as tactics to address such incidents, this chapter examines the pressures migrants encounter at the intersection of the demands for social repro-duction, the insecurity of work in this setting, and the ways these affect notions of masculinity and femininity. We can also gain a deeper under-standing of the gendered assumptions and rationales embedded within border-based humanitarianism.

A Note on Storytelling and Humanitarian Intervention

Writing about violence in the Thai-Burmese borderlands is anything but a neutral endeavor. For NGOs, it represents a form of storytelling that puts the narrator in the position of a witness empowered to translate migrants' or refugees' lived experience into language that is legible and useful for humanitarian funding proposals, for advocacy, and to a broader readership and public support for a cause. As Schaffer and Smith (2004, 27) write: "The kinds of stories [NGOs] choose—sensationalized, sentimentalized, charged with affect—target privileged readers in anticipation that they will identify with, contribute to, and become advocates for the cause. The frames they impose on stories are designed to capture the interest, empa-thy, and political responsiveness of readers elsewhere, in ways they have learned will 'sell' to publishers and audiences. NGOs harness their rights agendas to the market and its processes of commodification."

Schaffer and Smith's political and economic analysis of human-rights narratives is useful here because it reminds us that the priority for human rights or humanitarian NGOs is to advocate with policymakers, to fun-draise, or to design or evaluate programs—all of which require the work of showcasing narratives that have been revised to appeal to target audiences. The process of revising raw testimony involves applying interpretive frameworks, what is effectively a project of selection and translation to the language and interest of one's audience (Saltsman and Majidi 2021).

As an observer straddling the line between scholar and practitioner in Mae Sot, working with a Global North humanitarian NGO to implement an assessment of gender-based violence, I was acutely aware of the distance between the accounts and perspectives coming out of migrant neighborhoods and labor camps on the one hand, and the linguistic priorities of our Global North donor and our organizational headquarters in New York and Geneva, on the other. Crucially, at the start of my work, when submitting reports on my unit's progress on achieving programmatic objectives, I saw that my choice of the word "migrant" or "migrant worker" to describe the population of people with whom we worked on the border had been edited to "Burmese displaced in Thailand." When I probed this point informally with my supervisors, I was told that our donor was funding a response to a humanitarian crisis and that such crises produce refugees, implying that migrants, and the level of opportunistic agency often imposed on the term, were not associated with humanitarianism and were therefore not ideal recipients of aid. As Malkki (1996, 378) reminds us, through humanitarian representation, "refugees stop being specific persons and become pure victims . . . abstracting their predicaments from specific political, historical, and cultural contexts." In our project, such distinctions had important implications for how my colleagues and I listened to and translated the stories we encountered in our work. Significantly, a focus on "displaced Burmese" over "migrant labor" directed our analytical gaze toward individual acts of violence, applying a framework of victimhood and humanitarian protection. Echoing Malkki's analysis, such a lens did not make room for consideration of the broader structural violence of the borderland's labor-regulation regime or how migrants themselves navigated that terrain. Additionally, though we were working on gender-based violence, we were not focused on the production and reproduction of gendered subjects in the borderscape, even though such processes are, in fact, closely linked to the proliferation of or responses to gender violence.

The interpretive frameworks that powerful transnational institutions like NGOs apply to migrant narratives of violence and precarity are important because they constitute relations of power that impact those migrants' lived realities. They are part of migrants' political subjectivation, what enables "individuals to be described (by others) and identified (by themselves) in the public arena" (Fassin 2008, 533).[2] To Fassin, the humanitarian politics of testimony, including its emphasis on bearing witness, victimhood, and trauma, frames the terms under which the targets of intervention can exist politically. This framing is an important part of producing migrants' gendered border positionalities.

Thinking about position and subjectivity in this way, it makes sense to analyze migrants' accounts as arising in the interactive space between speaker and listener, the "subjective-in-between," as Hannah Arendt called it, "in which a multiplicity of private and public interests are always problematically in play" (Jackson 2013, 31, citing Arendt 1958). Storytelling is an agentic act, a "way of transforming our sense of who we are," Jackson writes. And when it comes to stories about violence, continues Jackson, the telling can be about "recovering a sense of ourselves as actors and agents in the face of experiences that make us feel insignificant, unrecognized or powerless" (17).

I offer this reflection at the outset of this chapter on narratives of violence in order to position my analysis between the power of telling as an agentic act and the power of translating testimony as part of the process of political subjectivation. That is, I look at Burmese migrants' accounts of violence as moments for the co-construction of subjective knowledge. To do greater justice to migrants' voices, I inductively ground my analysis in their narratives, asking what stories the speaker seemed to be telling us and why, and not just reflecting on how their stories fit into prescribed humanitarian or human-rights categories.

2. Here Fassin refers primarily to how certain figures emerge on the political scene in ways that are politically significant for how others think of themselves and the world around them. I have thus transposed his initial meaning to a discussion about how humanitarian discourse about migrants and refugees performs this work as well.

Gender and the Communicativity of Violence

To write about storytelling and violence as communicative in this way is to analyze narratives for their productivity, to look at what they reveal about the relationships among individuals, families, communities, states, and other actors. The communicative power of violence "may be contained in the family or staged in the public realm. It may demonstrate the presumptive immunity of the [perpetrator] to the state's interventions or call the attention of the state to its own inadequacy" (Morris 2006, 59). Visible violence is in the public view and threatens repetition and mimesis, while "acts of violence may [also] express power precisely to the extent that they prohibit their own revelation," including the violence of the home and that which is perpetrated by the state in a covert manner (such as torture or disappearance) (Morris 2006, 79). Sexual violence that is visible can be a symbol for many things, including a lack of law, for being beyond the law, or for a lack of social mores, structures, or community cohesion to prevent such abuses from happening. In the realm of the visible, sexual violence, such as that depicted in the scenes of torture at Abu Ghraib prison in Iraq, captured in photographs by British and US torturers themselves, can serve as a tool for stripping a man of his humanity through acts of emasculation (Razack 2005). Expert knowledge produced about violence in communities such as advocacy or humanitarian NGOs, state agencies, or scholarly publication, can have an essentializing effect, normalizing violence as inherently linked to an idea of culture or social dislocation (Cabot 2016). Such "expert" discourse can reify gendered images of victimhood (as I discuss further in chapter 6; see also Crosby and Lykes 2011). As a consequence, domestic and other forms of interpersonal violence become hypervisible under the lens of humanitarian programs. As well, in the state's interpretations of and responses to domestic violence, which often articulate the boundaries between private (home) and public (the state/community), authorities (whether state or otherwise) reproduce gendered notions of acceptable and unacceptable violence. This can bring an institutionalized legitimacy to masculine or patriarchal rule within the household, signifying the boundaries of what can or must not be discussed.

Even as sexual violence always involves a violation, the communicative force of violence shifts temporally and spatially in ways that are contingent on broader social factors, including widespread structural violence and precarity. Gender ideologies intersect with the representation of sexual violence as individuals and collectivities overlay horrific acts with moralized interpretations of good women and good men (Das 2008). For those who find themselves surrounded by multiple forms of violence (e.g., structural, collective, and interpersonal) and labeled as victims or as violent themselves, Das (2007) asserts that the conceptualization of this violence as ordinary or everyday often manifests as a fear of potential aggression that allows for management and certain forms of gendered governmentality.

For example, narratives that normalize violence against a feminized workforce are part of what produces what Wright (2006) calls the "myth of the disposable third world woman," which has been so central to ideologies of decentralized capital accumulation in a post-Fordist era. In thinking about how social actors become disposable, this book suggests that it is important to analyze how violence is conceptualized by those encountering it directly or spectrally on an everyday level. This, I argue, offers us a new way of seeing agency in the work of producing the gendered hierarchies that are so central to the productivity of feminized regimes of flexible labor.

Through this lens, we can begin to see how violence and its communicative power constitute important sites for the production and reproduction of precarious gendered subjects and positionalities in the Thai-Burmese borderlands. Situating this within a spatial analysis, looking at the "complex relationship between borders and violence" as a "space of political creativity," can open up new angles for thinking about both the spatiality of violence as well as the generative qualities of borderscapes in the ongoing production of subjecthood (Brambilla and Jones 2020, 291). As the previous chapter illustrated, Mae Sot and its surrounding areas developed into a border economic zone in part *because* of their reputation as peripheral, wild, and violent spaces. Both the idea of the borderlands as violent and specific instances of abuse lead to particular sets of experience for migrants and not others as they encounter state authorities, employers, NGO staff, and others.

Mae Sot, Seen as a Violent Borderscape

Much of the scholarly research and studies conducted by NGOs and scholars about Burmese migrants in Mae Sot over the last ten-to-fifteen years centers on the ways in which the structural violence of the borderlands manifests in forms of physical violence perpetrated by local authorities and employers against the migrant worker population (Amnesty International 2005; Arnold and Hewison 2005; Aung 2010; Campbell 2013; Caouette and Pack 2002; Human Rights Watch 2010, 2004; Kusakabe and Pearson 2010; Pearson et al. 2006; Pearson and Kusakabe 2012a, 2012b; Robertson and FTUB 2006; Saltsman 2012, 2014). Migrants, particularly those without documents, are subject to harsh treatment by Thai security officials, including extortion, verbal harassment, and even physical violence, which often takes place at the approximately half-dozen informal checkpoints set up in and around the town (Human Rights Watch 2010). Thai authorities have been linked to the trafficking of Burmese women into the sex trade and men into the fishing industry (Feingold 2013; International Labor Organization 2013; Leiter et al. 2006). Research describes employers who underpay and withhold pay from migrant workers, and who hold workers' identification documents captive. A 2010 report by Human Rights Watch contains a succession of tragic stories describing employers' physical abuse of their workers, especially in the context of negotiations for compensation (see for example 88–94). Through a "Profiling Urban Displacement" project I worked on in 2011, I found that 15 percent of undocumented migrants and 11 percent of those with documents reported experiencing harassment by authorities or employers in 2010.

With much research focused on the abuse migrants experience at the hands of authorities, there is a gap of information available about social conflict and interpersonal violence among and between migrants. A series of UN and NGO reports in 2006 attempted to address this gap by surveying refugee camps, which can provide some level of comparison with the migrant neighborhoods, settlements, and labor camps that are the focus of this book. According to a 2006 survey of close to 2,300 refugees in three camps (Mae La, Ban Mai Nai Soi, and Ban Mae Surin), 75 percent of camp residents identified problems related to alcohol consumption as a key protection concern ("protection" here a humanitarian term for access to human rights, including physical safety), and 60 percent pointed to the threat of physical violence (IRC 2006). Between 2003 and 2006, 350 protection incidents were reported to the UN refugee agency (UNHCR), an increase in the reporting of domestic violence, rape, and physical assault other than rape (UNHCR 2006). In a 2010 assessment of more than 2,000 refugees in Thai camps, an NGO found that 15 percent of refugees experienced violent crime in the two years prior to the survey, 12 percent experienced family disputes, 6 percent cited debt and loan issues, and 4 percent mentioned gender-based violence (IRC 2010). Only 2 percent mentioned abuse by camp authorities (who are refugees themselves) or by Thai authorities. This reflects a similar situation outside the camp, as documented by the Profiling Urban Displacement study, which notes that 10 percent of migrants (registered and unregistered) mentioned experiencing physical assault in the previous twelve months by a variety of actors, including authorities but also gangs, people within their communities, or family members (Saltsman 2011). Across all the studies asking about abuse, it is important to note that reporting is often extremely low because of the fear and mistrust of officials (International Commission of Jurists 2012; IRC 2011).

Some of these numbers might suggest that most migrants have not experienced physical violence. Indeed, in the more than 150 interviews co-researchers conducted with Burmese migrants as part of this book's fieldwork, few individuals reported physical abuse at the hands of authorities, employers, or others. However, such numbers are misleading for two key reasons. First, as Smith (1994) shows, making claims about the prevalence of abuse and violence from survey or even qualitative interview data can be shaky. Second, to draw conclusions solely on the basis of these statistics belies the link between the abuses experienced and their "social weight"—that is, their communicative capacity to remind migrants of their place in Mae Sot and in Thailand. Thus, while most migrants have not experienced direct harassment or physical abuse by authorities, a more than one-in-ten ratio for harassment by authorities or employers is more than sufficient to ensure that migrants remain aware of the prevalent risk to their safety. Affirming this, 64 percent of those interviewed for this project articulated in unequivocal terms their heightened fear of arrest, deportation, and other forms violence. It is this generalized awareness of violence that I focus on here. Thinking about violence as communicative and generative in this context allows us to contemplate how the structural violence of a border industrial zone is imbricated with the ways migrants reflect on and narrate the social disorder in their communities. Put another way, how does this fear, embodied in the circulation of narratives of violence, push migrants to make interpretations about self and space, to give meaning to social position, and to formulate ideas about how to survive and make order?

During fieldwork, migrants sometimes wavered between talking about violence in great detail and hesitating to discuss it at all. While some of this variance was between participants, some being more forthcoming than others, it was more often the case that the variance arose depending on the topic. That is, there were certain forms of violence that seemed to leap out of people's mouths, even (or maybe especially) when co-researchers had not even asked specifically about violence, while other types of conflicts or incidents, like intimate partner violence, remained more hushed. In the following section, I focus in particular on the forms of violence that participants wanted to make more visible for co-researchers, and I ask what their communicativity means in this context.

Verbalizing Fear of Thugs and Police

Direct encounters with authorities, and individual as well as collective fear of violent gangs or police, framed migrants' perception of their world and their options. Aside from the fear of Thai police or other state security forces, which all participants shared, how individuals expressed such concerns varied based on place, whether urban neighborhoods, informal migrant settlements, rural towns, or agricultural labor camps. Htone Taung, for example, is seen as a relatively safe mixed neighborhood having both migrants and Thai residents. There, the fear is directed outside the neighborhood's imagined perimeter: the police, as elsewhere, but also thieves, drug addicts, gangs, traffickers, Thai male teenagers roaming the streets, and others. In the Kyuwe Kyan slum on the outskirts of Mae Sot, on the other hand, residents described dangerous social problems related to drug consumption and trafficking within their neighborhood. In the rural sites of Pyaung Gyi Win/Rim Nam and Romklao Sahamit, the relative isolation of Phob Phra weighed heavily on conversations, and participants were quick to invoke images of aggressive men from other ethnic groups who prey on young Burmese women.

When it comes to police entering the neighborhood, "all of us are afraid," as a Burmese man in Htone Taung put it. "Even though we have passports, we try to stay away when we hear in advance that the police will come to our section." As indicated, local police have a reputation for disregarding official policy regarding legal status, stopping and often hassling even those migrants who have gone through the arduous process of securing passports and work permits. Many regard the police in Mae Sot as corrupt, demonstrated perhaps most frequently by shakedowns on street corners in open daylight. A participant in Kyuwe Kyan mentioned that the day previous to her interview her two children were returning from work when police stopped them. They each had to pay 1,500 baht—more than ten days' wages—not as a formal ticket, but as a bribe to avoid arrest. Another woman in Kyuwe Kyan mentioned: "I was imprisoned twice for forty-five days. I was arrested by police when I went to sell watercress." While police will often extract amounts ranging from 100 to more than 500 baht for a typical shakedown, those who cannot pay on the spot may find themselves detained and on the hook for an even higher amount, all typically exchanged informally. Other participants complained that police will detour from their law-enforcement mission to nab migrants, especially those without legal status: "The police tried to catch a guy who did drug trafficking. That guy ran into our dormitory, and the police checked the people in the dormitory and found that all of us didn't have legal documents. So the police arrested all of us in the dormitory."

The threat of police intervention that we see in these two examples not only inspires fear but also leads to mistrust of state authorities and a heightened sense of vulnerability to other forms of attack. Stories of murder and crime bear meaning about how police respond, and offer an interpretation of migrants' position vis-à-vis the state in a high-crime landscape. An imam in Kyuwe Kyan started by describing gang activity in his settlement: "They do drug trafficking and kill people. Last summer, women and a child were killed. Last month, one man was killed in that dormitory. Because of these cases, police come to our quarter frequently. This is not our country, so we can't do whatever we want. Police don't value Burmese people's lives." These words express frustration with both the high level of murder and other types of crime in the area as well as the police who come to the neighborhood when such violent crimes take place, but who, according to this imam, devalue Burmese migrants' lives.

Participants articulate their fear of multiple actors at the same time they attribute meaning to the spaces they inhabit. For many, predation at the hands of authorities or others informed how they perceive and move through the urban and rural spaces around them. One of the participants who was robbed expressed the fear she felt after that incident: "From that time on, I was afraid whenever I heard the sound of motorcycles. I dared not bring my mobile phone or money when I went out. But it is impossible to go out without them [and] so it happened to me again." Another woman participant in Htone Taung explained to a co-researcher:

> PARTICIPANT: In the past when they were caught, they would be released by paying 100 [baht]. Recently I went out to change something and I was caught. I was asked to pay 3,000 to 4,000 [baht] but was released with a 1,000 [baht payment]. So I am not happy to go out. If I need something I just try to find it around here. If it is important I go to the big market, and sometimes I am not caught. We have to be afraid of going out like that.
>
> INTERVIEWER: So people in the community cannot go freely because they are afraid that they will be caught by the police?
>
> P: Yes, the situation is like that.
>
> I: So can women and young women go out of this community?
>
> P: Those who have documents go out, those who do not have documents do not go out very often, only if there is some important issue, they go out.

Given the wages of participants in Mae Sot, the amounts mentioned in this excerpt can equal more than a month's salary.

During a community mapping exercise, when asked to articulate particular areas that generated fear, participants tended to refer to the entry points and other places along the perimeter of the community. For example, a group of women in Htone Taung discussed recent incidents in their area:

> PARTICIPANT 1: The robbery happened at the entrance road to Mae Sot Hospital. My necklace was stolen at that place. People heard that one girl was shouting for help, but they couldn't find the criminals. It happened yesterday.
>
> INTERVIEWER: Where was it?
>
> P2: Here. That road is also called Oo Htote Road. That road is the worst. Oo Htote road and the hospital road are the same.
>
> P3: There is no light. My purse was robbed near Kaw Yone one or two years ago. Money, wallet, and mobile phone were robbed. It happened around 2 pm.
>
> I: So can people go freely in this area?
>
> P4: It is impossible at night. But it is possible to use this road in the morning. Police make arrests, though. Everybody is afraid of using this road. Parents don't allow their children to go to this place. Even if they need to use this road, the parents allow them only when adults accompany them.
>
> P2: They've heard that rape cases have happened in the past. They are also afraid to be shot by criminals.

Participants mentioned whole areas that were off limits, demarcating hostile spaces according to the assumed presence of police or criminal outsiders. These expressions of fear show that violence can have the effect of imposing virtual boundaries all over Mae Sot that are contingent on legal status, time of day, and gender, with both men and women participants framing the consequences of violence as especially restrictive of women's mobility. One community volunteer recounted her own experience of witnessing her son being assaulted by "local drug users." They "hit my son on the head with their liquor bottle." This incident reminded her: "It's not safe for women and children to go out at night in this area, especially behind the *anamai* [subdistrict health office]." A community leader in Romklao Sahamit said: "Girls cannot go out freely, especially at night, even within our village. If they went out, they would have problems. Even we men have problems. A lot of Thai, Burmese, and Miao drunkards." He was alluding to the risk of violence frequently attributed to criminal gangs, drug addicts, and drunk men from other ethnic groups in Phob Phra, using "Miao" as a term for Hmong. When interviewers asked what the participant thought about migrants going outside the parameters of the village, he answered: "Cannot! Even worse. We would have to face robbery, the cutting of heads and necks." Participants circulated as a belief among themselves similar archetypes of dangerous characters lurking outside a village or property boundary. From this perspective, staying isolated and even locked in a house or compound appeared to many to be an ideal response to avoid such a threat.

Narratives of Violence at the Heart of Gendered Notions of Order and Disorder

Violence is intimately involved in shaping migrants' sense of positionality. Compounding the sense that "police don't value Burmese peoples' lives," as the imam put it, is a shared awareness of the likelihood that police will transgress the law they are mandated to enforce to mete out punishments particularly tailored to the Burmese population. In Pyaung Gyi Win/Rim Nam, a group of men discussed the danger they perceive when police come to their area:

> INTERVIEWER 1: What do people here do when the police come?
> PARTICIPANT 1: Everybody runs away.
> P2: If they were coming now, we would have to run.
> P3: When his [pointing to P2] father passed away, we had to run away during the funeral service because the forest rangers came.
> P1: If we do meet the police, we dare not talk with sign language or stand face to face with them. Sometimes they shoot at us.
> P4: If we think we can escape, we run. If not, we don't run and we don't stand with our backs to them. If we do, they will shoot.

I1: Have you experienced this?

P1: Yes, one of my friends was arrested when we ran away together.

I1: Do they shoot . . .

P3: Mostly, they do not shoot. They kick, punch, and hit us when they catch us.

P2: We have to keep our head down and sit when we are arrested.

INTERVIEWER 2: If you run away, they shoot you. If you do not run away, they may do the same or kick and punch you. So why do you run away?

P3: The reason to run is that if we are arrested, they will send us to Myawaddy and we may be sold to human traffickers or at least have to give money on that side. Police have contact with them . . .

P2: If we were deported to 999 gate[3] on the Myanmar side, we would have to pay at least 1,500 baht or 1,700 baht . . .

P1: If we cannot pay, we will be sold to human traffickers . . .

P4: In addition, it would be difficult for us to come back to this area. We'd have to give 100 baht to each checkpoint.

This account conveys clearly the multilayered fear migrants in this area have of police and other local authorities. Significant here is the extent to which ideas about the powerless position of migrants and their violent treatment at the hands of authorities have been interpellated as an awareness of status and life on the border. Also important to note is the mention of trafficking, as it relates to the total abnegation of an individual's agency through the loss of his or her freedom of movement and autonomy. It contrasts with the notion of smuggling, which, in referring

---

3. The 999 gate refers to one of the main piers along the Moei River just outside Mae Sot where Thai police deport Burmese migrants. Previously, the Democratic Karen Buddhist Army managed the gate on the Burmese side until they were absorbed into the Border Guard Force in 2010. Research has noted frequent abuses of deportees at this gate; those who cannot pay are sometimes subjected to forced labor or sold to traffickers (HRW 2010; HRW 2012).

to a "choice" made by migrants to travel illegally, contains an element of agency.[4] Romklao Sahamit lies near well-known smuggling and trafficking routes where agents and brokers bring migrants from Myanmar or elsewhere on the border to major urban areas, especially Bangkok. Participants referenced the prevalence of both trafficking and smuggling, expressing their fear of brokers who operate in the area.

Trafficking is also a highly gendered term, as Adrijasevic (2007) reminds us, where the violence of victimizing narratives about men and women manifests in different ways. For the conversation among Burmese men excerpted above, trafficking may invoke being pressed into forced labor and feelings of humiliation, loss, and emasculation, among other emotions.[5] For women, humiliation and loss are at the center of the discourse on trafficking too, but also the possibility of rape and violation, the subsequent loss of moral standing in the family and community, and victimhood. A self-described leader among migrants in Romklao Sahamit village told interviewers the story of a girl who had been trafficked to the center of Thailand and then raped by brokers when she tried to return to the border. He stated that he and others in the area try to "stop girls from going to Bangkok by crossing the jungle. But they don't care and some come back crying, and we help them with medicine and they go back home. Sometimes we have to rent private cars to send them back to Myawaddy. Sometimes Thai authorities then arrest the girls and make them to be like their wives. At that time we steal them back, hide them, and send them to Myawaddy."

There is a disciplinary undertone to the speaker's description of the trauma of trafficking and rape of young girls in that he emphasizes his warning to young women, their disregard as they leave the safety of the community into the hands of brokers, and the consequent sexual violence,

---

4. The notion of "choice" here is a complicated one and needs to be thought about in a way that takes into consideration the set of constraints on individuals who, under various forms of duress, might be choosing the "least worst" option from among a series of unpleasant possibilities.

5. See Stoakes et al. 2015.

potentially at the hands of multiple actors, including police. It reinforces the sense that there is a gendered morality affixed to the notion of trafficking, in which women who break the rules get raped and therefore are, at least in part, to blame for their own victimhood. With this interpretation in mind, the speaker's words, which note his role in rescuing the women—stealing them back, like property—imply a sense of saving women not only from traffickers but also from their own ethical errors. His words effectively convey a sense of the types of violence prevalent in his area, how these impact the men and women there, the informal ways in which he and others respond in an effort to save their fellow migrants, and how these mechanisms come with gendered implications.

The previous excerpt also illustrates a tendency among participants to articulate the involvement of authorities in trafficking and the sexual abuse of migrant women in order to highlight the inversion of ethics and migrants' place before the law. In a discussion about safety, some participants contrasted employers and police, believing that employers are sometimes patrons who protect migrants against the predations of the police who might wish to arrest or extort from them. At such moments in the discussion, participants overlooked the fact that employers frequently do not register their workers, thus keeping them vulnerable to arrest and deportation.

When asked how he thought communities should respond to sexual assault against women, a teacher in Rim Nam answered:

> I have seen a lot of cases like that. The girls have problems reporting to the police, since they do not have any legal documents. And then, they just come here two or three days after the rape and say they were raped, so we don't really know how to help them. At such a time, we have no idea how to handle the girl's health. Yes, we can manage to send the cases to the authorities, but the girls are afraid to see them because they do not have any documents. This is happening everywhere. In the end we have to solve this with our traditional way by going to the village midwife. Maybe these girls have to drink a kind of herbal liquid. We are not taking any legal action, but just protecting ourselves. We are so afraid to go closer to the authority's area, let alone take action against them [violators]. Because we do not have any legal documents.

Clearly people who experience rape in this context and the migrants who attempt to provide assistance are in a complicated position. The insecurity of the borderlands, both in government policies and the everyday work of local actors, leaves migrants like the speaker and the women in his story with limited options. This excerpt shows that people make certain decisions about care based on an assessment of choices, choices that are limited by the violence of precarity. The teacher implies that the only way to respond to the rape of women in the community is to try to help them get an abortion through "traditional" means.

As these narratives suggest, sexual violence seemed to communicate to the migrants several layers of gendered meaning about their precarious position in Thailand. Many participants volunteered stories about murders and rapes that had taken place over the years, either in their neighborhood or nearby. The images conjured up in these accounts are disturbingly detailed and full of meaning. At least three participants described one incident in particular: "A married girl was raped and killed at Myay Ni Road. She was a Karen girl. Her husband was also killed. We went and saw their bodies. They hit sticks into her vagina. As they are Burmese, what law will take care of them? They have no relatives [in the area]. If their relatives were here, they would open the [legal] case for them. We wouldn't feel as bad if they did this to a beautiful, rich young girl with relatives. But they did it to the couple that collected plastic for their livelihood. Her husband was disabled and she suffered from mental illness."

In addition to being told in horrific detail, stories like this one contained moral lessons on justice and injustice, victimhood and power, violent life and death, isolation and alienation, legality and illegality, and right and wrong. The stories underscore migrants' perceptions that they are on their own in Thailand and that they have no recourse to law enforcement or the judicial system. And, as the participants suggest, gendered acts of violence are especially egregious violations when layered on top of social, economic, and political insecurity. Though migrants' ethnic identity rarely came up, it is also noteworthy that this participant chose to point out the victim's Karen identity, positioning her within a borderscape that frames Karen experiences and histories in particular ways.

In such statements, rape is understood as the epitome of violation and erasure of sovereignty in the absolute negation of consent. In this, women's vulnerability comes to symbolize the hardship and marginality of migrants. Participants in Mae Sot evoke an image of an extraordinarily violent world for migrants there, especially those who are undocumented. Subject to arrest and extortion by police, they are also at risk for theft or worse at the hands of perpetrators they often vaguely refer to as "criminals," often Thai or Burmese gangs. And participants always make clear their sense that they do not have access to justice within the Thai legal system. These conversations and narratives, which invoke an image of violence on almost mythical proportions, convey migrants' sentiments that they are on their own in Thailand, where they are subject to many predations. Without anybody to look out for them, they must take care of themselves.

The production and reproduction of violent discourse in this way takes a complex context and boils it down to a few pairs of effective dichotomies with gendered implications. Inside a landlord/employer's compound and outside, safety and danger, community (Burmese) and foreign (Thai, Hmong, or other). Such binaries make it easier for people to understand their circumstances, what constraints lie around them and what tactics are best for protection. But at the same time, so much violence seems to also communicate that migrants' best hope to earn an income, keep it, and be safe is to be a good worker and stay in the labor camp.

While all the participants' narratives suggest that both men and women are at risk of violence, these accounts serve an especially cautionary tale for women. The narratives emphasize vulnerability, yet in all four settlements in Mae Sot and Phob Phra there is ambivalence as well in the way these narratives place some responsibility on women to constrain themselves or face the consequences. The solution, then, at least in part, is for feminized workers (both women and men) to not stir up trouble. Just under the surface in participants' stories is the notion that harsh treatment toward men has the effect of harming their masculinity. For women who experience abuse, these narratives reify their vulnerability. In both cases, violence as communicated is a productive force in the assertion of a certain kind of gendered precarity in the borderland space.

Violence at Home: Reaffirming Gendered Morality as Order-Making

If the stories in the previous section produce images of Burmese migrants vulnerable to many external threats, migrants' explanation of intimate-partner violence has a different tone. Whereas the narratives shared above first emerged in detail when co-researchers asked about challenges or problems in the community, participants spoke about domestic violence in general terms only when prompted specifically about this issue (though no participant was asked directly if they had experienced such violence). Domestic violence is, by definition, intimate and private, and is therefore less likely to be spoken of. Scholarly research has covered well the tendency in most places to silence domestic forms of violence (e.g., Das 2008). Co-researchers and other activists interviewed for this book repeatedly noted that this is the case on the border as well. That said, intimate-partner violence is communicative in this context in its own way, in the form of gendered morality that serves both an explanatory role in making sense of displacement and a prescriptive function, guiding men and women in particular ways in order for them to get by in this challenging space.

Reflecting this dynamic, the perspectives of workers, paraprofessionals, and community leaders on interpersonal violence tended to coalesce around three salient themes: (1) identifying links between precarity and violence at home, (2) discourse about gender identities as a way of explaining intimate-partner violence, and (3) gendered morality as explanatory of displacement. Across all three of these analytical categories is an important moral message: the violence around them or in their households communicates tactics for how best to negotiate the difficult circumstances of displacement. That is, through their accounts of and explanations for violence, migrants articulate gendered moral guidelines for how they can make do in this precarious context.

Identifying Links between Precarity and Violence at Home

Most common among participants' interpretations of intimate-partner violence were references to how precarious labor and living conditions constitute an environment in which interpersonal violence erupts more easily.

In the words of a woman in Kyuwe Kyan: "If they have work, they are fine. But if they don't have work, at that time there is a conflict between husband and wife and they beat each other."

Framing intimate-partner violence around migrants' insecure circumstances adds a layer of understanding to how precarity impacts individuals and households. Participants in all four sites invoked images of couples arguing because of insufficient resources for the family's survival. Such accounts are structured around gendered roles that generalize and caricaturize migrant identities, as the following example shows:

> Some husbands do not give enough money to their family. For instance, their household expenses cost 200 baht but they give their wives only 100 baht. So their wives are unhappy and blame their husbands. After that, the problem grows bigger and bigger. If the wives can't find the money to support their family, they borrow money from others without letting their husbands know. As a consequence, they have to pay a lot of debt. Even I do not let my husband know how much I borrow from other people. If I have 1,000 baht in debt, I tell him that I have 700 baht in debt. This is because I do not want to burden him to repay the debt. Sometimes, creditors arrive at the family's home when they get back from work. Then husbands know the real amount of debt. Then problems happen.

To this participant, violence stems from an untenable situation at home. Implicit here is the notion that husbands are the primary earners and that wives manage the finances. Both are prey to a context in which wages are not enough for the couple or the family to survive; the man does not earn enough and the woman cannot spread the income thinly enough to cover expenses, thus incurring debt. Keeping the borrowing and the debt secret reflects a reluctance to make financial problems known and also a desire to maintain the image of a competent partner. Thus the burden to uphold a counterfeit stability in an environment where stability is impossible falls onto women. Often, however, both heads of a household work. Even in such cases, participants explain that violence can happen when men place dual pressures on women to earn income alongside them and to play the primary role in household management and care, a common trend globally (Hochschild and Machung 2012; Hondagneu-Sotelo and Messner 1994; Kabachnik et al. 2013; Sinatti 2014).

Also ubiquitous in participants' accounts of how economic and social conditions relate to intimate-partner violence is men's dependency on alcohol, a problem that featured in interviews and focus-group discussions as a primary trigger for violence at home. Often mentioned is how wasteful men spent hard-earned money on whiskey and beer instead of the family. In Pyaung Gyi Win/Rim Nam, a forty-year-old woman explained why violence takes place in households in her camp: "I will tell you why. They get 100 baht per day. If they drink one bottle, it costs 60 baht. If they drink a half bottle, it costs 30, and the cost for food is 40 baht. So nothing is left for the family. These are the common problems happening here."

Participants considered drinking to be a common male response to the hardship they experience. They noticed that when the harvest season ends in Phob Phra and work dries up, drinking and abuse increase. "When there are many jobs here," a community leader in Romklao Sahamit said, "there is no problem. When there are no jobs, the problems start and men will drink. If husbands drink and there is no income and no savings, the wives start blaming the men." The narrative here of a drunk, abusive, and wasteful man is imbued with expectations of masculinity unmet. Men are failing in their earner roles, but they are behaving in a "masculine" way by being aggressive. Community workers in Htone Taung agree that "most of the domestic violence is caused by business; if the women make money like men, it can dispel the domestic violence." They believe the situation will be improved if both adults in a household enter the workforce. In the border space, this often means both adults in a household become flexible labor. Thus, at times, individuals proposing solutions to intimate-partner violence take as inevitable migrant precarity, just as they often take as inherent the biological traits and social roles of men and women.

Discourse about Gender Identities in Accounts of Intimate-Partner Violence

As the previous section begins to suggest, migrants' accounts of intimate-partner violence and solutions to that violence are intimately tied to a discourse about gendered notions of what it means to be a man and a woman migrant. Participants referred to a seemingly fixed relationship between gender and social roles or behavioral traits. At the same time, labor conditions and migrants' social exclusion in Thailand inform migrants' discourse about gendered identities. Participants' narratives make links between the challenges of life in border spaces, the demands to produce constantly for low wages, and gendered notions of morality. For a participant in Htone Taung: "If everything is fine, married life is prosperous. If there is a financial problem, conflict happens between the married couple. Wives totally depend on their husbands, and when their husbands can't fulfill the family's basic needs, problems happen."

Here, a male partner's failure to meet the household's basic needs becomes the source of stress that leads to violence. In reality, laborers might lose work or not receive pay in a number of instances. Workers are laid off, employers do not always pay employees, workers strike and forego pay, and the harvest and planting season ends. And yet it is possible for others to interpret the end result as unfulfilled responsibilities.

Men participating in a focus-group discussion in Pyaung Gyi Win/Rim Nam considered a man at another site who does not meet standards of masculinity. "He doesn't live like a breadwinner," they said. "He depends on his wife and does whatever his wife assigns him to do. He is always drunk. Therefore, she beats him." The role of violent aggressor is reversed here: the woman physically assaults her husband, who is a drunk, who presumably does not earn enough income or any at all, and who is dependent on his wife, instead of the other way around. Being passive (to his wife) and his lack of income together portray the man as feminine, a point underscored by the wife's abuse against him.

Other stories of the "bad/weak/unreasonable" man from men's focus-group discussions in Htone Taung and Pyaung Gyi Win/Rim Nam include these two: "He gets married and he doesn't do any jobs. He spends his wife's income. He doesn't do any household chores. He doesn't take care of his children. His wife has to do household chores after she gets back from work. He also beats his wife after drinking alcohol." And, "The husband wastes all of the earnings by drinking alcohol. There is no saving in their families." A woman interviewed in Kyuwe Kyan shared a similar narrative: "They [husbands] told their wives that doing household chores are the wives' responsibilities and working to support the family is their responsibility. They assign their wives to fill the tank for taking a shower for when the men come back from work. Although they love their wives, they order their wives to do household chores with authority. They are the breadwinners of the families and their wives have to fulfill the responsibilities of wives."

These excerpts convey an ideal of masculinity as well as what the caricaturized men lack in that department. Important points here are that men should be good earners and respectful. If they cannot fulfill their earner role, at least they need to help out around the house. Good men are fair and willing to share duties. Taking part in childcare and household chores does not affect their masculinity, as long as they also earn sufficient income. The point here is that migrants often seem to frame violence between partners, or how to prevent that violence, in a way that relies on some idea of fixed gender roles. For example, in contrast to the images of a bad man, a twenty-two-year-old woman in Kyuwe Kyan expresses this idea of a dutiful and appropriate woman: "I think the women play an important role in reducing the conflicts. As wives, they have to do household chores and fulfill the responsibilities of wives." While this may not be surprising, such notions about gender cannot be untangled from the social and economic reality in which migrants find themselves. Thus, I suggest here that these accounts of fixed gender identity and responsibility are sites where the insecurity, injustice, and inequality of the border context is displaced as migrants project a hardship they do not deserve onto themselves as men and women striving impossibly toward some constructed goal of "tradition."

Gendered Morality in a Context of Displacement

In addition to relying on gendered identities and hierarchies as a guide to behavior, participants also used gender as a metaphor to convey important principles about the individual and the collective in the context of displacement and liminality in order to explain and make sense of it. We see this in descriptions of dispute resolution and in explanations for why gendered violence happens.

The head of a migrant social-welfare organization in Mae Sot made clear to me the relationship between gender and a sense of tradition, loss, reassembly, and change in his analysis of migrant conditions and of why intimate-partner violence is especially prevalent on the border. He understands that interpersonal violence stems from migrants' need to leave their homes and come to Thailand, that dismal economic conditions compel emigration and that their extreme poverty in Thailand provokes abuse within families: "Why are people poor? For example, why can't a [Burmese] family stay in their [country] while others can? Because we have no food to eat. What does the father do? Drink alcohol. Hitting, beating up others in the family. Mother has to go out to work. I will tell workers, 'Why must you become slaves in another people's country? This is slavery. Doing the work for others. The work that they do not want to do.'"

Following this, he then highlighted five reasons for intimate-partner violence. First, he pointed to the family separation that comes with migration and displacement; men and women leave their families behind, enter new relationships without mentioning their pasts, and then turn on each other when they become aware that they have violated certain mores ("You are not a virgin!?" "You are not a virgin either and you are the father of how many children already?"). Second, the transient lifestyle of Burmese migrants in Thailand leads to promiscuity and conflict. Women get in and out of relationships too easily: "Some of them have family or relationships not even in their own village [in Myanmar] but just in another factory in Mae Sot. Stay with a man for one month . . . No parents around to watch over them. So they live as they like, and then she moves to another factory." In such an example, men get jealous and conflict among ex-partners, current partners, and the "promiscuous" woman ensues. Third is the consequent contentious dynamics of second or third marriages and dysfunctional stepfamilies. A fourth reason underscores increased alcohol consumption and gambling as a source of domestic violence. Men return home drunk in the evening, having spent most of the family's money on alcohol, only to find that their wives blew the rest on the lottery. The result: conflict and cycles of violence. Finally, the head of the organization points to the pressure that irregular employment places on the family: "Construction workers and farmers, unlike factory workers, do not have work all the time. Then they do not have money and wives complain, "I want to have money. Other people go to morning market, Sunday market, Wednesday market, but I cannot go. Why don't I have money?" Then the wife says, "Why don't you look for another job?" The husband says, "No, I only want to work with my current employer. Now there is no job for four, five days, so we just wait." "No I can't wait," says the wife, and then domestic violence happens."

Within his short analysis of Burmese displacement and reasons for intimate-partner violence, the speaker moves from a narrative of displacement to a loss of tradition and the destruction of the social fabric built on kin networks, to the pressures on the family generated by insecurity and the financial challenge that many migrants face when working in Thailand. Throughout these points, which are politically nuanced and include both structural as well as micro-level explanations for violence, the speaker emphasizes certain views of masculinity and femininity. The effect is to offer a gendered lens on displacement and migrants' struggles for survival in border zones. In his analysis, gender serves as a trope for talking about change, loss, and destruction. It thus lies at the heart of explanations for current conditions and theories for how migrants must behave to survive those conditions. As authorities and migrants performatively assert certain gendered identities through this discourse, the intersection of gender with tradition, community, and loss has implications for how migrants make meaning out of their experiences and forge distinct subjectivities in this border space.

Making Gender, Making Order

This chapter centered on how precarious work, the challenges of displacement, and gender traditions intersect in a mutually constitutive fashion in the homes and community spaces for Burmese migrants as opposed to the factory floor or the field. Migrants' narratives about violence outside their workplaces provide an important angle for considering how economic production and dispossession permeate all aspects of their social lives.

From this perspective, it is possible to see through the telling and retelling of stories of violence that gender takes on a productive force. At the same time, these stories produce certain notions of gender that are contingent on the experience of displacement and refracted through the power of collective memory. This is true for forms of violence that take on a high level of visibility as spectacularized accounts, as well as for those that migrants utter in language shrouded by moral opprobrium and guidance. The difference between visible and unspoken violence is important in that it reveals those narratives that migrants select to convey the hostility of their experience in Thailand and those that are not to be mentioned in detail but that contribute to certain gendered tropes.

Through an analysis of both the spectacularized and the barely spoken, I have shown how migrants' discourse on violence serves as an ordering mechanism for them, not unlike what Liisa Malkki calls "mythico-histories." These refer to "sets of moral and cosmological ordering stories: stories which classify the world according to certain principles, thereby simultaneously creating it" (1995, 54). Stories of aggressive police and sexual assaults indicate a fear of mistreatment that reminds migrants, especially women, that it is better to remain safely in factory dormitories, worker compounds, or homes than to be out and on one's own. Through the symbolic weight given to violence against women, stories reinforce the need for gendered orders within migrant collectives as they underscore a degree of exclusion, injustice, and lawlessness that define the border space. Women who restrict their movement and remain safe from rape are, in effect, protecting the whole community, since their violation at the hands of an outsider would be an annihilation of the sovereignty of the whole group. Listeners and interpreters in the research associated with this book became acutely aware that the experience of violence reverberates through migrant communities. What we then do with that information depends on our own position as actors in the social field of the borderscape.

At the same time that gender is useful for explaining and making sense of a violent social space, it is also the case that such explanatory narratives reproduce certain ideas of femininity and masculinity in a context of precarious labor. Such practices may be considered sites of what Shawn McGuffey (2008, 216–17) calls "gender reaffirmation," in which social actors "extract dominant conceptions of gender, race, and class from the macro world to interpret their personal experiences as they recover from trauma perceived as threatening to heteronormative gender identities." Although McGuffey was interviewing survivors of child sexual abuse, the concept translates well to this project's inquiry into the construction of gendered border positionalities. Certainly the concepts of masculinity and femininity range widely among migrant communities in these borderlands. The fact that conservative interpretations were so dominantly offered as part of—or at the heart of—explanations for what has gone wrong for Burmese in Thailand and how to put things back together is telling about the contested and shifting place of gender identity and questions of how a labor force reproduces itself. Migrants' stories here seem to suggest that as life becomes more precarious, pressure increases on men and women to live up to certain ideals rather than on oppressive structures that need to be changed. As the conversations were presented to an NGO research team, it may not be surprising that they centered on the individual lives of men and women instead of on the gendered structural violence of the borderscape's labor regulations that make life so challenging.

Looking at gender and production in this way is important because it reveals some of the nuanced aspects of the injustices migrants experience within the dynamics of capital accumulation in border zones like Mae Sot and Phob Phra. The ramifications of migrants' challenging work and living conditions relates not only to low or nonexistent wages, physical abuse, arrest, or deportation, but also to the way that migrants can at times project the violence of such experiences onto the identities and relationships of women and men. At the same time, my analysis sheds light on some of the gendered subtleties of migrant political subjectivity, which inform how people interpret and respond to the myriad technologies of governance deployed in border economic zones. One of these technologies was the gender-based violence assessment that I carried out with a group of co-researchers. As the next chapter shows, our collaboration and co-creation of knowledge generated ways of knowing the migrant population that had material consequences.

4

The Office of Knowledge Construction

There are thirteen of us crammed into this small room in a modular trailer, around two long and narrow folding tables that give us just enough room to sit but not enough to move about. It is March and approaching the hottest time of the year in Mae Sot. Outside, the pavement is baking, but we are insulated, kept unnaturally cool by the humming air conditioner perched above us on the wall. Bathed in florescent light that reflects dully off the matte-gray plastic walls are the signs of our prolonged discussion: scattered papers; flip charts with tables and notes in Thai, English, and Burmese; and laptops connected to a tangle of chargers that all seem to flow from one overburdened multiplug. This is where the co-researchers and I have been meeting nearly every day for months to assess gender-based violence in migrant settlements along the border.

In the cramped comfort of the trailer, the conversation centers on the daily evaluation of our findings and our interview questions, one aspect of our commitment to practice iterative data collection. Yin Tha Thu, a co-researcher, notes that in one-on-one interviews, when she asks about problems women face in the community, domestic violence never comes up. "To the people in the communities," she says, "violence will always be something that happens outside the home, on the road or at the edge of the community. It's not what's going on in people's homes or in the families." Others nod their heads in agreement. There is widespread feeling among co-researchers, many of whom have done health, education, and women's-protection work in those settlements for years, that during interviews respondents downplay the prevalence of domestic violence. As the ensuing discussion moves toward ideas to address this dilemma and get a clearer picture of what violence against women looks like in migrant-worker settlements, I realize that the group is debating more than a methodological approach; they are exchanging interpretations of what gender-based violence means in the communities where they conduct research. Further, they are articulating their own notions of gender-based violence through subtle gestures and verbal cues suggesting relations of power and influence among the research group members. As a technical term rooted in academic, social-movement, and transnational human-rights discourse, "gender-based violence" and its deployment among this team of researchers reflects the multiple discursive refractions that represent status and difference—both within the group and between us and the migrant-worker participants who are part of the assessment but have no voice in this discussion.

Our puzzling over divergent understandings of gender-based violence offers a glimpse into how our coalition produced certain ways of knowing the Burmese migrant population. At the same time, as this chapter illustrates, Yin Tha Thu's point reflects a knowledge-production process embedded in the inequality of our positionalities vis-à-vis the humanitarian industry and the borderland's precarious labor regime. Concepts of community, organizing, social change, gender, and gendered violence shifted constantly but quietly under the unstable terrain of our imbalanced dialogue. We not only gathered data about discourse, we also generated it in our own right, and the use of that information by the various organizations involved and by me in this book constitutes an exertion of power—that is, the power to amplify or submerge certain knowledges. Indeed, while our work aspired to ideas of community-engaged research, the modular trailer was in one sense analogous to a "research laboratory." Far removed from migrant settlements in a neighborhood of estates where well-funded NGOs had their offices, we fine-tuned our instruments, conducted analyses, and made interpretations on multiple levels. The crowded room was the space in which we rendered migrant workers and the topic of gender-based violence "legible" to the NGO community and to our donors. Recognizing our physical and social distance from the communities and the social problems on which the research was focused is an important entryway to an interrogation of participatory approaches in humanitarian contexts and the ways these can be part of (or a resistance to) humanitarian logics of order and governance.

Participatory Research and Humanitarian Governance

For nearly four months, the group met to adapt interview questions and finalize plans for sampling, recruitment, and data collection, and then, once we had started the research, to debrief about the day's interviews and focus groups, discuss any logistical or security issues, further adjust the interview guide, and reflect on the work we were doing. In addition to these elements of collaboration, I considered co-researchers as participants because, as I made it clear to the group, I was not only studying violence in migrant communities but also how research projects are implicated in generating important discourse as sites of humanitarian knowledge construction. During our daily meetings, I observed and took notes as we discussed the process of our project.

This form of collaboration reflects my intention to foster what Torre and colleagues (2018, 496) have called "the participatory contact zone," in which we "come together as research colleagues around a common inquiry" and in recognition of our vastly different positionalities. At the heart of this partnership is what Brinton Lykes (2013, 776) refers to as "informed empathy and passionate solidarity." As an "outsider" in many ways, including my geographic origin and my lack of direct experience with forced displacement and precarious labor, I aimed to accompany these activists and service providers in a collective effort to deepen our understanding and take action on gender-based violence in migrant settlements along the border. Participatory approaches are gaining prominence in humanitarian contexts; they are often considered a sort of remedy to the limitations of research in crisis environments, notably the ethical dilemmas and the power imbalance between aid workers and recipients (Afifi et al. 2020; Ager et al. 2014; Blanchet et al. 2017). Recent scholarship tends to affirm the possibility of participatory research methods in humanitarian contexts to foster greater trust and collaboration between local communities, including those with direct experience of the topic studied, and those with research expertise (Ormel et al. 2020). Afifi and colleagues (2020, 389) assert that community-based participatory research (CBPR) in crises can be tools for "recalibrating equity and power . . . restoring dignity, and rebuilding effective community."

However, such transformative change seems rather a tall order for participatory research in humanitarian intervention, the latter having been famously characterized as structurally "inhumane" (Harrell-Bond 2002) and as "powerful pacific weapons" for spreading empire (Hardt and Negri 2000, 35–36). Didier Fassin (2012) argues that even when mobilized as a technology of compassionate governance, humanitarianism constitutes a politics of inequality in the form of victimization. Others point out that to the extent NGOs are themselves a part of transnational governance regimes, the everyday practice of doing NGO aid work contributes to the production of neoliberal subjects (Bernal and Grewal 2014; Li 2007; Fisher 1997). This framing is certainly relevant in spaces of displacement like the Thai-Burmese borderlands, in that refugees and other dispossessed populations living in "extended exile" (Hyndman and Giles 2017) find themselves excluded from states' normative rights-based governance systems and are therefore ideal subjects of transnational aid interventions with a mission to "protect." As well, scholars note that UN agencies have increasingly integrated neoliberal tenets such as entrepreneurship and self-governance into their strategies for managing displaced peoples, a topic I discuss at length in chapter 6. Ilcan and Rygiel (2015) call this approach "resiliency humanitarianism," citing a shift in the aid industry toward holding forced migrants responsible as ethical and productive subjects. How NGOs implementing aid work analyze aid is a key part of how the social categories of "migrant" or "refugee" become emergent political groups in local and transnational policy arenas (Malkki 1992; Häkli et al. 2017). Forging self-governing, ethical, and productive apolitical refugee subjectivities is at the heart of contemporary humanitarian governance, which is deployed by an array of UN agencies and NGOs at different scales, and which offers a politics of compassion that in effect operates to depoliticize the dispossessed (Fassin 2012; Barnett 2013).

Given this power structure, can sharing ownership over the research process or recognizing power relations—or any other principle of participatory action research—really flatten or upend what so many consider to be an inherently unequal system? Is there something about community-based participatory research that creates space for forms of resistance, even as these research projects are funded by donors that are very much enmeshed in the Global North humanitarian logics of intervention? Do such approaches embrace and engage with critiques of the kind of power involved in forging neoliberal subjectivities? Or beneath the sheen of collaboration, might we find in participatory research practices the unspoken forms of oppression and political struggle that have been so characteristic of Northern humanitarianism?

Rather than offering an analysis that advocates for one form of intervention over another, I suggest, in keeping with this book's central assertions, that humanitarianism as a logic of order and a site of possibility is made and remade in the borderscape in ways that are not isolated from other forms of governance. This means seeing humanitarian aid workers and the discourses that guide them as part of a broader assemblage of forces, intentions, histories, agendas, narratives, practices, and policies that operate relationally, through which subjects are constituted and through which subjects constitute the social space around them (Deleuze and Guattari 1987). This assemblage includes elements associated with NGOs, but also the experience of precarious labor and dispossession with which many migrants continue to grapple. To focus on NGO work as a space of meaning-making, then, is to offer an analysis of how border humanitarianism, as a spatially situated technology of governance, is itself a lived experience that social actors performatively reproduce through discourse and interaction—a phenomenological approach that builds off of what Hilhorst (2003) termed "NGO-ing." In such spaces discourse matters, but so does positionality; we cannot isolate microsocial practices from the matrices of social hierarchy and the diversity of lived experience that inform how actors make sense of the world around them. As many diverse actors came together to carry out this piece of humanitarian research, we engaged in what Horst (2006) calls "dialogical knowledge creation," where a variety of perspectives and ways of knowing the world collide in a power-laden social field. Recognizing this, I center the voices of the individuals who were engaged in the work of co-producing knowledge and focus on the positionalities of actors involved in this action research project, considering our standpoint in relation to the context and to one another, and in consideration of how each of us relate to systems of privilege and oppression (Merriam et al. 2001; Ryan 2015).

Border Stories

The co-researchers and I fit into the context of border humanitarianism in unique ways, with different positions in the hierarchy of aid work, vastly different life experiences and perspectives, and different ways of identifying in terms of privilege and oppression along social axes of gender, ethnicity, and nationality. This includes the ubiquitous tendency in humanitarian practice to divide actors along global and local lines, with the former referring to technical expertise, often based out of NGO headquarters in the Global North, and the latter referring to governments and communities hosting displaced populations, the people directly and adversely affected by disaster and conflict (Richey 2018; Attanapola et al. 2013; Morse and McNamara 2006). While scholars have rightly critiqued these unrooted geographic categories that are in fact surrogates for geopolitical positions often situated along North-South lines (e.g., Roepstorff 2020; Mac Ginty 2015), the aid industry continues to be framed in that way and has in recent years pushed forward campaigns for "localization" in a display of rebalancing power relations (Al-Abdeh and Patel 2019). As the following pages illustrate, the co-researchers and I certainly had to navigate these categories, but also important here is how the notion of "local" can often, in humanitarian spaces, supersede and erase other boundaries that may be more significant but that are less visible to Northern actors holding management positions.[1]

For example, in our group's assessment team, Ko Reh, who identifies as Karenni and who was in her mid-twenties when we started to work together, was relatively new to humanitarian labor in Mae Sot, having previously lived and worked in one of the refugee camps in Mae Hong Son

---

1. One of the reasons for this is the often extreme pay difference between staff considered "global" or "expatriate" and those who are "local," a trend that has been well documented (e.g., Carr et al. 2010). As Carr and colleagues show, the economic inequality imposed on these categories of humanitarian workers can have a detrimental impact on program implementation.

Province further north along the Thai-Burmese border. However, because she was a "local" staffer with the Northern NGO funding this project, in our assessment she found herself in a leadership role over participants from migrant-led organizations. This put her in a difficult position. As she put it when I spoke with her six months after the project ended: "At that time, I was not very familiar with those kinds of assessments, but I just jumped in and facilitated trainings and was then running interviews. Huh? What?" She was surprised and discomforted to be in that position relative to others in the group who had more experience doing action research. Assumptions about Ko Reh's "local" status might have led the NGO to overlook her relative lack of experience and her relative outsider status in a network of border-based activists and service providers compared with other co-researchers. At the same time, Ko Reh's position with an "international" NGO and her English-language proficiency constituted a level of social power in this space.

The deployment of social categories like "international," "global," and "local" in this context is important for subtle articulations of power, as the following pages show. De-centering these categories means looking critically at how humanitarian organizations use them, and it also means de-centering the Global North as a reference point. It means paying attention to how status and knowledge are situated relationally among co-researchers, who are themselves embedded within the organizational and operational assemblages that constitute humanitarianism. This reflects what Mac Ginty (2015) calls a "critical localism" that privileges a post-territorial recognition of the fact that populations are mobile and that connections between spaces and people are dynamic and relational.

In my conversations with co-researchers, I asked them to share stories with me about their childhoods and how they ended up in Mae Sot. Since this place is defined by transience for many forced migrants coming from Myanmar, or from elsewhere on the border, I was interested in learning more about why my collaborators had chosen to live and work in this city, what their relationship to it was, and how their past was linked to their perception and approach to work on gender violence. The experiences co-researchers shared varied widely and depended on which part of Myanmar or Thailand they came from and the time period in which they grew up. Together, they provide an image of positionalities that are intertwined with dispossession and structural violence, ethnic identity, and an ethics of social activism, including aspirations of freedom for the Burmese migrant population. To begin, Naw Klo, who identifies as S'gaw Karen, is in her early fifties and works on migrant access to healthcare. She left her home in the early 1980s and was essentially mobile for twenty years:

> My father worked in construction and my mother was a teacher. They had to pay to support the family and there was never enough. They borrowed money, and after the debt increased they couldn't pay it so they moved all our family to Mae Thawar village and we stayed there. But then, because of the fighting—the Burmese army was fighting with the KNU—we moved to Waw Lay. Then there was fighting near Waw Lay, so we went to Maw Ku, and then I moved with my husband and my children to Baw Noh camp.

The debt that Naw Klo's family faced continues to be common in southeastern Myanmar, particularly in those areas affected by conflict; it is a result of the heavy taxes imposed on the population by the Burmese military and other armed groups and spiraling inflation (Brenner 2019). Moving to Mae Thawar in Hlaingbwe Township under the KNU's control provided some reprieve initially, but during the 1980s Naw Klo and her family were increasingly caught in the fighting between the Tatmadaw and the Karen National Liberation Army. Like many thousands of Karen displaced from their villages, Naw Klo fled to Waw Lay, in the border area across from Phob Phra district, where she and her family could quickly escape to Thailand if the situation became dangerous. Impermanent makeshift settlements dotted both sides of the border, informal camps to house these forced migrants under the authority of the KNU. For more than a decade, families moved back and forth across the border, uprooted during most dry seasons when the Tatmadaw launched their offensives against the KNLA. Amid these cycles of displacement, Naw Klo married and settled temporarily in Baw Noh camp in Thailand. Her unsettlement continued, however, when the Democratic Karen Buddhist Army burned that camp in 1995, forcing her to move again to Mae La, the largest camp on the Thai-Burmese border. Naw Klo's words reflect the shared experiences of many ethnic Karen migrants along the border where mobility and displacement are enmeshed with the course of a life, including childhood and marriage.

Even for those not directly uprooted by war, political violence, and militarism, the impossibility of making ends meet was a common experience. Ko Reh was in her mid-twenties when we first started working together for the same Northern NGO. She grew up in Loikaw Township in Karenni state:

> I lived there until I finished high school. We grew up in a small, poor section of the Township. In Loikaw, I stayed with my relatives and in the boarding house, mostly because my family—my mother, my father— were working in Thailand as migrants and I was alone. After high school, I left for Thailand.

Ko Reh's stay in a boarding house, a kind of youth dormitory, was a consequence of her relatives' precarious situation in Karenni state while her parents were in Thailand. This period, she explained, was challenging and formative. Ko Reh received a bilingual education in Karenni and English and studied Christianity as well as the political history of the Karenni struggle for self-determination, a course of study not available for those attending schools under the state's educational system. Nevertheless, she was separated from her parents and had to figure out how to cope on her own.

Another co-researcher, Soe Soe Mya, also told how her pursuit of an education changed in light of her family's stability. In her early thirties at the time of my interview with her, Soe Soe Mya identified as Bamar and worked with a labor-rights, migrant-led, border-based organization for several years. She told me a little of what it was like to grow up with four siblings in a rural area in Pago:

> We didn't have rice fields and my parents did not have a regular income. My father did day labor, so he would get paid when he was called, but on the days he didn't get a call, he wouldn't get paid. When I was in high school, I had to start working. I worked in the rice paddy and picking beans. I made only 300 kyat [US $0.31] per day. Sometimes 250 kyat. I couldn't help my family, and that's the reason I am here.

In addition to describing conditions of extreme poverty, both Soe Soe Mya and Ko Reh note that migration disrupted, or at least impacted, their education, an experience shared by many. Soe Soe Mya left school to work, and ultimately to move to Thailand, where she found employment in a garment factory. Ko Reh was able to finish high school in her country but had to deal with living in a boarding house and being isolated from her parents, who were working in Thailand to support their family.

Soe Soe Mya's experience of growing up in a family struggling to survive in rural lower Myanmar is similar to the challenge faced by millions of Burmese, including many of the hundreds of thousands who left Myanmar to find work in Thailand. Soe Soe Mya grew up in a Myanmar (still Burma at the time) afflicted by the crippling economic disaster of the thirty years of dictatorship and mismanagement by Ne Win's "Burmese Way to Socialism." Government financial decisions eradicated people's savings overnight.[2] It was an era marked by almost complete public dependence on black markets. She describes her situation as particularly difficult because her family was poor even relative to others in her village who did not have much; her family was landless and dependent on irregular day wages or sales from lottery tickets. After dropping out of school, and faced with the prospect of earning less than 50 cents per day working as a farm hand on rice fields, Soe Soe Mya decided to join the ranks of the industrial workforce just starting in Mae Sot, where she could earn more than ten times as much (though still far below Thailand's minimum wage).

Other accounts of forced migrants living and working along the Thai-Burmese border often echo these experiences. They present a complex and overlapping set of reasons for families to leave their homeland to seek refuge and opportunity in Thailand, including war and militarism, family reunification, and livelihood (Saltsman 2011). Having themselves come from a background of multilayered dispossession, most co-researchers

---

2. For example, in 1963 Ne Win decreed that 50-and 100-kyat notes were no longer legal tender. In 1987 he acted on the advice of an astrologer and eliminated many of the larger kyat notes. Both acts resulted in the sudden loss of savings for much of the public (see Matthews 2006).

quickly empathized with the dynamics of family separation, isolation, uprootedness, and scarcity that were so common among the migrant communities we assessed. It was not hard for them to imagine the stress and trauma that individuals and families were dealing with.

When co-researchers discussed their upbringing or their early years in Thailand, it became clear that on top of their experiences of displacement and movement they sometimes had multiple encounters with violence. For co-researchers who began their time in Mae Sot or elsewhere in Thailand performing labor-intensive low-wage work, exploitation and employer abuses were almost a given. Soe Soe Mya arrived in 1999, getting a job in a garment factory. She changed her employment four times due to workplace conditions: "First I worked in Champion factory. After Champion, Ban Song Khwae, then Mae Pa, then Ban Nuer behind Tesco Lotus." As we saw with Pyaung Gyi Win—Baldy's land—in Phob Phra, Soe Soe Mya's references to factory names vary between the official name, such as Champion, and the spatial moniker. Ban Nuer and Mae Pa refer to subdistricts and neighborhoods in the border area; for migrants, precarious labor is inscribed into the geography of Mae Sot. Soe Soe Mya's experience as a factory worker in Mae Sot resonates with the stories told by many migrants. In Mae Sot, garment factories open and close with regularity as mobile capital deploys, shifts, and redeploys rapidly. It is not uncommon for factories in Mae Sot to shut their doors overnight to cut losses during a dearth in orders, leaving workers surprised the next day, without wages from the previous month(s), and with little recourse to justice (Zaw Aung 2010; Campbell 2018a). When workers face problems at one factory, such as closure or a failure to pay wages (or a host of other issues), they must often scramble to find a job at another factory that happens to be expanding its workforce. For six years, Soe Soe Mya worked the line at garment and knitting factories. Each of the factories she mentions are large producers. The buildings are concrete structures with slats in place of windows and high ceilings and fans for ventilation; adjacent are the worker dormitories. Workers remain within a high-walled compound except for their monthly or weekly day off (depending on the factory). At least two of the factories where she worked—Champions and Ban Nuer—were also sites of large-scale worker protests and strikes (Campbell 2013).

As she suggests, Soe Soe Mya was mobilized by the action at Ban Nuer. When her employer refused to pay workers their wages, "we held a demonstration; Yaung Chi Oo helped us to negotiate and solve our problem," referring to a labor-rights organization that does outreach and training and supports workers to take collective action. She continued:

> While in the process of solving the problem, in 2005 I was able to attend the BLC [Burma Lawyer's Council] trainings. After the trainings, I was selected as their volunteer. Then they observed my attitude for one week, and after one week I became staff. When I started with BLC, my role was office assistant, and from office work I eventually moved to legal aid.

For Soe Soe Mya, the exploitation she faced at the garment factory in Ban Nuer precipitated her transition from an assembly-line worker to staff member at a border-based, migrant-led organization. It was her involvement in the protest there that connected her to the Yaung Chi Oo Worker's Association, a proxy for a garment workers' union on the border, and the legal-aid group Burma Lawyer's Council, both of which work together to organize workers and train them on topics such as labor rights and human rights. She had shown herself to be particularly capable, and perhaps her interests aligned with the work of these organizations; among all the workers on strike, she was one of only a few who became volunteers. She remained with BLC for nearly ten years, until the organization closed its office due to a lack of funding, and then she worked with Yaung Chi Oo as legal staff and helped to manage a safe house for workers who faced workplace abuse. Soe Soe Mya's narrative conveys a story of workplace abuse but also struggle, a turn to activism, and recruitment by a migrant-led, community-based organization. Also noteworthy is that BLC was a home for Soe Soe Mya, nurturing her professional and personal development, a common activity of border-based humanitarian organizations.

Co-researchers dealt with other kinds of violence in the worker dormitories, labor camps, urban neighborhoods, and informal settlements in which they lived. The activist Ko Min Thu's story in chapter 3 is illustrative of this. While doing construction day labor in the late 1990s, the violence he witnessed in his Mae Sot neighborhood—drug trafficking, neglected children, child mortality—ultimately pushed him to action. He explained:

> When I saw those problems, I thought, "These children are Bamar. One day they will become adults. Then they will go back to their country. If these kinds of children from different areas go back, there will be many bad people." Then what came to my mind was that I must do something about this. I discussed with the adults. I asked if it would be a good idea to do some education for the children. They said it would be. I arrived here in 1997, and since 1999 I have been a teacher. We worked for our own income and we also taught the children. Me and one of my friends. We took turns. When he taught, I went out to work. With the income we made we bought the teaching materials needed. As for our daily food, the thirty households took responsibility to feed us. Our own income was used for teaching.

Ko Min Thu stresses the grassroots nature of his transformation from migrant worker to organizer and service provider, which, as we saw in the previous chapter, may have been fueled by the idea of repairing the frayed social cohesion of displaced Burmese migrants in Thailand. Seeing immense social need, he organized the neighboring households, developed a plan to provide the neighborhood children with education and childcare, and sacrificed his own well-being by donating his now part-time earnings to the school and living off his neighbors. Indeed, a service-provision consciousness rooted in immediate problem-solving has been a consistent theme in Min Thu's narrative of humanitarianism on the Thai-Burmese border. Importantly, he saw the connections between social problems in the worker settlement, ethnic identity, and possible negative implications for a future with "many bad people" in Myanmar, as he put it. This way of thinking about ethnicity and national identity informed co-researchers' positionality on the border, even if it was often left unspoken as an underlying sentiment. In the next two chapters I will pick up the thread of how the response to violence and a sense of national identity in exile are linked.

While Ko Min Thu's organizer identity arose explicitly in response to the social problems he witnessed and the need for community order and protection, others had to find ways to navigate their own individual encounters with abusive circumstances. Let us return now to Naw Klo's story. She started working in the Médecins Sans Frontières health clinic at her first refugee camp in Thailand. "The clinic had KNU nurses, but they could not speak English," she remembered. The head nurse implored Naw Klo, who could speak some English, to get involved. At first, she said, "I was very shy to speak, but besides me there was no one. They were going inside Karen State to help, so I saw that it was really necessary to work in our community." Starting as a translator, she quickly gained knowledge and experience, becoming a paraprofessional healthcare worker before long, and eventually a midwife. But when the Democratic Karen Buddhist Army (DKBA) attacked and burned the Baw Noh camp, her family had to flee and she had her own domestic problems:

> In 1995 we moved to Mae La camp, where I was the head midwife for the SMRU health clinic.[3] And right from the beginning, my husband drank more and more. After coming home, he'd be violent. This shocked the children. At first he didn't beat me. His mother had said, "Don't beat your family," so he always kept this in mind. But the way he would talk! It was very, very painful for me. Like emotional violence. Yes! So sometimes I took some Promethazine or the Chlorphenamine tablets to sleep, and sometimes—well, not during pregnancy—I also drank Regency [alcohol] and I slept. A whole bottle! Like I wanted to commit suicide. I was thinking about religion and also ethnicity. Most of the women, normally if asked [about domestic violence], they cannot answer, they don't dare answer, but sometimes I share my experience and then after that they also speak out.

Naw Klo's story of community work is interwoven with her experiences of abuse and cycles of displacement. Her time in the camp crystallized her awareness of a responsibility to help her "community" of displaced Karen people, and so she joined the international NGO Médecins Sans

3. SMRU stands for the Shoklo Malaria Research Unit, a field station of the faculty of Tropical Medicine, Mahidol University, Bangkok, Thailand. As Naw Klo indicates, SMRU serves as a source of healthcare for Burmese displaced on both sides of the Thai-Burmese border.

Frontières, eventually becoming the head midwife in charge of labor and delivery for that health facility in the camp. Her husband's drinking and abuse worsened after the DKBA attacked and burned Baw Noh camp and they were forced to flee to Mae La camp—displacement layered on and resonating with cycles of domestic violence. Naw Klo's story of abuse explicitly conveys her desperation, how close she was to killing herself with sleeping pills and alcohol. Courageously, she continued working as a midwife despite the horror she faced at home and she survived. Her story also touches briefly on religion and ethnic identity as social institutions that structured her sense of opportunities and constraints, including the stigma around divorce in her strictly religious Baptist S'gaw Karen community. Such factors are bound up in Naw Klo's ideas about gender and gender violence, about social expectations for women, and about potential solutions for survivors. At the same time, in referring to her husband's abuse as emotional violence, she exhibited a level of intellectual engagement with concepts to analyze and categorize gender violence.

During my interview I had not asked Naw Klo about her experience with violence, but she chose to share this with me. In fact, it was not the first time that I heard her describe this part of her life; the previous year she had stood up in front of a workshop on domestic violence and told her story. When she told me that most women don't dare answer questions put to them about domestic violence but that they speak out after she shares her own experience, this implied an informal role as a kind of counselor and caseworker alongside midwifery. She uses narrative as a tactic to inspire strength in other women who have experienced abuse, and then she works with women who express the need for resources to help them seek medical attention, safety, shelter, justice, or any other solution. Though such interventions are not part of her everyday duties as a health worker and trainer, Naw Klo fulfills the role of counselor and caseworker informally: "Even when I give trainings, it doesn't stop there. They always communicate with me if they have a problem. They call me at night." Through her formal training and activities, she expands her network and makes herself available to provide assistance. She left me wondering if this work, done on the side of her work as a trainer for the Northern NGO, was in fact a priority for her over the kinds of health-oriented activities she was actually hired for. This layering of informal case management and formal health-program assistance is somewhat similar to Ma Sandi's role discussed at the start of chapter 1.

Naw Klo revealed that she arrived at her agenda for social change through her years of health work and her particular strategy of turning her own abuse into finding ways to care for others. She identifies herself as a different kind of organizer than Ko Min Thu and Soe Soe Mya. While Ko Min Thu's development as an organizer arose explicitly out of a need for social order and protection, Naw Klo became a midwife with a northern NGO but then built on that network, using her knowledge of healthcare and her own traumatic experiences as a resource to informally counsel and organize response services for victims of violence. However, Naw Klo's organizing work had to be on the side because, while there are a number of women's protection organizations in Mae Sot, her official work does not encompass such activities, and the women's protection organizations do not recognize her autodidactic caseworker skills as valid. These skills were gained during waves of displacement and her own efforts to make meaning out of the violence inflicted on her and act on that meaning. Her experiences caring for others constitutes a form of situated knowledge that takes constraints upon agency and works them into opportunities for social and personal healing.

These three co-researchers—Naw Klo, Soe Soe Mya, and Ko Min Thu—narrate distinct accounts of displacement and violence. Their stories are linked to political persecution, years of conflict, economic destitution, dictatorship, domestic and sexual violence, and workplace exploitation. They convey different avenues for transitioning to activist, organizer, and service provider. Other co-researchers shared their memories of growing up on both sides of the border, or of being raised as the son of the director of a migrant-led health organization, or of going through the Thai school system and negotiating both Karen and Thai identities, to name but a few experiences. Most co-researchers pointed to inflection points where exposure to or awareness of interpersonal or structural violence propelled them into service or activist work.

While this means that co-researchers were able to ground their approach to work in migrant communities in their own lived experience, knowledge acquisition and the constant evolution of one's positionality always involves multiple layers of perception and learning that shift through time and space. Contrary to the trends in humanitarian programming and scholarly research, shared experiences like these do not necessarily translate to what are labeled "insider" or "local" status. Co-researchers for this project were representative of the broader migrant population in this area and at the same time different; there was a border between them and the rest to the extent that as service providers they were influenced and guided by NGO or social-movement discourse and training. This distance enables co-researchers to maintain an analytical eye, but at the same time it may lead to agendas not fully rooted in the needs and interests of the diverse migrant populations in and around Mae Sot. As intermediaries (Merry 2006), they are migrants themselves, and yet they have stepped away from the everyday precarity in which they once found themselves, and in which the majority of Burmese on the border still live and work, and into the safe space of programmatic analysis, budgeting, the allocation of limited resources, and organizational thinking. To the extent that their organizations—or the northern NGO funding the project—maintained an expectation that co-researchers be both representatives of "migrant communities" and semi-detached or objective staffers, my collaborators found themselves straddling a socially constructed and performatively reproduced insider/outsider divide, a challenging place for them to be situated. Indeed, Merry (2006) reminds us that being cast (or casting oneself) as an intermediary is fraught with ambivalence, given the expectation of loyalty to the aid industry and the potential for mistrust from the broader migrant population. I am especially interested in how our collaborative project affords a lens for seeing that ambivalence and tension and may contribute to certain ways of seeing and knowing Burmese migrants and gender violence.

Policing Participation

Given my own background, points of privilege, assumptions, and agenda, I of course had a significant impact on how our group performatively reproduced social hierarchy, both within our collaboration and among the broader population of Burmese migrants. I approached our collaboration with an agenda rooted in the academic principles of Participatory Action Research—namely, an aim to co-produce the "participatory contact zone" where different ways of seeing the world can converge over a shared commitment to human rights and the specific goals of our gender-violence assessment. To do this requires some level of democratic praxis in the research space and a clear consensus privileging the knowledge and voices of those with lived experience of the social problems and injustices that brought us together. Despite these aspirations, the contradictions of my own position exerted a kind of force, complicating things. As a program coordinator for the NGO funding this project, where I leveraged my power in this project was often my choice, though I also reported to my superiors. Aware of the tension between my official job duties, which privileged efficiency over participation, and my own goals for the gender-violence collaborative assessment, I placed myself in the position of being a different kind of intermediary than what Merry (2006) suggests above. While my superiors saw me as an outsider and a representative of global knowledge who could "speak their language," I used the power of my autonomy to stretch out the gender-based violence assessment far beyond what the NGO had anticipated in its proposal to our Global North donor. I had to articulate the details of the project to managers and donors in the language of humanitarian reporting, but in an effort to create space for co-researchers and I to have adequate time to do the work, I also used this language to shelter our project from my managers' inquisitiveness and their commitment to short-term gains. In so doing, I may have "bought time" for a more participatory project, but I simultaneously contributed to a discourse that located valid knowledge in some idea of the "global," relegating local knowledge to the realm of lived experience, raw data in need of expert analysis, as it were.

Within our research space, during sessions to deliberate our approach to the collaborative assessment, including where we wanted to do research, who we would speak with, and what we wanted to ask them, multiple tensions surfaced across varying perspectives and positions. Sometimes this tension reflected divergent vantage points or different relationships with contacts in migrant settlements. While co-researchers showed cross-ethnic solidarity in their efforts to co-create the project, some tensions around gender arose intergenerationally or along disciplinary lines (e.g., a health worker vs. a social activist or social-work approach to responding to GBV).

I also embodied a set of contradictions. First, I found myself (gently) pushing co-researchers to engage in dialogue; sometimes I was on my own in a "crusade of participation," while others on the team, pressed by time and busy schedules, were ready to forgo discussion and consensus in exchange for speed. I grew self-conscious that, rather than doing my part to create space for democratic praxis, I was at times being a bit of a research autocrat and replicating some of the very same dynamics from which I wished to move away. This was particularly palpable in my discussions with Thai and Karen staff from the Global North NGO who had led research projects before. They had other ideas about what participation meant and were critical of my overly flexible, inductive, and iterative approach.

Second, as a program coordinator my use of professional power cannot be divorced from the other dimensions of my privilege, including my class, race, and gender identities. This is certainly true in contexts of humanitarian intervention that invoke elements of colonial relationships between Northern and Southern actors, most notably an extreme inequality between aid workers from the Global North and those from the refugee community or host country. The extent to which the racial and gendered aspects of my social identity formed barriers with my Burmese, Thai, or American colleagues is important to take into consideration as part of my positionality. I share a brief ethnographic snapshot that illustrates the complexity of these identity attributes in the practice of our assessment, and their connection to our work of producing humanitarian knowledge.

꩜

It was early 2013 and we were four days into a mix of training and dialogue about research methods, gender violence, and humanitarian response in the Thai-Burmese borderlands. Co-researchers, the leadership from their organizations, and Thai, Burmese, and US staff from the Northern humanitarian NGO funding this assessment were all sitting around large, rectangular, cloth-draped tables in the center of a meeting room. A scattering of stained cups, instant-coffee and Ovaltine packet wrappers, and dirty plates were piled on one side—the remnants of meals during short breaks to give us some semblance of relief in the course of so many hours seated in conversation. The co-researchers and I would carry out the everyday aspects of the GBV assessment later; this broader group had come together that day to help us reflect on the conceptual components of the project. We were attempting to communicate in Burmese, English, and Thai. Even though this had become somewhat standard for our group as a way of making sure that we were all on the same page (I could speak Thai but not Burmese; Karen participants were fluent in Burmese), interpretation and translation themselves constitute a "process of meaning construction" (Spivak 1993, 177). The words we used and our choice of vocabulary were, to some degree, sites of struggle, domination, or resistance among different ways of knowing and different social positions (Alarcón 1989, 62). As was the case in that meeting, and throughout the project, much of the translation work was between divergent ways of seeing and knowing, this in addition to the need to literally translate between the multiple languages represented in our group.

As was common in our dialogues, conversation that day moved non-linearly; different group members shared their perspectives through anecdotes as we circled toward the question of how to conceptualize and discuss gender violence. San, a woman in her forties from Thailand who identified as ethnically Karen, jumped in and described a case she had encountered the day before. In a community near Kyuwe Kyan, she explained, she had received a call about a toddler whose parents had left him with an older woman in the neighborhood while they went to find work in Bangkok. When others in the neighborhood informed San that the older woman was abusing the child, she made the decision to remove the boy and place him with caretakers affiliated with the neighborhood mosque. San's story implicitly asked, Might we consider stories like this examples of social problems related to gender violence? Subsequently, Naw Klo pointed to the prevalence of "unwanted pregnancies" on the border, and Hla Gay, a Karen woman with a background in reproductive health, stressed the importance of including alcohol and drug consumption in an analysis of gender-based violence. Moving around in this way, co-researchers and other meeting participants added dimensions to the group's focus on gender violence, deepening our knowledge of what they had witnessed in the borderlands and thereby piecing together ideas of how we might conceptualize gender violence or situate it among other manifestations of social suffering.

However, with each story or contribution, I could see that Rachel, a US aid worker who specialized in violence against women, was getting increasingly irritated. Finally she spoke up with an exasperated smile. She quickly shut down the idea that alcohol was a cause of violence and she offered a definition of gender-based violence that paraphrased the World Health Organization's definition of violence against women.[4] The room fell silent. As Rachel looked to me, the other Global North person (and the other white person) in the room, for backup, I silently fumed and scrambled to figure out how to respond. I tried to move the conversation along, tabling for the time being what had suddenly been cast as oppositional viewpoints in tension, and I made some comment about the importance of multiple perspectives, to which Rachel responded with an expression of incredulity. Later that day I kicked myself for not handling the situation better.

What bothered me in that moment was not the fact that Rachel had brought up WHO definitions, which was a valuable piece of information for the group to discuss. Indeed, this resonated with the views of some co-researchers and meeting participants. Rather, I was annoyed that her words, spoken with the authority of the "global voice," had stifled deliberation in that moment, and had perhaps left some in the room with the sense that they had just been told their ideas were wrong. This was a missed opportunity to dig into what might have been emergent meanings and understandings of the complex and multifaceted ways that violence materializes for migrants here. I felt that Rachel had presented her ideas not as her own but as *the* official way of conceptualizing gender violence, giving the impression that it was the only correct way to approach this complicated topic. Indeed, an approach to gender violence rooted

---

4. WHO 1993 "UN Declaration on the Elimination of Violence against Women" refers to violence against women as "any act of gender-based violence that results in, or is likely to result in, physical, sexual, or mental harm or suffering to women, including threats of such acts, coercion, or arbitrary deprivation of liberty, whether occurring in public or in private life."

in transnational definitions tends to privilege consideration of individual encounters with abuse on the interpersonal level over approaches that recognize the contingent relationship between structural oppression and individual experience (Ticktin 2011a).

I grew anxious in that moment, thinking about how this interaction might impact the group's efforts to produce a shared approach where many ways of seeing and knowing could coexist. This encounter reflected "the power of discourse to produce effects through reiteration," wherein that discourse is situated in a matrix of social hierarchies (Butler 1993, 20). But this was far from the first time participants had been in a meeting where a Global North aid worker had spoken over them with an air of expertise. I had witnessed this myself many times, and have probably unwittingly been that aid worker at some point too. Indeed, as part of the UN's "localization" commitment in 2016, the former UN Secretary General Ban Ki Moon reiterated that "international partners" need to provide "expertise and good practice and add capacity and capability" to "local partners" (UN 2016). From the humanitarian industry's perspective, asserting expert knowledge is part of what it means to engage in "localization."

At the same time, I would argue that the co-researchers' response to Rachel with a silence that neither affirmed nor confronted her words represented, at least in that moment, a form of everyday resistance through the appearance of passivity, as if Rachel's words had just washed over them and flowed right out of the room (Scott 1985). How the encounter ultimately impacted the ways our collectivity perceived and deployed ideas of gender-based violence is impossible to discern. Nevertheless, the exchange is a useful example of how multiple positionalities collided over questions of knowledge production. And as the subsequent section shows, we should analyze this encounter in the context of NGO professionalization and imbalanced knowledge politics. Also left unspoken were the gendered politics of my professional relationship with Rachel and the ways in which my lack of support for her contribution in that exchange could have tapped into broader—and quite valid—concerns among the Violence Against Women team that other units in the organization disregarded their input, a sign of their marginalized position within this prominent and transnational NGO.

Such moments represent my attempts to police and manage the collaborative process to create space for co-researcher knowledges to emerge and comingle. At best, these partial attempts were not without their limitations. However, thinking of this exchange as one among so many interactions in border-based humanitarian intervention, where ways of knowing and seeing meet one another in an unequal playing field, it becomes possible to see how collaborative research and action can, in their own right, produce knowledge about violence and what it means to be displaced. As I show, such moments cannot be unyoked from how actors make meaning of the social space of the borderscape. Moments like this in our project discussions reflected our own performativity—witting and unwitting—in the production of gendered border subjects and understandings of gender violence itself.

Translating Violence, Making Meaning

This ethnographic snapshot reveals the messiness of collaboration when it comes to knowledge production. It illustrates the ways that different perspectives and positionalities encounter one another and collide in the space of co-creation. However, when we add other moments of dialogue from this project to the analysis we begin to get a clearer sense of the politics of knowledge production regarding gender violence and humanitarian aid in the borderlands. A dialogue at the conclusion of the assessment when co-researchers and their senior colleagues discussed our findings and identified next steps elucidated some of the ways we had come to "know" the migrant population. What our group called the "Interpretive Focus Group" (IFG) discussion (borrowing the term from Dodson et al. 2007) took place in June 2013. It was an opportunity for co-researchers to present their findings and discuss the challenges we faced and the tactics used to navigate them. The group then interpreted the meaning of the study's findings together. In the excerpt below, participants in this interpretive dialogue reflected on the prevalence of gender-based violence in the settlements and neighborhoods where they conducted research:

SU HLAING: One factor is discrimination by employers. For example, Burmese are discriminated against and they sometimes do not get paid or they get paid later than other employees. As well, there are family problems. For example, a husband went to work in Bangkok and left his wife and kids. He did not contact or support his family. Some women were pregnant and their boyfriends did not marry them, so they had to get an abortion. Do other people have opinions?

SAN: Actually there are many problems in kilometer 42. We did not ask specific questions. We did not know the real issues, so when we asked, we just asked generally. If we took the time and sat together and talked with them, they would start talking about men drinking alcohol and then continue on from there . . .

SOE SOE MYA: When we went to interview a person, she would not talk on behalf of her community. She would just say that nothing happened with her marriage, and that is all she'd say. If she talked on behalf of her community, there would be a lot of issues.

SU HLAING: When we asked a question, some talked about issues in their environment, whereas a few would reply that nothing happened. But one or two people mentioned everything, all the individual cases. They also shared their experiences and feelings.

HSER DEE: When we went to kilometer 48, we arrived at a funeral house where men were gambling upstairs and women were gambling downstairs. There may be many houses like that. If there is a lot of gambling, a lot of violence will also exist.

SOE SOE MYA: When we observed 42, we saw that this Phob Phra community was completely controlled by community leaders. So workers cannot go out much and they do not have many problems. But in Kok Kwai, there is no control, so there are more problems.

This excerpt is telling. San and Soe Soe Mya both reported challenges in approaching sensitive topics related to gender violence, lamenting the structure of our assessment. While co-researchers like these two individuals generally ran semi-structured interviews and focus-group discussions with flexibility, letting participants to some extent guide the conversation, a more familiar setting—perhaps one without the inherent formality of an interview—would have led to a greater level of comfort among participants. Particularly important here are how this focus group of co-researchers and other migrant activists tended to analyze gender violence. They do not appear to limit their interpretation of our assessment's findings to the kinds of dominant ideas rooted in Global North humanitarianism that Rachel offered. Hser Dee, a Karen woman who worked in a border-based, migrant-led health clinic, affirmed the point about alcohol and also called out gambling as a cause of violence. As well, it was clear that Su Hlaing embedded gender violence in a social field defined by forms of structural and interpersonal violence. She pointed to the relevance of labor precarity, family separation in migration, and unwanted pregnancies. Moreover, Soe Soe Mya posits that reduced freedom among forced migrant workers and greater control by forced-migrant community leaders could actually be linked to a greater perception of safety and fewer incidents of gender violence among those community members. Such an interpretation—which runs somewhat contrary to a transnational human-rights-centered approach that would privilege personal liberties—can only stem from an intimate awareness of how insecure life is for Burmese migrants in the borderlands, especially those without documentation. It also resonates with some of the views we saw in the previous chapter, wherein the threat of GBV was from outside the community, suggesting a demand for security.

Given co-researchers' awareness of how structural and interpersonal violence overlapped in migrants' lives, it is important to revisit Yin Tha Thu's remarks at the start of this chapter. When she said that "violence will always be something that happens outside the home," and as she expressed frustration, was she referring to a limitation in our assessment's methods, to narrowed definitions of gender violence that missed tapping into the lived experience of migrants, or something else? In looking through the dozens of interviews with migrants, it turns out that something more subtle was going on. A pattern emerged at the instance when co-researchers asked participants about violence in their communities. As Yin Tha Thu indicated, participants often answered that this was a nonexistent social problem, but there is more to the story, as the following excerpt from an interview with a forty-year-old woman who has lived in Htone Taung for more than fifteen years suggests:

> INTERVIEWER: How about violence between husband and wife?
>
> PARTICIPANT: Between husband and wife, it does not commonly happen. There is no such violence in this section between women and men.
>
> I: Then in this section, is there any bodily harm occurring between couples?
>
> P: No.
>
> I: How about psychological violence?
>
> P: No.
>
> I: When husband and wife fight, what are they doing?
>
> P: If husband and wife fight, they shout and scold each other.
>
> I: They shout and scold each other. What do they say?
>
> P: They say, "You are what?" "I am what?" "You take a stick, I take a knife."
>
> I: Do they beat each other?
>
> P: Beat, they beat.
>
> I: They beat, they shout.
>
> P: If the women are beaten by men, they shout, they cry.

Aside from the number of observations one can make about this excerpt, I focus here on the interview style and the transformation of a "no" answer to a question about violence to a "yes" answer. At first when the interviewer asks about violence, the participant explains that it "does not commonly happen," as "there is no such violence." But a moment later when the interviewer asks if partners beat each other, the answer is yes. What changed in the interview for the participant to make her decide to discuss the nature of physical and verbal violence between couples in Htone Taung? Did the interviewer's repeated questioning wear down the participant? Or is violence somehow not the same as physical beating?

Consistently in almost every interview when this type of interaction took place, interviewers used the Burmese word *ajanpet mhu*, which literally means "violence." One finds this term in Burmese-language media headlines describing riots and military conflict or attacks. It is also a term commonly used in NGO training on women's rights, human rights, and gender-based violence, but less so in everyday life.[5] It was only when interviewers used the term *yaigt* ("to beat"), that it was possible to achieve understanding during interviews. It is not that participants do not consider what goes on in their neighborhood to be violence. Rather, there appears to be a language barrier between the professional Burmese that interviewers used and the Burmese that participants could understand. This may also be a conceptual barrier, to the extent that *ajanpet mhu* ("violence") is an abstract term, whereas *yaigt* ("beating") is concrete. This gap between the abstract and the concrete is analogous, I suggest, to the difference between the professionalized knowledge of NGO discourse and the everyday knowledge of local community members, a difference that erects borders between communicants. In our collaboration, there are likely many more moments where we iteratively worked to translate the experiences of migrants into data legible for NGO gender work.

Such examples demonstrate the way in which humanitarian assessments are infused with technical terms that can lead to particular understandings. The term "gender-based violence" is itself rooted in academic, social movement, and international human-rights discourse (Merry 2009). In the context of our collaboration, the use of and meanings attributed to "gender-based violence" reflects the emergence of status and difference among our team of researchers (and other experts and advisers that weighed in on our project). As well, our reliance on technical language constituted a barrier between us and the migrant-worker participants who were part of the assessment but had no voice of their own in this discussion. Writing on NGOs and gender programming, Millán (2016) points out that the shift of meaning through translation also works to bring local notions of gender and gender violence in line with "global" conceptions of these terms. Examples like those shared in this chapter are windows into the everyday practice of "NGO-ing" (Hilhorst 2003) wherein social actors navigate and reproduce the pressure to professionalize and privilege "expert" knowledge in development and aid work (see also Lang

---

5. Personal correspondence with Chotayaporn Higashi (August 15, 2014).

2012). The assertion of "expert" or "global" ways of framing violence over descriptions rooted in lived experience is one of the ways the humanitarian industry attributes greater value to perspectives that locate violence in migrant bodies and not in the unjust social structures around them. This complements the tendency for Global North humanitarianism to focus on gender-based violence through a more medicalized lens, as Miriam Ticktin (2011b) has pointed out, referring to perspectives primarily focused on medical and health care for victims. A focus on both individual resiliency and medical care direct attention away from structural forms of violence that might require systemic political solutions.

Excerpts and ethnographic accounts from our collaborative process, subtle as they may sometimes be, are important to analyze because they reveal how different ways of knowing interact in this field of unequal power relations. Beyond that, though, the performative reproduction of knowledge politics in our assessment as well as in other areas of humanitarian intervention can have material consequences for migrants in the borderlands. That is, our gender-violence assessment generated knowledge about how residents of the four sites where we did our assessment talk about and respond to forms of gender violence. Such considerations ultimately factored into our interpretive focus-group discussion about which sites were in need of which kinds of interventions. The group devised a broad list of possible projects, but the majority fall under the umbrella of "gender transformative approaches," which are primarily focused on behavior change and which frequently feature in humanitarian programs (Brush and Miller, 2019). As chapter 6 elaborates, such activities are designed to insinuate particular values around individual and family norms into migrant household life as a way to decrease instances of domestic violence. Indeed, some co-researchers interpreted responses like the one quoted above as a sign of participants' acceptance of violence: "According to their answers, they are used to these problems. They don't report it as a family problem." The assumption that intimate-partner violence is part of the banality of everyday suffering affixes violence to the people and the communities in which they live in a way that speaks less to participants' lived reality and more to the research team's expectations and interpretations. Echoing the critique of humanitarianism above, this assumption also runs the risk of shifting the burden of responsibility for violence solely onto the forced migrants who are already struggling with displacement and multiple forms of insecurity. The circulation of assumptions, values, and definitions in this manner in humanitarian arenas fuels the production and reproduction of "migrant" and "refugee" social categories in the borderlands. As noted earlier, in a place like Mae Sot, where migrants are excluded from so many of the Thai state's social and political institutions, we cannot discount the significance of how transnational or Northern agencies perform the work of sovereignty among the displaced, including political subjectivation.

Humanitarian Knowledges and Border Positionalities

This chapter has pointed out some of the ways that different vantage points relate to making meaning of migrants' experiences with gender violence in the borderlands. Our assessment group consisted of actors that came together at a particular juncture in time and space because of their individual trajectories, their organization's shifting position in a political arena of contested resources and legitimacy, my own agenda and politics, and the arrangement of donors and Northern NGOs to produce a particular kind of knowledge that would facilitate more humanitarian programs. By looking at a sampling of co-researchers' backgrounds and perspectives regarding violence and activism on the border, as well as snapshots from our collaboration, I have shown that knowledge construction in arenas of participation is complex, translocal, and cannot be reduced to local/global configurations. Each co-researcher approached the partnership with an unspoken individual history of dispossession, mobility, violence, activism, and professionalization that informed their approach to the topic. In many ways their life trajectories overlapped with those of the hundreds of migrants with whom we spoke during the work of carrying out our humanitarian assessment of gender-based violence. Their histories, and the years of experience that they accumulated working in migrant neighborhoods, labor camps, factory dormitories, and informal settlements along the border provided them with rich and layered knowledge of the kinds of struggles migrants encounter in their precarious lives here. At times, co-researchers could draw on related life experiences to empathize with the participants, and therefore in many ways they appeared to embody the methodological concept of "peers." And yet at other times our collaboration essentialized participants, and the logic and language of Global North humanitarian intervention clearly impacted how we interpreted migrant experiences and perceptions of violence. Wavering in this way between empathy and reliance on a reductionist lens to analyze experience may in fact be one manifestation of how co-researchers and the rest of us doing this work internalized the tension between what we observed, felt, and knew, on the one hand, and the structured analytical categories of Global North humanitarian logics within which we believed we had to operate, on the other. That is, our ambivalence and navigation between different ways of knowing in this project speak less to a divide between the knowledge of lived experience and expert knowledge and more to the subtle workings of the humanitarian-aid industry as a technology of governance in which particular narratives and logics emerge as more valid or salient than others.

Rather than seeing this tension or ambivalence cast in "local" or "global" terms, I have, building off of Mac Ginty's (2015) "critical localism," proposed an assemblage lens for thinking about how multiple emergent subject-positions, discourses, and practices come together in a social field shot through with power relations. That is, instead of analyzing the narratives, histories, and viewpoints in this chapter as examples of already-existing positions on social hierarchies, I think about how these subjective phenomena are interlocked in what Deleuze (1988, 32) calls "constitutive relations." How actors come together, the ways they interact and make meaning in their social space, how they perceive and engage with overlapping technologies of governance are all part of an assemblage of emergent agency and political subjectivity that structures and reproduces material conditions for migrants as well as others (Ghoddousi and Page 2020). Co-researchers' ways of describing their backgrounds, and their affective interpretations and actions, illustrate how dispossession, violence, precarious labor, and ideas around identity, ethnicity, and social change were all key forces informing the way they see and engage with the social space and relationships that surround them.

This includes the way co-researchers related to and were part of the practice of humanitarian research, and how that practice, as a microcosm of the broader aid industry, reflects a form of power in the borderscape. As this chapter shows, it is possible to tease out the overt and subtle ways in which NGO discourse about gender and violence insinuates itself as a materialization of hegemonic Global North power to translate and structure how we see and analyze targets of humanitarian aid. In this chapter, I have highlighted three examples of how humanitarianism and its logics are performatively reproduced and asserted: (1) my own efforts to render the work of our assessment legible for donors and NGO supervisors, (2) Rachel's intervention in our planning dialogues and my policing of participation, and (3) co-researchers' reliance on a professionalized and abstracted lexicon for discussing violence with migrant respondents. Together, these reflect a form of power over whose knowledge counts as valid and how such knowledge is represented. The assertion of social hierarchy in this way constitutes the "epistemic violence" that is endemic in institutional research (Castro-Gomez and Martin 2002) and is "essential to projects of rule and a site of rule itself in the form of epistemic governance" (Janes 2016, 77). In this way, we can start to identify humanitarian research projects like this as one form of order-making in migrants' lives in the borderlands, alongside others discussed elsewhere in this book. Amid migrants' various efforts to find safety and security, this mode of governance operates in part by reflecting particular images of what it means to be displaced and vulnerable back to migrants in precarious positions. This, in turn, opens certain avenues to mitigate violence, while closing others.

An assemblage lens to focus on the politics of knowledge production in humanitarian aid work reminds us to consider the relationality of space and social actors. In offering a conceptual framework that centers the idea that space and subjectivity are mutually constitutive, this book enables a critique of Global North humanitarian logics while also providing for a deeper understanding of how different actors in the borderlands make meaning of their experiences and arrive at vastly different interpretations of displacement and violence. Instead of thinking about precarious migrants, employers, landlords, and aid workers as social actors *in* a border space where violence is happening, I suggest a more topological approach that considers these actors, their subjectivities, and the space they inhabit

as intertwined in the iterative work of performatively producing and reproducing the borderscape (Paasi 2011). This allows us to move away from an
analysis rooted in assumptions of unchanging social categories in static
spaces, like "local" and "global." Put another way, rather than envisioning
an already-existing reality of migrant experiences and perceptions of violence to be captured through our research, I am arguing that our research
actively produced and affirmed ways of knowing and acting on violence
in migrant communities by attributing certain meanings instead of others. In the Thai-Burmese borderscape, then, positionalities are emergent
and constitutive of the border itself, situated in histories of coloniality and
the experiences of displacement, refuge, and precarious labor. They are
part of the performative enactment of a social space defined as violent in
certain ways and not in others.

5

Make Big Problems Small and Small Problems Disappear

The Adjudication

My distinct feeling at this moment is that we are not supposed to be where we are. Against the front door of a two-story concrete townhouse, 5 meters from a bustling street in Mae Sot, three elderly men sit behind a desk. They face a crying woman and a man we assume to be her partner, who is soothing a toddler in his arms. I was with P'Kind, a Karen woman who worked with me as a research assistant in 2014. We were five minutes early for our meeting with the People's Volunteer Association (PVA). A young Burmese staffer greeted us quietly, not wanting to disturb the proceedings, and before we could suggest that we come back later, he directed us to a bench to the left of the desk and then turned and disappeared into the building to find Maung Law, the organization's public liaison. We were stuck.

Behind the desk signs distinguish this space as official and transnational. We see a "no unauthorized entrance" sign in Thai and Burmese, a stamped letter from the Islamic Committee of Tak Province granting this community-based organization the power to mediate social conflict, a photograph of the Thai king, and a poster of Shephard Fairey's depiction of Aung San Suu Kyi with an expression of benevolent authority.

P'Kind and I sit at a right angle to the proceeding, witnesses to a very intimate discussion. Speaking softly in Burmese, the men behind the desk issue a judgment to the couple. They cannot accept the woman's explanation that she was defending herself and declare that she is guilty of physically abusing her husband. One of the adjudicators produces a handwritten promissory note for her to sign saying that she will not act out in this way again. As soon as she signs the paper, one of the men files it in a large binder of similarly handwritten pages, and the adjudication is done; the men disperse with barely a word—one climbs onto his motorbike and drives off. Volunteers gather and move the desk to the side, and the space of authority dissipates, leaving only the front door of the office and the signs on the wall reminding us that the PVA resolves disputes.

This temporary assembly of an adjudication team at the offices of the PVA, a proceeding that brought together a representative from the Islamic Committee with Burmese activists living in exile, reflects a form of gendered order-making that materializes in multiple forms on the Thai-Burmese border. The moment's seemingly fleeting and ad hoc tone underscores the fragmentary character of migrant tactics to deal with the violence around them, and especially within their communities. Who comes together to respond to gender and sexual violence and the form this response takes is contingent on space and the arrangement of power in that space. Migrants in an isolated farm-labor camp in Phob Phra, in a Mae Sot factory dormitory, or in an urban informal settlement on the land of a wealthy owner are all on the periphery of the Thai state and are likely to experience the resolution of social conflict and the deployment of the law in different ways. Social order here is more of a "hall of mirrors," as Comaroff and Comaroff (2006, 34) put it, describing the multiple refracting power relations that provide shifting notions of order on the political margins.

Moreover, migrants in each of these locales also confront varying constructions of their political and social identities. Given the focus on sexual violence, gender becomes a prevalent metaphor for migrants' shifting positionalities on the border as they inhabit and move between spaces where "risk and (in)security are embodied" differently (Johnston 2017, 4). As well, there are important commonalities underlying the disparate experiences of access to justice. And the responses migrants encounter—and the assemblages of power that come together behind such responses—are very much a product of migrants' precarious positions, their lack of legal status, their exploitability in the workplace, and the perception among state officials that they are outside the law.

As this book shows, though, the perception of total legal exclusion is at odds with migrants' lived experiences, which contradict ideas of legal uniformity or dichotomy. Burmese migrants here are, as Wendy Brown (2008, 16–17) writes, in the interstitial space "between law and non-law." To the extent that law is an enforced construct for maintaining order, the Thai-Burmese borderlands suggest a level of legal pluralism, "a living law growing out of fragmented social institutions" (Teubner 1997, 7; see also Merry 1988). In this legally in-between arena, social conflict and its resolution are interactive moments for making meaning and producing notions of collectivity (Rössel and Collins 2001; Simmel 1955; Wagner-Pacifici and Hall 2012). Studying such moments can tell us a lot about how populations on the margins attempt to get by.

Structured around two narratives and excerpted dialogues from my conversations with heads and staffers of migrant-led, border-based organizations, this chapter explores what the resolution of conflicts and the responses to sexual and gender violence reveal about governance for Burmese migrants in the borderlands and about the place of gender in migrants' efforts to make meaning of their dispossession. How social actors handle and discuss conflict and the resolution of sexual and gender violence is, I suggest, a form of "everyday bordering," as Yuval-Davis and colleagues (2019) call the quotidian forms of making exclusion felt and known. However, whereas they limit their analysis of everyday bordering to the practices that *directly* implement exclusion (e.g., police checkpoints or language requirements in schools), I suggest that in a borderscape where the state has designated a population alien, criminal, illegal, and otherwise "other," aspects of everyday life that seem unrelated to migration, integration, and exclusion should in fact be analyzed for how they might constitute the work of bordering. As previous chapters have shown, fear, violence, and discourses around security redraw the maps of these border spaces for migrants, turning neighborhoods and roads into a shifting checkerboard of constraints and possibility. And gender plays a central role in this as the expectation of violence against women works to constrain the movement of women and girl migrants in particular. But far from being passive inhabitants of this terrain, migrants are actively engaged in the work of producing stability and order—and thus space—where there appears to be limited room for their agency; migrants "use, manipulate, and divert" dominant relations and spaces in their deployment of what de Certeau (1984, 30) calls "tactics" to carve out a place for themselves that lies outside the restrictive arena of low-wage intensive labor regimes. These tactics are not necessarily a form of resistance to the state; they seem to reflect a myriad of responses to the social unruliness of exploitation, criminalization, and exclusion. Often they resemble aspects of how actors and communities practice "everyday justice" in state-controlled, semi-autonomous, and autonomous territories under the control of Ethnic Armed Organizations, armed insurgent groups in Myanmar (Kyed 2020; Denney et al. 2016). As the following discussion with the PVA staff, P'Kind, and me illustrates, the discourse used to both legitimize these responses and explain gender violence is equally as important as the structure of these responses for what they say about migrants' place in overlapping regimes of governance on the border.

Ma Say and Maung Law:
Gendered Discipline for Migrant Workers

Both Ma Say and Maung Law are volunteers with the PVA, which identifies as a migrant social-welfare organization founded by a former member of the armed student group All-Burmese Students Democratic Front (ABSDF) in 2004 to protect Burmese migrants in Thailand and help them gain access to crucial services, including healthcare and education. PVA is part of NGO networks in Mae Sot that meet regularly to coordinate on child welfare, women's protection, and labor rights. It operates openly on the border, primarily in Mae Sot. It is a membership organization and boasts a volunteer base in the hundreds in Tak's border districts as well as unique relationships with Thai authorities. It is not uncommon in Mae Sot to see young Burmese men cycling to work wearing army-green PVA T-shirts with the image of a dove inside a six-pointed star. It also has a social-media presence on Facebook, which links to other social media sites that mention the PVA and carry news coverage of the organization.[1]

---

1. See https://www.facebook.com/People-Volunteers-Association-199415453432990 (accessed February 11, 2021).

The PVA works in multiple migrant settlements in Mae Sot, but for this study, the PVA is particularly relevant for Htone Taung and Kyuwe Kyan. In recent years, it has increasingly worked with predominately Muslim communities, coordinating with Tak Province's Islamic council to address social problems. The PVA does not appoint local leaders, but works with them or directly with the migrant workers who file complaints. Though it works openly in Mae Sot, it is not a registered organization and most of its members are not documented, so they occasionally face arrest.[2] Participants in both Kyuwe Kyan and Htone Taung noted that the PVA plays a central role in resolving disputes. Although some participants consider the PVA a primary actor in dispute resolution, findings in both sites suggest that the PVA is more engaged as a backup to the Burmese leaders embedded in communities. Local authorities we interviewed also explained that they rely on the PVA when parties to a conflict reject their orders. This is because the PVA can mobilize their volunteers and because certain members and the organization as a whole have connections with local police.

The following excerpt is from an interview in Burmese with English interpretation. When relevant, I include the voice of P'Kind, who helped with interpretation. Ma Say works on the rights of women and children and Maung Law is responsible for volunteer management and communications.

> ADAM: What is the method for dealing with domestic-violence cases?
> MA SAY: For example, a man beats a woman. He beats her one time, two times, and more, so women who suffer cannot stand it any longer and come and inform us. If we get informed, we get the man to come with us. I want to give you a real example, of a Karen man and his mother, who is a school director. He beat his wife. So I'll tell you how I dealt with that.

---

2. While the close relationship that the PVA's director presumes to have with the Thai police doesn't always prevent volunteers from being arrested (especially if they are not wearing their PVA T-shirt), once in detention, volunteers often call the PVA office, which is able to prevent deportation and secure the volunteer's release.

I said to the man, "Why do you drink alcohol all the time? How many bottles do you drink each day?" "Five bottles," he said. Apa! [Oh my!] So I said, "If you drink five bottles a day, can't you reduce it to three bottles a day? From three to two, from two to one, to one-half bottle, and at the end if you can completely stop drinking, your family will be peaceful. In your family, in order for your wife and children to respect you, you must be a good person. You don't have to be in our office like this. Your wife does not have to feel pain like this. Men are the head of the household. If the wife and children who depend on the head of the house do not love but hate and are afraid of the head of the house, this is not good. They must love and respect you." That's the kind of thing I tell people. When I said this, the man cried.

This is not the first case. I saw many cases like this. He looked at me and said, "I know, my mother is also a teacher." So I said, "If your mother is a teacher you must know a lot. You must feel sorry for your mother, as it affects her dignity when you get drunk and make problems." I told him that and he was so quiet. He promised me, but I don't know if he will keep his promise. He said he would reduce the amount he drinks and eventually quit drinking. He will not make trouble at home any longer. Six months have passed and his wife hasn't come again.

ADAM: Are there other ways you talk to the people involved in such a conflict?

MA SAY: First I ask, "What is your religion?" "Buddhist." "How about parents? Are they wild like you?" "Not wild." "So why do you have to speak like this? If you speak like this and people hear it, it is not good for your own dignity. Even if you get upset, pretend you don't see. It can reduce your emotions. It can reduce a lot of your stress too. It is not the right thing to shout. When people hear, don't you feel shame? As you have children, if you are wild like this and your children see this every day, you cannot say your children will not speak the same way you do. And when your children are growing, they will have to socialize with people around them. People will say, 'Don't go close to this girl,

this boy, their mother's personality is very wild.' The children
will experience that kind of exclusion from people around them.
Then these children will become wilder."

MAUNG LAW: In all issues we use culture and religion to discipline
them, as the clients are from many different religious backgrounds. If they are Muslim we have to mention the teachings
of Islam, we have to talk in terms of their religion so that they
like to hear what we say. We also let them know the legal aspect,
which laws they are breaking and what the punishments are. In
religion, for example in Buddhist teaching, what kinds of evil
they will receive. No one likes what they do [when clients commit violence], our families don't like it, others also don't like it,
so when we do something that no one likes, it's like they cause
problems, and so they have to face the consequences . . .

MA SAY: Religious, legal . . .

MAUNG LAW: We discipline them with religious teaching, legal
teaching, cultural teaching . . .

MA SAY: Social . . .

MAUNG LAW: Socially also. As you do things that people around you
cannot accept, you are guilty. They must understand this. Okay,
go ahead.

MA SAY: The reason is, when a man becomes the head of the family,
he has responsibilities as the head of the family. There must
be enough food and clothing for his family, and if they live
in another country they have to rent a house, there is no way
to own a house. He'll have to pay rent for the house and give
enough for the water and the electricity bills. Food and clothes,
and food for babies. Those are the responsibilities of a father.
However, here [in Thailand] people do not distinguish between
the father's role and the mother's role. Mom works, father also
works. The income of both will cover the cost for the family's
well-being. If they have extra, they will keep it as extra. They
may eat better food, wear better clothes, or give donations.
Like that. Man has a responsibility as a man and woman has a

responsibility as a woman. This is what you already know too, Adam. [laughs]

ADAM: So, what about the cultural side?

MAUNG LAW: About culture. According to our Burmese culture, a woman as a housewife has five duties; a man also has five duties according to Buddhist teaching. The five duties of a wife and the five duties of a husband . . .

MA SAY: In Burmese traditional culture.

MAUNG LAW: The five duties of the wife and the five duties of the husband. Since we have those kinds of rules, we use them to control people and discipline people.

ADAM: I see. Okay. Do you know what those five are?

MA SAY: The five duties of the wife in our Burmese culture: Treat your husband as your master. Keep and use your husband's money efficiently. When your husband comes back from work, talk sweetly to him and prepare nice food for him. Prepare and maintain the bed and yourself according to the desire of your husband. Be loyal to your husband. Deal with your husband with full honesty. As a woman, these are the five duties, but it can be translated to a lot of meanings.

ADAM: And what points for the man?

P'KIND: For the man, find money and give it to your wife. Second is give your time and love and care to your wife. Third is be kind to your wife as you would be kind to your mother and your sister.

MA SAY: Then be loyal to your wife. Be with only your wife. Then don't betray your wife.

MAUNG LAW: Anything relating to Burmese cultural teaching are in the *Lawkaniti Kyan* [Burmese collection of folk wisdom; from *lawki*, a term for the secular realm].

This excerpt from our conversation is rich with meaning about the kinds of ideas that circulate in the work of intimate-partner dispute resolution—ideas relating to gender, honor, dignity, family, culture, social norms, and religion, to name a few. While the outcome of the PVA's adjudications typically involves some form of compensation or community service work, as the speakers suggest, the PVA also emphasizes moral disciplining.

Ma Say and Maung Law highlight four disciplinary methods of instilling morality into offenders. First, they appeal to a cultural-religious narrative derived from religious texts to explain rules and roles. Although Maung Law refers to the man's Karen ethnic nationality in his example, religion is clearly a more salient factor in his approach. Second, they refer to a sense of social dignity; this is an attempt to make offenders aware of how parents and people in a surrounding community might see them based on their behavior. Third, they ask offenders to recall their reason for being in Thailand, reminding them that they are there to pursue financial gain and that excessive drinking or social conflict is counterproductive to that goal. And finally, the PVA mediators rely on particular interpretations of gender roles to guide offenders to see how they should reform their behavior. They deploy idealized images of men and women to push offenders (who are men in the above narrative) to reflect on how their behavior upholds or degrades their masculinity. The mediators seem to see their role in the migrant community as a protective one, arguing that they address the social problems and conflicts of Burmese migrants that nobody else will and provide migrants with moral lessons, instilling in them the will to improve themselves.

The rather static and patriarchal interpretations of religion, culture, and gender that Ma Say and Maung Law offer resonate across the labor camps, informal settlements, and urban neighborhoods where I did this research, and can be found in both urban and rural parts of Myanmar (e.g., Lwin Lwin Mon 2020). Several other mediators and migrant authorities made similar reference to rigid notions of gender as a tool to deal with domestic conflicts and other social problems. Such notions formed a set of rules to live and judge by, for a popular discourse capable of persuading or mobilizing the average migrant worker, whether Christian, Muslim, or Buddhist. Buddhist monks in Phob Phra, for example, used Buddhist teachings to solve marital problems; a pastor in Romklao Sahamit used teachings from the Bible for the same purpose; and participants note that imams, elders, and other respectable people in Mae Sot's Muslim community often handle family cases for other Muslims in their communities, sometimes in conjunction with the PVA. Such tools in dispute resolution are considered to be "customary" or "traditional."

In some ways, this appears to be a logical strategy because multiple participants—nearly half—cited religion or cultural customs as a guide for or explanation of their situation.[3] Numerous Buddhist participants mentioned that they use religion to find peace amid difficulty, advising themselves "according to the Dhamma when problems happen," for example. However, many on the border reject the notion that religious ethics work as a framework for responding to gender violence. Even migrant authorities who rely on such methods are not always in favor of them, and some are quick to say that they wouldn't mediate conflicts this way if they had a choice. A Muslim religious leader in Kyuwe Kyan complained that Thai village heads and police placed the expectation on him to govern his neighborhood because he was an imam, but that he is reluctant to do this work because he feels unqualified for the task and does not feel it is his responsibility: "Whenever the police and headmen come, I never try to avoid them, because I am not wrong. I feel hesitant because I am doing religious work, but nonetheless if the community members commit the crime, the police and headmen will definitely ask me, "Don't you control them as their religious leader?" Although I try to control them, they do not listen to my words. The officials know I am responsible for the community, but I don't do it, so the officials are mad at me. It's not my business. It is the government's business!"

This imam's frustration is not surprising. From his account, it appears that government officials have thrown the responsibility for security in this settlement to him and that he is expected to use his religious authority to maintain order, and they blame him for his apparent shortcomings. While many leaders acknowledge using morality, culture, custom, and religion as tools to solve intimate-partner violence among migrant workers, they tend to agree that cases of serious crimes or serious violence—especially

---

3. It is noteworthy that participants typically referred to "culture" in a general sense and only occasionally as specific ideas of ethnicity. In these latter cases, this was more often a reference to religion as associated with ethnic nationality, like Baptist or Seventh Day Adventist for S'gaw Karen, or a reference to an ethnopolitical institution.

murder and sexual assault—should be handled through formal legal channels. However, the data reflect that formal legal action happens only a fraction of the time, meaning that informal authorities instead use custom, such as a code of ethics, and local interpretations of the law to mediate for people who have suffered gender violence.

It is also the case that migrants do not always prefer to have their social problems dealt with by resorting to religious language or appealing to custom or traditional ethics. A resident of Htone Taung who works for a Burmese border-based social-welfare organization for women and children attacked the use of religious or "traditional" language: "Gender discrimination occurs *because* of the religious belief. That conservative thinking still influences Burmese people. For example, women are born to do household chores and men are born to do business. Women need to have domestic skills to support their family after getting married. The qualities and abilities of women decrease after getting married because women have to do household chores and men have to find money. Men think they are the only ones responsible for finding money to support their family. Thus they don't value their wives." For this participant, the use of religious doctrine to solve problems related to gender violence needs to be changed, not reinforced.

The fact that it is inevitably often up to Burmese community and religious leaders to try to restore order, issue justice, or piece back together a torn community in the wake of violent crime is no doubt a product of migrants' insecurity before the law. A Burmese lawyer working in Mae Sot told me that while intimate-partner violence is a criminal offense in Thailand, "the problem is that our Bamar people do not have the capacity to address the violence in the legal way. They cannot afford to wait, they cannot afford to do it." He specified that this is because of fear ("if they hear about the courtroom, the police, then they are already worried") and insufficient money, and because they have no labor protections they cannot afford to take time off from work. Thus, a lack of free and fair access to the criminal-justice system relegates migrants to having serious problems solved—or left unsolved—by informal authorities who explain their work as more of a necessity than a choice or a desire for power. This lack of access to justice resonates with the common assumption among Thai officials that Burmese migrants prefer to manage domestic cases through religious authority. The result is a normalization and naturalization of migrants' use of religious doctrine to solve intimate-partner violence, as if it were universally preferred as a method.[4] Even if such methods are not

4. In the case of religion and custom, what is commonly referred to as "traditional law" and "Burmese Buddhist customary law" are in fact constructions of the British colonial era that have left a lasting legacy on legal and social discourse. Since, initially, Burma was a part of the British Raj, the British extended the Anglo-Indian laws developed and applied there to the Burmese. This included a system of legal pluralism that allowed for different religious-moral laws to be applied to four main religious categories of Buddhist, Christian, Muslim, and Hindu for cases relating to inheritance, marriage, divorce, and adoption (Hla Aung 1968; Ikeya 2012). Ikeya (27) notes that this had the effect of reifying ethnic boundaries in colonial Burma. This designation, which was part of the Burma Laws Act of 1898, meant that family issues were not subject to the formal Anglo-Indian legal system but rather to a notion of "religious customary law" (Maung Maung 1963). Institutionalizing the informality of family law was born from two false assumptions, in addition to gross generalization. First, the English divined that Burmese family conflicts were best dealt with outside the legal system, that "in the Burmese family system the reasonable is to precede the legal" (Jardine 1882, 197, quoted in Furnivall 2014, 131). Second, the British supposed that the "custom" on which the Burmese relied to decide family cases was from a religiously derived text, the Dhammathats, when in fact this was more legal and ethical material, the annals of Burmese rulers' principles and beliefs, than religious doctrine, even if these rulers were influenced by Buddhism (Hla Aung 1968; Davids 1932). In their Orientalist approach to understanding Indian and Burmese societies and social structures, the British appropriated and adapted local knowledge to fit their conceptions (McGeachy 2002). The British also constructed plural legal regimes in colonial Malaysia, designating Muslim law as the preferred source of authority for deciding cases related to marriage and inheritance. It is worth noting here that during the colonial epoch, as Siam attempted to assert control over all the various peoples within its designated territory, the government enacted a similar legal pluralism in the predominately Muslim areas in the south that was modeled after the British colonial system. See Loos 2006, who argues that the vestiges of this pluralism can be found in contemporary Thailand's southernmost provinces.

This inaccurately conflated a sense of custom and religion in the British colonies, dividing different ethnicities and religions from one another. In addition, it cemented as law the preference for customary law to deal with family disputes. And finally, it simultaneously romanticized and exoticized local methods for dealing with disputes as "traditional" and static.

uncommon in Thailand and Myanmar, it is but one of many forms of legal pluralism, one of the many means for community-based dispute resolution (Kyed 2018). An important difference for migrants in labor camps or factory dormitories is their lack of mobility—that is, their lack of choice in how they wish to pursue recourse to justice.

Because religious or ethics texts have the potential to limit the rights of women, leaders' reference to faith-based doctrines to solve intimate-partner violence has serious gendered implications, as the participant who works with a women's rights organization indicates. A frequent issue participants noted in this regard pertained to divorce. Several women recalled the pressure some religious groups (or groups who rely on religious texts) placed on victims to stay with abusive partners, citing Buddhist, Muslim, or Christian "custom." That said, mediators we interviewed who mentioned divorce referred not only to such doctrines but also to their responsibility, and the responsibility of organizations like theirs, to not separate people but to keep them together. In that this suggests a perception that divorce only leads to further social atomization and alienation among displaced persons, the burden of social cohesion and unity ends up disproportionately on the shoulders of those who face abuse. In this sense, religion as a set of ordering discourses constitutes a gendered response to the conditions of precarity.

Ma Say's and Maung Law's references to "Burmese cultural teachings" appear to perform a similar role. While their use of these ideas in disciplining offenders and adjudicating conflict might fit what they think migrants want to hear, the gendered concepts of morality seem to underlie a particular narrative explaining why violence has taken place and how couples (and migrants more broadly) can reorder their lives to restore harmony. Gender becomes a verb here in the service of fostering a sense of a community striving for order.

The specific cultural guide to which Maung Law refers, the *Lawkaniti Kyan*, is a good example of this. It is a collection of maxims recorded and revised over the last five centuries during the pre-colonial period. The *Lokanīti* is a Sanskrit-language text that includes 109 sayings originating in India (Sternbach 1963; see also Gray 1886). A Burmese version of this text, the *Niti Kyan*, contains 211 maxims; at least at the time it was translated into English in 1858, it was thought to be in everyday use in monastic teachings. It provided a foundational code of ethics in the precolonial and early colonial system of Burmese education (Fowle 1860). The collection contains chapters on "the wise man," "the good man," "the evil-doer," "friendship," "women," "kings," and "miscellaneous" (Sternbach 1963, 332). Here are some sayings: "(38) A woman separated from her husband for thirty days endangers her chastity. (73) A woman is the best and sweetest of blessings. (76) A good mother teaches her son to speak fairly, and a good father teaches him to act honestly. (127) Trust not a woman who has separated three times from three different husbands. (134) A good wife is as a brother to her husband when he eats or dresses, resembles a sister in modesty when in private with him, a slave when he is preparing for a journey, a friend when in difficulties; she comforts him quickly to sleep, she attires herself neatly to please him, she forbears kindly when he is angry. (149) A man who is married and has a family, but stays at home without working or exerting himself for their benefit, is lazy and good for nothing" (Fowle 1860, 255–62).

The *Lokanīti Kyan* has remained a source of important—or at least prevalent—sayings in Myanmar. More recent editions (Sein Tu 1962) have been printed as small booklets and widely distributed by the government and government-associated groups (e.g., New Light of Myanmar 2003). That the military government in Myanmar, which has a reputation for the perpetuation of conservative patriarchy, was circulating the text through state-sponsored media is telling.

The ideas of the *Lokanīti Kyan* resonate widely, surfacing unnamed in migrants' voices on the border, as when this forty-year-old Burmese woman in Htone Taung, who occasionally manages couples' disputes, explained her strategy: "A girl must understand her husband's work. I said to the girl, 'When your husband gets back from work and calls you, this is your duty to make sure you respond. Maybe he needs to drink water, or eat rice—those are your duties. Setting the bed is your duty. If he takes a shower, giving him a towel and *longyi* is your duty. If you fulfill all your duties, then your husband won't have any problem with you. He is responsible to feed you. Your welfare is his duty. Because he is responsible for ensuring your well-being, listen to what he says, as he also must listen to what you say.' That is how I handled couples' issues."

Somewhat similarly, a couple in Romklao Sahamit that works as a team to respond to conflict explains that they offer different moral guidelines to the men and women they counsel. For men, they appeal to his responsibilities as a father and his identity as a man:

> FEMALE MEDIATOR: I tell him, "You go gambling, you drink alcohol. You also have children and a wife. They have to eat. You do not bring them food. Instead you ask her to find money for you to go gambling. So, what do you think of yourself?"
>
> MALE MEDIATOR: Here money problems are the most common, so I talk about money. "Little brother, today how much did you spend on your alcohol? You still have a future to think about and your health too. Today you worked and made 100 baht [US $3.00]. Little brother, you drank up 60 baht. Sometimes you may even drink up 100 baht with friends. Your wife at home has no food to eat. Your children at home have no food to eat, so they will cry, and if they cry, can you put up with hearing it?" As a man, we discipline them in that way.

For women, the male mediator refers to women's responsibilities and duties, while the female mediator encourages the woman to be patient:

> MALE MEDIATOR: I say to her, "Little sister, it is not nice to behave in that way. Your husband is working to bring income, so when he comes home your role is to cook and give him food. You have to treat your husband nicely. Keep everything neat and tight. Treat a man as you should treat a man. Female roles must be fulfilled."
>
> FEMALE MEDIATOR: I try to discipline them as if I were them and this is how I would feel if I heard these words. The people here listen to me and that is why it works. What I do is listen to both the man and the woman. Then I tell the wife, "Try staying with him for three months or six months. Then if you are not fine, come back to me." Then when she agrees, we make a promissory note for them. After we make the promissory note they get together peacefully again.

While the tendency for migrant authorities to apply such gendered narratives as disciplinary measures is significant in its own right for what it indicates about the types of ordering influences imposed on migrant minds and bodies in the context of domestic conflict, it also raises questions about how such narratives fit into migrants' and mediators' tactics to manage and survive displacement. The particular combination of references to economic stability, gendered norms and maxims, and references to the social and community fabric in migrant authorities' narratives suggests that scolding offenders and victims to be better men and women is more than a tactic to resolve disputes according to a notion of tradition. Rather, it appears to be a way to create a sense of tradition to help strengthen ties, foster a sense of community based on shared values, and maintain order among a population on the move and affected by poverty, separation, and displacement. But these settlements, full of transient migrants, do not generally resemble the kinds of socially cohesive communities where one is more likely to find such dispute resolution tactics in Myanmar. That these strategies echo everyday justice practices in Myanmar means it is not surprising that we find such tactics here in Thailand, along the border (Kyed 2020; McConnachie 2020). However, that they are deployed here among precarious and mostly undocumented workers in the borderscape, in spaces largely defined by exclusion and social disorder, lends weightier significance to the resolution of social problems.

By looking at the intersection of gendered discourse and the resolution of social problems among migrants, we can start to see how gender becomes a tool for producing particular modes of social organization in this border context. Gendered discourse helps migrants make sense of their experience, at the same time that it has an ordering effect. The conservative moral overtones invoke once again the concept of "gender reaffirmation," reasserting some idea of the traditional to keep together a social fabric perceived as torn (McGuffey 2005, 2008). As such, the deployment of gender in religious, ethical, and cultural narratives via custom are part of the complex arrangement of governance on the border. The resolution of intimate-partner conflicts and other incidents of gendered violence among migrants, and the discourses buttressing and legitimizing those methods, becomes a lens to understand how the dynamics of capital accumulation and questions of family, morality, memory, and tradition are interlaced in the fashioning of a new kind of worker "suited to the new type of work and production process" in this context (Gramsci 1971, 286). As this next excerpt demonstrates, how these assemblages of power form to bring together particular actors and narratives, and how such networks interface with the state, has significant implications for the ways migrants experience sovereignty and borders.

Hsar Moo: "Organizing" Karen People in Exile

Hsar Moo is a Karen man in his forties who grew up as a refugee displaced repeatedly along the border, and who worked as a Thai-Karen translator for a Thai legal-aid organization until early 2015.[5] But he was also a representative of the Kaw Mu Raw Karen Youth Organization (KMR-KYO), a group that has operated on the border since 1979.[6] High-ranking members of the Karen National Liberation Army and the Karen National Union formed the KMR-KYO not as a branch of the government in exile but as an informal network of governance. The name Kaw Mu Raw refers to the place in Karen state where certain key military figures in the KNU apparatus are from. These senior officers formed the KMR-KYO as a way of extending the reach of the KNU into Thailand, though not explicitly. From its inception through the time of this writing, the KMR-KYO reported directly to the central level of the KNLA. In practice, the KMR-KYO maintains a low profile in Thailand, particularly since it operates as an unregistered organization and a somewhat decentralized informal network. It operates only along the border areas in Tak Province and in Phob Phra, Mae Sot, and Mae Ramat districts. It does not receive outside

5. Hsar Moo was arrested in 2015 and convicted of drug trafficking. He is currently incarcerated in Thailand.

6. This group is not to be confused with the Karen Youth Organization, which operates primarily in the Karen-majority refugee camps along the border. The KMR-KYO shares only the name with the camp-based KYO. Whereas the Karen National Union formed the KYO to organize youth activities in camps and educate youth on a particular historical narrative of Karen history and politics, the KMR-KYO, despite its name, does not actually have a focus on youth at all.

funding, and its members do not officially draw salaries. P'Kind and I interviewed Hsar Moo together, in Thai and in Karen.

HSAR MOO: Our purpose is to go and organize Karen people who fled from Burma and spread out everywhere unorganized. And our role is to go and organize them, put them back together, let them know that we have to be together. The scope of the KYO is to work for people who are not only Karen but are also Burmese people who stay together in the community. The KNU has their own law, but they cannot operate fully and they have no court here. So we only handle the case traditionally, as village heads have done for their villagers since long ago. Like leaders of the community who help with mediating cases. For example, when fighting occurs between couples, they mediate for them, have them sign promissory notes that say they will not do it again. The offenders may have to pay a fine if they repeat the violence. They have to promise they will not use violence again. That is the method that is used. This is only for small fights between a couple or in the family. But the next stage is if they repeat an offense or if someone breaks the promise. Then they'll have to pay a fine. If we don't do it this way, they will not be afraid of us. When a criminal offense has happened any place along the border area, we ask KYO people who stay in that area to refer it to the Thai village head first. If the village head decides to refer it to the police, then the case will go through the Thai justice system because we are in Thailand and the event occurred in Thailand. Sometimes if the case is not too serious, the village can mediate it. This is how we work. But we do have authority to mediate all smaller cases. The method of mediation is easy. Our principle is to make big problems small and to make small problems disappear.

Debt and loan cases where people don't pay back their debt are very common. We deal with such cases to protect the migrants. If a debt and loan case is between migrant workers, and we do not get in and help out, sometimes it can lead to a murder case. Because they can murder when they get angry. Sometimes such cases between migrant workers don't involve big money—only 400 or 500 baht [US $12.50–15.50]—but for them, they have to work many days to make up that amount.

Sometimes there are also adultery cases. This is also a big problem. Just imagine the husband of a woman is not happy, he gets angry, and commits a serious crime. We sometimes use negotiation for this. For example, we ask if she can forgive him and stay together with him. The man who commits adultery may have to pay her compensation. We don't decide how much the compensation is; that is the result of negotiation between the two parties. We just produce a promissory note for them to sign. It is written that they are not going to repeat this behavior. But if they repeat it we have to think how to punish them, so we may have them pay a fine or have another form of punishment or community-service order. We talk about those possibilities first, then we make a promissory note.

You see, problems like this, like debt and loan and adultery, if we do not do it ourselves and we bring it to Thai justice, the Thai government will not accept those cases. Because when problems occur there is no evidence. When there is no written document relating to debt and loan, the police cannot proceed with the case. With adultery cases, police also do not know how to charge them. Therefore, we have to use the method called "community wisdom." What we are doing is helping Thai village leaders in their work; we help deal with small issues.

ADAM: And what about bigger issues?

HSAR MOO: Even robbery for a small thing, we can mediate it too. This is for robbery or theft between migrant workers. We have the robber pay compensation. For example, we negotiate how much they will have to reimburse the victim when they steal their bike. This is a criminal offense, but we mediate it because it is not serious and the parties are both Burmese migrant workers. But if the theft is between Burmese migrant workers and non-Burmese, we do not dare interfere. That case we will refer to

the Thai justice system because we are afraid that more problems will follow later. In any case, if both parties do not agree,
we cannot force them. Only if both parties agree, we can produce a written document about their agreement just as a kind of
evidence. We can do that.

ADAM: And how about a divorce paper or something like that?

HSAR MOO: Divorce paper, we don't do. If a couple is fighting, and
the man continues to commit violence against his wife, we have
to plan a punishment for him. It can be a community-service
order or a fine that becomes a community fund.

ADAM: Like what kind of work?

HSAR MOO: Depending on the community. What kind of thing will
benefit the community. Sometimes they have to clean the learning center or some other place. We just do it like that. We don't
really know how to punish an offender. We have to use many
forms of punishment so that the problems will not be big. If you
ask, "Do we do every process legally?" we may not in some cases.
But if we don't do it our way and only refer the case to the Thai
justice system, the police won't accept some cases. They do not
give protection to some cases, so if we let it be, then domestic
violence can be more violent.

ADAM: So, if the KYO were not present on the border to help . . . I
see that there are a lot of problems like domestic violence and
other issues . . .

HSAR MOO: True, true, a lot. An example from yesterday: We call
it sexual abuse, though not rape. The mother of the victim
came and reported it. I said, "You need to report it to the police
because we cannot mediate this case." The mother was afraid
to, since she was in charge of a gambling outfit. If an investiga-
tion started and the police found out about the gambling, then
both parties would be guilty by law. So the KYO asked, "How
do you want to do it? What do you want to be satisfied?" The
mother of the victim said she would like 300,000 baht [US
$9,300] as compensation. Oh ho! We asked why that much, and
I say, "Can you talk and agree on an amount so both of you can

be satisfied? Because the man has no ability to pay that much. If you go to the justice system, both parties will be guilty." So finally the mother of the victim agreed on 5,000 baht [US $150] as compensation. The man paid 5,000 baht. If we look into it, both are legally wrong. We don't say that we did the right thing here, but as long as they both agree, we don't say anything. If one party cannot be satisfied then we must proceed to the legal system.

Hsar Moo's narrative moves between justification and a detailed account of how his group navigates the complexities of legality and authority. Explaining his group's existence as a consequence of Karen displacement, he makes important references to tradition and community. He tells a simplified version of a story in which people are uprooted and lost in Thailand. His main point is to underscore the need for a group to "organize" the wandering Karen refugees for their own benefit and well-being and "put them back together." Implied here is a notion of a once-cohesive community of Karen people; this is part of a historical, social, and political narrative that has particular strength among the networks of Christian (particularly Baptist) Karen people on both sides of the Thailand-Myanmar border (Horstmann 2011). Horstmann (2011, 86) points out that "while the physical space of a Karen homeland *Kawthoolei* has been gradually lost, the spiritual idea of a 'homeland' is still alive," though at the expense of the actual sociolinguistic and religious diversity of the Karen population in Myanmar and Thailand.[7] Part of this narrative is the need for Karen people to reorganize in a diaspora and together maintain the idea of *Kawthoolei*[8]. However, Hsar Moo suggests that over time, this mission has changed to one more focused on governance and only

7. *Kawthoolei* (lit. "a land without darkness") is the S'gaw Karen-language term for the Karen nation.

8. Hsar Moo's account portrays what Charles Keyes (2008) refers to as "ethnofiction," a version of Anderson's (1991) "imagined community," in which groups assert particular notions of history that privilege certain collective ethnic identities over others. As Anderson argues, whether these bonds are factual or based in fiction is less important than the way or style this construction takes place (1991).

sometimes directly includes the work of maintaining ethnonational identities. This is likely because, as Hsar Moo indicates, increasing numbers of non-Karen people from Myanmar have joined the displaced Karen in Thailand, broadening or diluting the mission of this network.

Describing his group's reliance on mediation, promissory notes, and forms of community-based punishment that respect tradition clearly gives some level of legitimacy to the work Hsar Moo's organization does to resolve disputes, especially as he stresses that KMR-KYO practices have been used in "villages since long ago." He links mediator practices to convention and custom. While it is possible that KMR-KYO's work to resolve conflicts relies on tactics learned in KNU-controlled areas in Myanmar, Hsar Moo's comments gloss over what is in reality a complicated zone of mixed control due to decades of political violence and displacement (Harrisson and Kyed 2019; McCartan and Jolliffe 2016; Smith 2007; South 2011). In this sense, his reliance on "tradition" not only justifies the work of his group but is also in the service of the broader goal of defining a notion of "homeland" or "nation." In addition to material symbols of nationhood that are prevalent in refugee camps and Karen-migrant villages in Thailand, perhaps it is also possible to consider dispute-resolution tactics as part of an "invented tradition" that conveys a factitious sense of continuity between current practice and a historical order of things in the homeland (Hobsbawm 1983).

A second device Hsar Moo deploys to justify the work of his organization is the repeated reference to violence. He states explicitly that due to the Thai government's reluctance to solve petty crimes among Burmese migrants, and because of the precarious conditions in which migrants find themselves, a small problem can often erupt into physical brutality. Debt and loan cases, Hsar Moo argues, can become murder cases, even when the amount owed is only 400 or 500 baht. Spouses can take revenge on unfaithful partners. Stressing the desperation of migrant conditions, leaving migrants in what he describes as a lawless space means that violent chaos will be rampant. He depicts a tense scenario for migrants on the Thailand-Myanmar border, where serious violence is always a possibility and never far off. The KMR-KYO is there to address this issue and to "make big problems small and small problems disappear," instead of the other way around.[9] U Winn, who acts as mediator for this network in Phob Phra, seconded this perspective. "In the past I was fighting alone for the Burmese people. At that time, there was no organization." But he felt that "the KYO must be organized because in our Phob Phra township child-trafficking occurred, rape occurred, killing occurred, so on and so forth, and we have to face all that." Like Hsar Moo, he portrays a story of origin that begins with a violent and out-of-control landscape in need of an entity to make peace and order.

As mediators legitimize their networks by referencing tradition and violence, it becomes clear that these two themes are relevant to the assemblage of power in which the individuals affiliated with the KMR-KYO are embedded. If the violence and disorder of the border space precipitates a need for their network, notions of tradition and custom serve as a framework for migrant realities and possibilities that helps make sense of the perceived disorder and insecurity. And it appears that these discursive concepts play an active role in shaping the notion of "order-making" as well. These ideas are themselves actors in a network alongside individual migrant workers, families, informal migrant authorities, and Thai security officials acting in their formal and informal capacities.

Hsar Moo's account positions the KMR-KYO in a political network that spans the Thai-Burmese border and includes both the KNU's ethnopolitical juridical system and the Thai-state apparatus. Like the formalized refugee camps on the border where the KNU continues to have an implicit influence in everyday governance (including conflict resolution),[10] labor camps represent another space where members of the Karen political

9. This was said to me by an informal mediator of disputes in Phob Phra. It corresponds to a well-used saying in Myanmar to "make the big cases smaller and the small cases disappear" (*kyi te amu nge aung, nge te amu pa pyauk aung*). See also Denney et al. 2016.

10. As McConnachie (2014) shows, the linkages between the KNU and the Karen authorities that manage everyday life in the predominately Karen camps along the Thai-Burmese border are ideological and relational. In previous research I demonstrated the connections between camp management and the KNU and the KNLA, as camp-security members in more than one camp noted they were formerly combatants (Human Rights Watch 2012).

and religious network feel the imperative to involve themselves. Legally, it appears that Hsar Moo positions migrants in-between Thai and Karen juridical systems. On the one hand, he recognizes that Thai authority should apply to the migrant population, affirming a sense of territorial sovereignty, but on the other hand, he underscores the lack of access migrants have to Thai police or courts. When Hsar Moo opines that police don't take migrant cases because of a lack of evidence, he refers to both the logistical and ideological barrier to migrant access to justice. Thai police complain of a lack of Burmese-Thai interpreters and have relied on community organizations with international funding to supply translators. Police and the courts in border areas have complained that they have a difficult time dealing with crimes and conflicts involving migrants, in part because suspects tend to disappear across the border and evade capture, a common occurrence in Mae Sot. At the same time, migrant community leaders report that Thai authorities under-police petty crimes and civil conflicts between migrants, and that migrants feel they cannot report their crimes for fear of arrest and deportation.

As Hsar Moo puts it, migrants' marginalization from and simultaneous persecution by the Thai justice system creates the need for what he calls "customary" and "traditional" tactics derived from the KNU's governance in certain territories in Myanmar. In his portrayal, his group reluctantly gets involved in solving conflicts, and he also makes clear that the KMR-KYO knows its limits: when cases involve Thai nationals, Hsar Moo's network calls the Thai authorities. In this framing, the KMR-KYO is an intermediary bridging the gap between the informal space of chaos and violence into which a precarious system thrusts migrants and the formal space of Thai law. This is notably different from the way everyday justice tends to be organized in Myanmar, even under Ethnic Armed Organizations where community-based dispute resolution can reflect a form of state evasion (e.g., Scott 2009).

A Multiplication of Borders

In an effort to make legible a complex arrangement, Hsar Moo portrays a clear system of parallel governance. In his account, the border is broken up into clear sectors of sovereignty and governance, and there is an identifiable boundary between the formal and the informal. The everyday reality for migrants, however, seem only to suggest murkiness, complexity, and fluidity. The sexual abuse he refers to at the end of his narrative confirms that his network's rules don't always apply: though he says earlier that his group refers sexual-assault cases and other serious crimes to the authorities, it appears that Kaw Moo Raw mediators begrudgingly negotiated the case to protect the illegal gambling business of the victim's mother, engaged in a calculation of moral equivalency, and even brought down the amount of compensation she initially requested. It would appear that laws for Burmese migrants are made and remade in practice by an overlapping arrangement of power, which is, of course, part of what constitutes the border space as structurally, and not just physically, violent. To the extent that "the law is produced and elaborated every time it is invoked in the scene of its anticipation," as Judith Butler and Ana Athanasiou (2013, 129) write, migrants' place before the law is performatively constituted through interaction and discourse.

Beyond the Kaw Moo Raw network, sources of order are often not in concert with one another, and, moreover, come not only from Karen and Burmese living in Thailand. Migrant workers described arrangements in which retired Thai police officers who spoke Burmese and Thai seemed to mete out discipline for conflicts; others referred to gangs headed by a Thai police sergeant,[11] and, as noted earlier, several religious figures played such roles, especially in Baptist and Seventh Day Adventist Karen communities and in Mae Sot's Muslim quarter. In all four sites migrant-worker settlements rely on a Burmese leader to act as an interlocutor with an employer, landlord, the police, or an informal group. Three of the grassroots migrant-welfare organizations interviewed confirmed that they also appoint such leaders to keep order, as they have identified that maintaining order is crucial for the well-being of their target populations. One director of an organization in Mae Sot reflected: "In the past when this kind of case occurred, people thought, 'It is not my business,' and they

11. Human Rights Watch 2010 interviewed a Karen man from this gang who noted that the police officer in charge had him extort and intimidate other migrants, but also provided protection from deportation, since he was undocumented.

would not get involved, as they were afraid. But now, we have community leaders in those communities. Community leaders have to deal with social affairs. We trained some people to become community leaders and they inform us when cases arise."

In the two Phob Phra sites employers and landlords usually chose the leaders in individual labor compounds; some participants stated that their leader was in charge because he had been in the compound the longest. A Thai employer and landowner in Pyaung Gyi Win explained that in response to intimate-partner violence, he "mediated and asked them to stop quarreling because that is very noisy." According to him, migrants will report social conflicts to "employers, the village head, civilian-preparedness volunteers, or the police," and he acknowledged that typically migrants handle problems within their own families or households. On the other hand, a migrant in Pyaung Gyi Win/Rim Nam who also worked as a volunteer for multiple NGOs explained: "I can't speak Thai. The village leader can't speak Burmese. So they can't solve the problems. The Thai village leader selected a Burmese leader to solve the problems."

In fact it is not uncommon in Thailand or Myanmar for people to rely on community-level solutions that are similar in process to what I have outlined above. Indeed, many scholars consider village-level justice to be the "traditional" way of solving most conflicts in both these countries (Kyed 2020; Callister and Wall 2004; MDR and Kempel 2012; Kittipong 2003). Using the Thai term *yutitham samarn chan* (lit. "justice for social harmony"), Kittipong (2003) laments the loss of such traditions by an increasingly centralized system of governance in Thailand, but notes that contemporary decentralization efforts create space for a revival of community justice and restorative justice. The Thai Ministry of Interior and the Ministry of Justice have both initiated nationwide programs to train village-level authorities on mediation techniques; several dozen villages now have government-established community justice centers where Thai village residents can have their disputes heard and resolved. Wanchai (2010) studied local dispute-resolution methods in Thailand's deep south in Pattani, and in the Isan region in the Northeast, and found different but equally effective mechanisms to maintain peace and order—in the predominately Muslim south relying on religious networks and in the Northeast on kin networks. Wanchai also observed in Phetchabun Province a system implemented on the subdistrict level where residents of seven participating villages approved a set of rules to govern themselves, including fines for disrupting festivals, excessive drinking, and loud noise after 11 pm. A committee of elders adjudicates such offenses.

In 2007, in response to criticism that the criminal-justice system had failed both victims and perpetrators, the Thai government created a legal mechanism that allows for intimate-partner violence to be handled in the court or to be resolved within the community or extended kin network, opening up a "formal" space for a community and restorative-justice response for such issues (e.g., Angkana et al. 2004; Kittipong 2003; Chitruedee 2006 for background pre-legislation). As in the complaints of many Burmese migrants in Thailand (and reflective of a global trend), studies showed that police hesitate to get involved in such cases because of the view that intimate-partner violence is a family problem. Police involvement, according to a community leader interviewed by Angkana and colleagues, "leads to divorce. In cases where the accusation is taken to the police, it is difficult to reconcile because it destroys the honor of the husband" (Angkana et al. 2004, 9). Many see restorative justice as an ideal alternative, as it allows for the option of maintaining family unity.

Thailand's "Domestic Violence Victim Protection Act, BE 2550 (2007)," states: "The court shall . . . cause the parties to settle the case for peaceful cohabitation of the family," albeit with the protection of the rights of the victim as a priority (Section 15). This law codifies a restorative outlet for intimate-partner violence cases, empowering the court to impose a sentence of rehabilitation for the offender (Section 12). Section 16 allows for "a mediator which is a person or a group of persons who are fathers, mothers, guardians or relatives," or a variety of other actors, including social workers or a social-welfare agency, to resolve such disputes as long as they submit a report of the result of the mediation to the court and the judge deems the results fair. An emphasis on protecting the honor of the parties involved, a preference to keep families together, and effecting a legal area for informal familial management of intimate-partner violence reflects not only the recognition of the role of local justice mechanisms but also the utterly gendered and collectivist nature of such processes in Thailand (as elsewhere). In addition, it is inevitable that in practice, a wider variety of actors than those mentioned in the law are involved in mediating such conflicts, they do not do so as a court-sanctioned remedy, and they rely on methods and networks of power that are beyond the normative legal framework. In my own fieldwork, I found that village-level justice centers in the border areas of Thailand were often minimally run, with greater reliance on informal but respected individuals to deal with problems.

In Myanmar, the great diversity of governance mechanisms, including highland spaces controlled fully or partially by a multitude of ethnic armed groups, divides the state into hundreds of smaller territories controlled by patrons offering security for local residents (Harrisson and Kyed 2019; Jolliffe 2014; Karen Human Rights Group 2010; South 2011). For a large part of the country, particularly in the lowland areas that have historically been less affected by conflict (such as the Aeyeyarwady Delta and the Dry Zone), it is quite common for village tract or village-level authorities to resolve minor disputes, or even sometimes more serious issues, outside the criminal-justice system. Village tract dispute resolution relates to the official duties of village administrators as stipulated in the "Ward or Village Tract Administration Law" (2012).[12] The law provides for village tract administrators to resolve disputes, maintain peace and order, and to manage disciplinary matters for residents. In recent years, research has documented the practice of village-level management. Although village tracts are the smallest administrative unit in Myanmar today, most of the work of maintaining order and resolving disputes takes place on the village level with village administrators (those in leadership positions over one hundred households), area leaders (ten households), village elders, religious leaders, and other respected persons all playing a role in this work, with much variance from village to village (Lwin Lwin Mon 2020; Denney et al. 2016). There are also village militias throughout the country involved in maintaining security and enforcing local rules (Buchanan

---

12. A village tract is the smallest rural administrative division and can contain up to eight villages. For an outline of administrative duties at this level see chapter 7, "Functions and Duties of the Ward or Village Tract Administrator," http://www.asianlii.org /mm/legis/laws/wovtalh2012669.pdf.

2016; Myanmar Development Research and Kempel 2012). Such actors are sometimes proxy agents of the state in Myanmar, unlike village heads operating in areas still mostly controlled by ethnic armed groups who are part of those ethnopolitical governance structures. Nevertheless, both maintain significant autonomy when it comes to the day-to-day management of local affairs and often push for *nalehmu* ("reconciliation," lit. "an understanding") over punishment and rely on the kinds of promissory notes, or *kahn won*, discussed in this chapter (Rhoads 2020).

A key difference between the legal or administrative mechanisms in Thailand and Myanmar discussed above and the practices for Burmese migrants on the border is the extent to which the latter are rooted in networks of power that are connected to, but largely detached from, the power structures of the state or even Ethnic Armed Organizations in most cases. This jumble of overlapping hierarchies and mechanisms for making order are contingent on local, translocal, and cross-border relationships. A look at these networks shows that authority is constituted in connection to the state but not necessarily under the state's bureaucratic, political, or institutional power structure. In some ways the state's power is felt through its absence or mutated presence (Das and Poole 2004). Instead, authority is constituted via a series of interlocked power-saturated networks of which local Thai officials are one part, though not necessarily the head. The work of restorative justice for migrants has been outsourced to a series of well-connected powerbrokers. There are clientelistic aspects of these relationships: among other services, migrants rely on authorities to serve as intermediaries with the Thai state apparatus in exchange for being "good" subjects, whether as employees, neighborhood residents, or participants in NGO programs. For undocumented migrants, these authorities are just as instrumental in facilitating a political identity as they are in providing shelter or protection.[13]

---

13. The relationship between migrant political identities and clientelism differs from how scholars have tended to analyze patron-client relationships in Southeast Asia—that is, as a central component of how state political systems function (e.g., Scott 1972; Tomsa and Ufen 2013). Migrant political subjectivities are constructed as peripheral to state political systems, which designates them as "external" to the nation-state. Consequently,

A proliferation of local leaders appointed by various actors engenders, as these arrangements suggest, a multiplication of borders between different groups of migrants with different authorities and often different rules and methods of maintaining order. From this perspective, it becomes necessary to envision governance on the border as stemming from a multitude of groups, many operative only in one cluster of houses, one labor camp, or in two or three villages. As Comaroff and Comaroff (2006, 20) point out, when "governance disperses itself and monopolies over coercion fragment, crime and policing provide a rich repertoire of idioms and allegories with which to address, imaginatively, the nature of sovereignty, justice, and social order."

This chapter has centered migrant narratives about responses to and the resolution of gender and sexual violence in order to illustrate how an analysis of their discourses serves as an important lens into both order-making and meaning-making in precarious borderland spaces. The voices of Hsar Moo, Maung Law, Ma Say, and others quoted here bring nuance and complexity to questions of how populations experiencing displacement and social and political exclusion survive and organize themselves. They reflect that rather than a well-established parallel system of governance developed by Burmese political actors in exile, the tactics of order-making, discipline, and conflict resolution among Burmese migrants on the border are fragmented, contingent, and generative.

How incidents of gender violence are dealt with and the language used in the process are directly related to an expressed imperative among informal authorities, especially migrant social-welfare groups, to maintain some sense of social cohesion and to organize migrants who have "spread out everywhere unorganized," as Hsar Moo put it. At the same time, the methods described in this chapter and the narratives deployed to legitimize them appear to be a product of assumptions among many, including

---

migrants' political networks, many of which resemble forms of clientelism, exist or thrive specifically as a result of migrants' exclusion from the everyday processes of social order in Thailand.

actors in the Thai state, that Burmese migrants are better off managing their conflicts through "customary" means. Whether such assumptions are rooted in an essentialism of the migrant population or are just a convenient way to mitigate risk to the bureaucratic Thai state apparatus, they manifest in a sense among migrants that they do not have access to formal justice and must therefore look to other actors who appear ready to discipline the guilty, aid the wounded, and keep the peace. In this way, such order-making tactics and the gendered discourses that often accompany them speak to how sovereignty and governance for precarious populations are contingent on the landscape of low-wage production systems, cross-border political networks, translocal ideologies, and the micro-level clientelistic relations of power. In this space where sovereignties and boundaries have proliferated and shattered the border's geography, migrants appear further constrained by this disorderly array of orders, which carry out the work of border-security management in intimate ways the state never could. It is in this way that the everyday resolution of disputes, including those related to gender and sexual violence, are also instances of "everyday bordering." Such moments are idiomatic of exclusion and the constitution of state authority at the margins at the same time they suggest political assemblages that are translocal.

As well, ways of dealing with these gender-violence incidents contribute to the production of shifting gendered positionalities; ideas about how to survive and manage displacement that are themselves linked to ideas of femininity and masculinity. There is a resistive quality to these ideas in that they circulate in the interstices of multiple sovereignties. Yet these ways of instructing individuals how to see themselves and how to be in community with one another must be thought of as part of the work of reproducing the social order of humanitarianism and precarious labor on the border. That is, to the extent migrants adjust themselves and regulate their bodies on a biopolitical level in accordance with the circulating notions of custom and gender identity that are themselves embedded in border-based humanitarian logics, they also live up to implicit standards of a migrant work ethic that corresponds to the demands of mobile capital. Large-scale spatial practices that give rise to Special Economic Zones, including those on borders, are thus not only gendered but also influence gendered subjectivities in various ways, including how women and men relate to one another, think of themselves, navigate moral and civic structures, and participate (and are expected to participate) in local and global economies as well as in the social fabric and care structures of communities. These are among the most intimate ways that global capital has transformed spaces, insinuating itself into households and the practices of social reproduction, rendering both into forms of surplus labor (Bryan et al. 2009; Nagar et al. 2002; Pollard 2012). It is also through these mechanisms that migrants produce space in ways that forge networks for survival, order, meaning, and mobility. As the next chapter shows, the logic of humanitarianism and the structure of aid interventions on the border offer their own set of constraints and opportunities for security, mobility, and the contestation of gendered assumptions about what it means to be both a vulnerable refugee and an exploitable low-wage migrant.

6

Border Humanitarians

On the first day of the Core Concepts of Gender-Based Violence work-shop—part of a training package aimed at educating and empowering Burmese women in Mae Sot—the lights go down and participants move their chairs closer to a portable screen for a short film. When the facilitators—a Burmese and a Thai woman—switch on the projector, images of women's faces framed by an equal sign move across the screen. The participants see that they are watching a foreign film that does not take place on the border or in the region. The actress Eva Mendez is shown looking intently at a group of black women, while her voiceover declares: "Power and control are the reason rape happens in the first place." Another voice continues the narrative as global statistics about violence against women flash across the screen. "At least one in three women have been beaten, coerced into sex, or otherwise abused in their lifetime." Different snapshots of women of color in Africa, South Asia, and the Middle East are synchronized with the words "beaten," "coerced into sex," and "abused" that pulse into view. At this point, the former US ambassador-at-large for global women's issues Melanne Verveer appears, calling violence against women "regrettably a global epidemic." The rest of the film shows how the International Rescue Committee responds to this malady in Sierra Leone through "social empowerment," activities aimed at personalized care for survivors as well as changing men's attitudes and instilling in them a sense of responsibility.

When the film is over and facilitators ask for feedback and reflections, participants share four key themes that they noticed: the importance of empowerment, the link between violence and the abuse of power, the need to struggle for equal rights, and the prevalence of gender-based violence in many countries. As a co-facilitator for the subsequent training module on research methods, I sit in the back of the room and wonder which of the themes will feature in these training participants' work, and what other aspects of the film they absorbed, perhaps subconsciously. What about the racialized associations between gender violence and "Third World" women of color that resonates with Northern NGO portrayals elsewhere (e.g., Dogra 2011)? How about the use of medical language to discuss this violence? And finally, did participants take note of the emphasis on individual care and the absence of a broader feminist discourse of change?

These questions point to a dilemma of humanitarian politics, one that I was struggling with at that moment. While humanitarianism is foremost a moral concept, it has also become more overtly political in the last two decades, whether as a growing part of the rationale for military intervention or as a way of defining governance in ethical terms (De Waal 2007; Fassin 2012). But there is also the unspoken politics of what kind of ethics humanitarian intervention and the aid industry promote. Indeed, as noted earlier, Hardt and Negri (2000) locate humanitarian and human-rights work in the spreading of empire. Unspoken politics are what Susan Lindorfer (2009, 355) calls the "ideological substance" of intervention, and as the facilitator for the GBV assessment, including trainings on research methods and ethics, I was often filled with a sense of unease, wondering what types of relations or identities we were peddling unwittingly as part of our activities broadly designed to "protect and empower" Burmese men and women displaced in Thailand. Part of my ambivalence had to do with the welfare of the individual migrants who would participate in our activities; wouldn't our subtle—or not so subtle—emphasis on certain knowledges and values over others have an impact on their lives and on how they think about themselves, about displacement, and about what their opportunities and constraints might be? On another level, maybe the activists involved in this project harbored some ambivalences as well, given their histories of arduous political struggle, often at risk of persecution by the Burmese government. How do such histories and beliefs intersect with the kinds of humanitarian discourses emanating from Global North aid agencies and donors, which tend to universalize refugee populations as suffering, and in so doing, "leach out the histories and the politics" of individuals (Malkki 1996, 379)? That is, what happens to the situated struggles for political transformation of these Burmese activists in exile—whether in terms of the vibrant pro-democracy movement or the decades-long battles against and resistances to patriarchy—in this space of international intervention and supply-chain production?

To ask these questions is to recognize an alternative border-based form of humanitarianism that is intimately bound up in cross-border and regional politics and political histories. This chapter is about the ambivalence and subtle politics of humanitarian intervention and the complex and dynamic ways in which it is interwoven in the political subjectivities of Burmese activists in exile in a booming border industry town. Building on the previous chapter's look at the fractured nature of governance on the Thailand-Myanmar border and the importance of gender and ethnicity tropes in making meaning of violence and maintaining order, here I compare activists' narratives of gender justice with migrants' perception of NGO activities on the protection and empowerment of women. I am especially interested in how the ideologies of humanitarianism infiltrate and "haunt" migrants' and activists' efforts to navigate the violence of dispossession (Gordon 2008).

The Ethical Subject and the Politics of Women's Empowerment in Humanitarian Assistance

Toward the end of the twentieth century and in the early decades of the twenty-first, violence against women has increasingly emerged as a focal point for humanitarian intervention, which the industry often characterizes as gender-based violence. This trend reflects a response to growing recognition in the United Nations of various manifestations of such violence as human-rights violations, war crimes, and crimes against humanity.[1] Given the common interpretation of humanitarianism as a moral commitment to relieve human suffering, Miriam Ticktin (2011b) outlines

---

1. This includes a number of UN Security Council resolutions, including 1820 (2008), 1888 (2009), 1960 (2010), and most recently 2122 (2013), which recognize sexual and other forms of gender violence as war crimes and crimes against humanity in certain contexts, and which mandate states and the international community to respond to such violence and assist survivors.

a history whereby humanitarian NGOs, with Médecins Sans Frontières at the forefront, formulated primarily medicalized responses to gender violence in contexts of war, displacement, and disaster. This medicalized response, Ticktin writes (251, 256), rendered gender violence the "exemplary" humanitarian problem, as NGOs address "epidemics of rape" (to echo the words of Melanne Verveer) by healing one wounded body at a time, womanhood becoming synonymous with victimhood. Indeed, today, the most common types of humanitarian responses to gender violence are those characterized as "survivor care strategies," which include medical assistance, counseling, or advocacy for survivors of rape (Spangaro et al. 2013; see also Tol et al. 2013). A study by Spangaro and colleagues (2015) argues that NGOs consider care work combined with activities focused on raising public (or target group) awareness of available services to be the most effective intervention to reduce the risk of gender violence.

While such individualized and medicalized responses to gender violence signify the moral imperative of humanitarianism to restore a universal notion of humanity, Ticktin (2011b) points out that this tends to separate these acts of gendered violence from a necessary structural analysis of power and gender. This effectively depoliticizes forms of violence that are inherently political, as they are rooted in unequal gender relations and the social construction of gendered hierarchies. Ticktin (251) argues that humanitarianism's medical approach precludes "the ability to address this violence in all its manifestations" and fails to consider gendered violence "as part of larger histories and expressions of inequality which are inseparable from histories of class or race or colonialism" (255). To eschew structural analyses of gender and power in formulating responses to gender violence is, in fact, a highly political act, offering a particular interpretation of feminism as biowelfare. This book has included multiple examples in which migrants and migrant activists struggled between structural and political critiques of gender violence and a "global" humanitarian focus on GBV through the narrowed lens of individualized suffering.

However, in the second decade of the twenty-first century, humanitarian responses to gender-based violence extended beyond the bounds of physical care to consider an imperative to social change and to evaluate their own shortcomings in practicing gender equality. This was part of a broader shift from post-conflict reconstruction to more of a rights-based approach to development (Barnett 2011). A number of different factors have encouraged this change, including UN Security Council resolutions regarding women's participation in peacebuilding; the Sustainable Development Goals; and a growing body of evidence that gender inequality results in women being disproportionately affected by war, displacement, and natural disaster.[2] The Inter-Agency Standing Committee, a coordinating body for humanitarian assistance and policy, published its gender handbook for humanitarian action called *Women, Girls, Boys and Men: Different Needs—Equal Opportunities* in 2006, effectively taking the position that violence against women cannot simply be treated as another type of wound, given the gendered power relations that underlie such violence.

The creation of UN Women, the United Nations Entity for Gender Equality and the Empowerment of Women, in 2010 signified an attempt to bridge humanitarian responses to emergencies and the practices of the development industry, especially as related to gender violence. At the center of this effort is the concept of "women's empowerment," which, like the UN Women's mandate, inserts the development industry's approach to gender and gender violence into humanitarian practice. As the UN Women's inaugural director and former president of Chile Michele Bachelet explained, women's empowerment means going beyond "gender-responsive protection" and "gender-sensitive relief" so that humanitarian response can promote "longer-term resilience of communities and sustainability of humanitarian action" (DARA 2011, 7). Operationally, the term "women's empowerment" refers to programming decisions and activities

2. See UN Security Council resolution 1325 (2000) and 1889 (2009), which affirm the importance of involving women in peace processes and post-conflict recovery. Sustainable Development Goals include specific provisions for women, embodied in goal five: "achieve gender equality and empower all women and girls," and mention the importance of "investing in women" as agents of change. In addition, handbooks on humanitarian practice stress the importance of disaggregating data by gender to determine the gendered nature of conflict and recovery (see, for example, Sphere 2011). UN Women argues that humanitarian practice must also engage in processes of reflection to analyze its own gender practices with regards to recruitment, workplace culture, and staff policies (UN Women 2014).

that place decisions about the provision of humanitarian assistance, as well as the resources associated with that assistance, more frequently in the hands of women (IASC 2006). UN Women (2014, 2) writes that crises create opportunities such that "women may assume new roles in providing for their families, they may emerge as leaders and decision-makers in their communities, girls may get a chance to go to school, boys may be protected from recruitment to armed forces or forced labour and men may take on new roles in child care. Opportunities can arise during crisis to build back better in terms of the capacity of local institutions, livelihoods, service delivery and inclusive decision-making." As this excerpt shows, the notion of "women's empowerment" pushes humanitarian actors to think beyond the language of suffering and relief and more in terms of long-term development. Yet, as the following brief outline shows, humanitarianism's efforts to "empower women" belie the industry's ongoing tendency to erase gender politics from work with women.

Women's empowerment as a transnational concept has its roots in 1980s and 1990s feminist-organizing, subaltern struggles against class-race-gender intersecting domination, and Freire's (2000) idea of "conscientization" (*conscientização*), or critical consciousness-raising, in the context of popular education (Batliwala 1994). Women's empowerment involved calls for the transformation of unjust social, political, and economic structures, and as such was essentially a process of collective mobilization against both patriarchy and coloniality (Batliwala 2007). It was also a response among Global South feminists to what they perceived to be the largely economic strategies of Global North development discourse in the 1970s, particularly the Women in Development (WID) approach, which relied on economic-efficiency arguments to advocate for the channeling of more resources to women but did not address unjust gender relations (Batliwala 2007; see also Cornwall and Rivas 2015; Pittman 2014). However, as Srilatha Batliwala (2007) sadly witnessed in India (and as many other activists experienced elsewhere), the life of women's empowerment as part of the development lexicon exemplifies the development industry's success at depoliticizing and decollectivizing the language of struggle. According to Batliwala (560), South Asian feminist organizers initially conceived of women's empowerment as: "A process that shifts social power in three critical ways:

by challenging the ideologies that justify social inequality (such as gender or caste), by changing prevailing patterns of access to and control over economic, natural, and intellectual resources, and by transforming the institution and structures that reinforce and sustain existing power structures (such as the family, state, market, education, and media)."

Batliwala describes a trajectory in which this multilayered approach went from a highly effective organizing tool for grassroots women's groups in rural India to a phrase donors, governments, international NGOs, and private corporations used to champion principles of neoliberalism, which was on the rise in India throughout the 1990s. That is, Batliwala and others witnessed the transition of women's empowerment from a collective means to struggle for social, political, and economic change to a series of mechanisms primarily focused on producing economically self-sufficient women.[3] As Cornwall and Rivas (2015, 405–6) put it, the contemporary uses of women's empowerment "primarily concern the acquisition of material means through which women empower themselves as individuals and of the benefits that come when they put their spending power to the service of their families, communities and national economies." In this sense, development initiatives empower women to be independent and efficient producers and consumers within a capitalist system, one that will still exploit dominant gender hierarchies to extract a maximum of their labor power. From this perspective, the many thousands of Burmese women who join the ranks of underpaid and overworked garment-factory workers in Mae Sot are empowered, simply as a result of their participation in the labor market.

This individualized and neoliberal interpretation of women's empowerment is what one increasingly finds in Global North-led humanitarian action, where it serves as a reminder that women are a "good investment." The underlying assumption here—and a fundamental dilemma with the contemporary uses of women's empowerment—is a gender analysis that

3. For example, Oxfam's evaluation of its own poverty-reduction programs from a gender perspective notes that they primarily implement empowerment activities on the livelihoods level, urging economic change as the primary means to effect broader gender justice (Bishop and Bowman 2014).

divides women and men into categories based on their access to opportunities and resources, a move that defines gender as a set of "hierarchical and oppositional relationships between women and men in which women are structurally inferior" (Cornwall and Rivas 2015, 403). Rather than viewing gender relations as contingent and intersectional with hierarchies of race, class, and citizenship, this simplified analysis locates the problem and the solution to gender inequality on the level of local access to resources and markets. This narrowed conception of gender and gender inequality lends itself nicely to Northern humanitarian and development programs that seek to intervene on the level of the individual and the family and not on the level of unjust political-legal structures, exploitative economic systems, or patriarchal social orders. A struggle against the broad and diverse dimensions of patriarchy fall to the background as the dynamics of "case work," professionalized care, and individual empowerment take center stage. Susskind (2008) finds that humanitarian actors are often so focused on individual encounters with violence that they do not see or prioritize the widespread structural violence facing their clients, even when there are indicators suggesting causal links between these and individual cases of abuse (Dominguez and Menjívar 2014). The tendency to focus on women's biowelfare, as suffering or economic subjects and not as political actors, enacts a discursive slight of hand: their hypervisibility as survivors of rape and other gendered violence supersedes and renders invisible the reality of many women's poverty, inequality, and struggle (Crosby and Lykes 2011).

The emphasis in humanitarianism on individual self-care, including in terms of women's empowerment, reflects a broader trend of governance through moral principles and standards, what Nikolas Rose (1999) calls "ethopolitics," and part of what Foucault (1991) refers to as "governmentality." By "ethopolitics," Rose means the sets of "sentiments, values, [and] beliefs" that link individuals to notions of good governance (477). Ethopolitics is a "technology of the self," as Foucault (1988, 18) refers to it, "which permits individuals to effect by their own means . . . a certain number of operations on their own bodies and souls, thoughts, conduct, and way of being, so as to transform themselves in order to attain a certain state." Such technologies of self are part of neoliberal modalities of governance in which economic reason increasingly supplants political, social, or cultural consciousness. "Ethopolitics" refers to subjects who strive to be "rational, prudent, and entrepreneurial . . . actively making decisions about . . . conduct in the pursuit of self-improvement" (Inda 2006, 35). The ethical subject is thus engaged in a constant project of self-making toward standards of humanity evaluated in economic rather than political terms: productivity, self-reliance, and above all, efficiency. Ethopolitics is embedded within Foucault's (2008) interpretation of biopolitics, an individualized relationship between the state, sovereignty, and the individual on the level of management of the self. Biopolitics, argues Foucault, is instrumental to neoliberal governmentality, as "methods of training the body in the form of habit, in behavior" (Foucault 1977, 131) help construct the entrepreneurial and ethical self.

While ethopolitics, biopolitics, and governmentality are most often discussed in the context of "liberal" societies (see, for example, Brown 2015), their infiltration into the discourse of humanitarian actors and interventions to rescue the displaced reveals how entangled this ontological perspective is in the work of relief and development.[4] In fact, Judith Butler and Ana Athanasiou (2013) contend that Global North humanitarianism plays a purposeful role in the refashioning of dispossessed individuals into productive neoliberal subjects. A logic of empowerment predicated on the economic rationality of self-sufficiency becomes part of how subjects make and remake themselves in a context of repair and reformation. This, argue Butler and Athanasiou, gives a double meaning to dispossession. While the humanitarian imperative is about helping the displaced, it is inevitably also engaged in dispossessing individuals of their political and

4. See for example Fassin (2012) and Hyndman (2000). Didier Fassin (226) stresses that biopolitics is intimately intertwined with humanitarian action on multiple levels, including "the techniques of management of populations in setting up refugee camps, establishing protected aid corridors, making use of modes of communication around public testimony to abuses perpetrated, and conducting epidemiological studies of infectious diseases, malnutrition, trauma, and even violations of the laws of war." My concern in this chapter particularly regards the manifestations of biopolitics one finds in the strategies of recovery, empowerment, and self-development, because these help explain the role of humanitarianism as a technology of governance imbricated with the disciplinary regime of supply-chain production systems.

social histories, rendering them universally suffering, structurally inferior, and in need of an individual economic, not collectively political, notion of power (see also Fassin 2012). This ethopolitics constitutes an aspect of the "humanitarian border" (Walters 2011), offering particular technologies of governance situated within the space of intervention.

But such processes are anything but straightforward and run up against migrants' various agendas, relations, and networks. Since they are far from passive recipients of humanitarian aid, it is worth asking how the self-making technologies of governance I discuss here intersect with migrants' multiple, sometimes conflicting, interests, including those that relate to their own situated political histories and the disciplinary regime of supply-chain production systems in which they find themselves. In some cases, activists offer their own concept of humanitarianism that differs from that proffered by Global North agencies and is rooted in their agency and mobility. How migrants' histories, varying perceptions, and multiple identities engage with assistance programs that promulgate the "ethical subject" can reveal as much about how social actors negotiate the politics of displacement as it does about the nature of humanitarianism. Such an analysis can point to the importance of "theorizing from the borders," as Mignolo and Tlostanova (2006) write, when it comes to identifying the forms of humanitarian action that can not only assist but also enact solidarities and empathy with the migrant population.

Narratives of Struggle and Service: From Guerrilla Humanitarians to "Everyday Politics"[5]

For border-based migrant activists, there is an element of resistance simply in their presence and work in Thailand, as they "overturn cartographic power by carving out a space of refuge on the Thai side of the Thai-Burma

---

5. "Everyday politics" is conceived here following Kerkvliet's (2009) interpretation, which recognizes a resistive quality to certain quotidian actions among peasants or other populations grappling with systemic marginalization. In positions of extreme political and economic vulnerability, the tasks of survival can sometimes constitute violations of oppressive laws or norms and are therefore subversive, even if the actors engaging in such behavior do not necessarily define this behavior as resistance for a variety of reasons.

border" (Soe Lin Aung 2014, 33).[6] This view renders political the everyday life of running grassroots Burmese organizations, most of which are unregistered and thus illegal in Thailand.[7] Being an unregistered organization in Mae Sot means an office "hidden" in plain view in a house without a sign, where a discerning outsider might notice only an exceptional number of bicycles or motorbikes parked out front and an array of sandals at the door, where staff deposited them before heading inside. Such locales constitute subversive spaces, spaces appropriated from their intended purposes and just invisible enough from the broader public for local authorities to allow them to remain operational (Boyer 2006). This level of invisibility varies; some organizations strictly prohibit visits from outsiders other than donors (a precaution against attention by both Thai and Burmese authorities), others occupy a whole complex of buildings with a steady stream of people coming in and out at all times. Some offices pay off police for their invisibility, others work to stay out of sight, and in other cases, Thai district and municipal officials recognize a need for Burmese paraprofessional services and tacitly permit them to operate.[8] Acts of expression or amplified voices among unregistered organizations can mean a violation of the informal requirement to remain invisible. For example, in 2008 staff from the Karen Women Organization in Mae Sot told me that the day after they issued a press release condemning the Thai government's unlawful deportation of residents from refugee camps along

6. O'Kane (2006, 233) points out that in order to pursue political agendas through advocacy with state and UN authorities, it has been necessary for women's rights activists to "escape the incapacitating incarceration of refugee camps and other intergovernmental refugee regimes to act independently." Thus, in an ironic turn, these activists must subvert not only the Thai state's border enforcement policies but also the policies of the humanitarian system that maintains isolated refugee camps from which it has not been possible for activists to participate in feminist conversations taking place on more of a global level.

7. One of the few exceptions to this is MAP Foundation, which is a registered Thai NGO but is staffed by Burmese and Thai activists.

8. Mae Tao Clinic is a good example of the latter; their care for thousands of Burmese patients every year relieves the already overburdened government-run Mae Sot General Hospital.

the border, Thai security officials raided their office, leaving with boxes of papers and laptops that the staffers never saw again.

Beyond the political act of disruption,[9] activists manage multiple political identities and tensions that span moments of time and locales on both sides of the border. They balance political and activist agendas, marginal legal and social positions in Thailand, and the demands of Northern donors and NGO partners. At the same time, the participants in this project are women and men in exile, transnational migrants with families spread across multiple locales, refugees in the eyes of the humanitarian apparatus, and activists whose aims for effecting social, economic, and political change are rooted in their own complex histories. Their narratives of how all these layers manifest themselves in their work and life reveal an important series of tensions between discourses of resistance and ethopolitical governance.

While feminist organizing around rights and nationalism in Myanmar goes back at least to the early twentieth century, most of the women's rights organizations working in Mae Sot today started only in the mid-to-late 1990s, around the same time NGOs—both local and international—began to concentrate in the town.[10] All of the NGO representatives interviewed

9. The notion of disruption as political derives from the work of Mouffe (2005) and Rancière (2010).

10. Chie Ikeya (2012) provides an in-depth discussion of the role of women in the leftist and nationalist struggles that took place in colonial Burma in the 1920s and 1930s. This includes groups like the Burmese Women's Association, which advocated for the institutional expansion of women's rights. BWA and other groups, such as the Young Women's Buddhist Association and the Wunthanu Konmaryi Athin (Patriotic Women's Association), were heavily involved in student boycotts and other nationalist activities. As Ikeya points out, even as some of these groups offered feminist critiques of the status quo, they also embraced the role of "supporter" and moral guide for the wider movement, and not as leaders. Finally, it is also notable that within Burmese women's organizing during this period, there was a complex relationship with the growing "internationalist" feminist movements. Important "South-South" linkages informed Burmese feminist work, while at the same time the support for an imperial notion of Burmese women's "emancipation" through colonial intervention among many European and American women members of international feminist organizations, such as the International Alliance of Women for

primarily defined their work in terms of women's protection, and though some made explicit mention of women's rights, none referred to a more expansive notion of gender to include minoritized gender and sexuality groups. The place of politics was not always clear or direct. For several women activists in Mae Sot, their everyday work was textured by decades of resistance to the Burmese regime and their navigation of patriarchy's myriad manifestations.

Ma Thaung, the founder of a local Burmese group in Mae Sot, participated in the 1988 student protests in Rangoon, joined up with the All-Burmese Student Democratic Front (ABSDF)—an armed group that fought alongside several ethnic armed groups against the Burmese government—and then fled to Mae Sot after a decade at war. During her time with ABSDF, she worked as a medic and pursued an autodidactic social education by reading the works of revolutionary leaders like Che Guevara, Ho Chi Minh, and Aung San. She said that as a medic-combatant, "I saw underdeveloped ethnic places. I saw them suffering from civil war. I saw women and children abused." However, moving from student protests to armed resistance, Ma Thaung may have encountered a change in her own status. O'Kane (2006) explains that although many Burmese women activists recalled a fairly egalitarian protest movement in the late 1980s in Rangoon, they noted a shift when the same students fled to the highlands to wage armed resistance against the government. Suddenly fellow male cadres expected women who had played leadership roles in various parts of the movement to cook, clean, teach, or work as medics. The role of soldier was not an option for most. Naw Htay Paw, the head of another grassroots women's rights organization in Mae Sot, echoed this experience: "In the whole ABSDF organization, there were only two women in leadership roles. Only two! The rest of us were medics, teachers, . . . or communication officers." Filled with aspirations of revolutionary change but pushed to the margins of the movement, many women were determined to work against patriarchy on all levels and to focus on the needs of Burmese

---

Suffrage and Equal Citizenship (IAW) and the International Council of Women (ICW), created some tensions.

women and girls in particular, who they identified as disproportionately affected by conflict and displacement. Several women activists left armed resistance to pursue transformation by other means, including service and advocacy. When Ma Thaung came to Mae Sot in 2000: "I found that many women were in trouble in this border area. Many babies were left in the clinic. Women who experienced abuse also came to seek help. Forced sex workers also came to seek rescue. The clinic could provide only health services. It asked if we could do something and I decided to open a shelter. I gathered together others I knew and we founded a social organization."

Ma Thaung's work clearly derives from an urgent vocation to relieve suffering and save women from trouble, as indicated in her use of words like "abuse," "shelter," and "rescue." In this it reflects the language of humanitarianism, the recognition of a moral imperative. It also resonates with the humanitarian logics prevalent on the border at least since the mid-1980s when Christian aid workers arrived to provide assistance to the predominately Baptist Karen refugees. The growth of Mae Sot's women's rights sector was also contemporaneous and interdependent with virtually unceasing waves of involvement from transnational agencies committed to women's rights. Indeed, The 1990s marked a proliferation in women's rights organizing on a global level (Keck and Sikkink 1998) and in Thailand (Falk 2010). This was the decade of the Fourth World Conference on Women in Beijing and the Declaration on the Elimination of Violence Against Women. During this period and into the 2000s, a Burmese women's rights movement in exile burgeoned in a way that capitalized on these intersecting factors, heavily influenced by multiple discourses linked to transnational feminism, women's rights, resistance, and humanitarianism (O'Kane 2006). One set of initiatives brought Burmese women together from up and down the Thailand-Myanmar border regularly over a six-year period starting in 1997 to attend workshops on empowerment, counseling, gender, women's rights, and domestic violence (Norsworthy and Ouyporn 2004). Looking at the interconnected levels of patriarchy, the goals of these collaborative processes were to "develop culturally relevant solutions and action plans for social change," and to "help participants prepare to take the liberatory workshop methodology back to their home communities" (265–66). In this period advocates founded prominent Thai organizations to promote gender equality, including the Gender and Development Research Institute. Such organizations fought for the rights of Thai women workers, and as their director, Ruengrawee Pichaikul, framed it, saw the rights struggle for women migrant workers and Thai labor as inextricably linked.[11]

From the perspective that the border constitutes a space of subversion and escape, the work of social and biowelfare is, in and of itself, not just a professional activity or a moral imperative but a kind of resistive act for many who are involved in it. Talking on the second floor of a wooden house that served as an unmarked safe house, I asked Win Aung Lwi, the head of a social-welfare organization, about his vocation. Why, I asked, did he choose that sort of work when he came to Thailand? "In '88 I joined the uprising when I was only sixteen. Later when I arrived in Mae Sot, I saw many poor Burmese people, so as I was once involved in the revolution, I decided to continue that history and contribute. We know this Burmese government is not doing good. But as Burma is the military government, it isn't easy to fight against them through armed struggle. Therefore we're responsible for helping our people to be more knowledgeable. So I decided to do this work."

For activists like Win Aung Lwi and Ma Thaung, the humanitarian agenda of healing and teaching the wounded does not contradict a commitment to resistance or a broader feminist agenda. Alongside the emphasis on repairing and protecting damaged bodies, Ma Thaung called for structural change in Myanmar, "to be able to persuade men and the government not to discriminate against women so that the root cause of gender inequality can be dealt with." Here, the broader goals of dismantling patriarchal dictatorship in Myanmar meet the quotidian objectives of biowelfare in Mae Sot in the sense that these unregistered grassroots organizations are building up a constituency of women and men who will one day return from exile to change their country. Similarly, Alexander Horstmann (2015, 60) uses the phrase "humanitarian economy" to describe how humanitarianism has produced opportunities on the

11. Interview with Ruengrawee Pichaikul, December 2, 2019.

Thailand-Myanmar border to refashion weakened armed resistance movements as ethno-political and religious civil society. This enables the Karen political establishment to continue asserting autonomy through the provision of assistance and nationalistic teachings to displaced Karen (not unlike the KMR-KYO). This notion of empowerment signifies a commitment to an informed populace with a consciousness of change, a consciousness that subverts efforts by the Burmese government to cultivate a notion of citizenship characterized by compliance and silence rather than agency, inquiry, and criticism (Fink 2009).

Navigating Collective Struggle and Biopolitics

Despite the various ways in which activists identify a resistive nature to their lives on the border, their discourse does surface an important contrast between political work aimed at Myanmar and biopolitical social welfare in Thailand on behalf of the migrant population there, a gap that only seems to grow as time goes on.[12] This difference emerges in the types of activities organizations run and the varying narratives they reference in each. While several activists explain that they deliver feminist consciousness-raising activities to Burmese women living in migrant

12. The gulf between a politics of collective feminist praxis in Myanmar and individuated social-service provision in Thailand appeared to be widening during the political changes in Myanmar that took place between 2011 and 2021 when the military staged a coup. Donors were increasingly interested in funding only projects that could be implemented directly in Myanmar. Burmese women's groups in exile also encountered an expanded space for advocacy and activism in Myanmar as they waded back into the arena of political opposition. Their work there included population mobilization (through demonstrations, rallies, and protests), legal advocacy, and network-building with other organizations. Such activities have limited place on the Thai side, where migrants' precarious status precludes vocal struggle against the Thai government's criminalized exclusionary immigration policies or garment factories' severely exploitative treatment of their workers. Perhaps because of this context, Burmese NGOs' primary advocacy priority in Thailand has remained the achievement of greater rights for migrants there; in such a discourse an agenda of feminist struggle is apparently secondary. It remains to be seen how the discourse and practice of women's right work among Burmese migrant-activists in Thailand will shift in the long term after the 2021 coup in Myanmar.

labor camps and refugee camps, most of these have to do with understanding women's rights in a Burmese legal framework or the ways in which international human rights applies to Myanmar. "We use Burmese law," one activist explained. "As for Thai law, we got training about it too, but we don't know much."[13] Trainings by groups like the Burmese Women's Union also include content on the Convention on the Elimination of All Forms of Discrimination against Women (CEDAW), to which Myanmar is a signatory, as well as UN Security Council resolutions 1325 and 1889, which relate to women's representation in peacebuilding and the resolution of armed conflict. As the activist Naw Htay Paw explains it, these educational interventions serve a dual purpose: "Our training goal is to let women know that they own their rights. They must be able to make decisions on their own. We must own the knowledge of women rights. We also must enjoy these rights. That means we must be able to make decisions about our lives, like whether we want to have a baby or not. Our women so far are not like that. They know that they will depend on their husband, and so they must follow their husband's decisions. We redirect their knowledge. Women must have self-confidence. From our observation, they begin to have confidence, they dare to speak. They dare to go to Mae Sot market. In the beginning, they did not even dare to get out of the factory."

Several of the Burmese women's rights activists participating in this project defined women's empowerment in ways that spoke to both women's political consciousness in Myanmar and their personal lives in Thailand as workers and members of families governed by unequal gender relations. This reflects an artful management of divergent subjective spaces that intersect in the lives of displaced Burmese men and women. Narratives like this signal activists' abilities to navigate donor priorities, given that funding for Burmese human-rights organizations in Mae Sot has typically sought to support the growth of an independent civil society in

13. An important exception here is with regard to Thailand's labor law, about which migrants have substantial access to information as a result of the many dissemination campaigns local and international NGOs conduct in Mae Sot via radio and workshops.

military-controlled Myanmar rather than an international movement for workers' rights in Thailand.[14] Nevertheless, it does not mean that workshops about rights in Myanmar cannot build solidarity among Burmese women in Thailand. In Naw Htay Paw's words, one finds a cross-fertilization of political-mobilization tactics as she appropriates the discourse of women's rights aimed at change in Myanmar and applies it to the achievement of increased confidence among women in Mae Sot to work individually and collectively to seize power in their lives and workplaces.

The projects donors specifically fund in terms of gender work that is explicitly part of humanitarian assistance for Burmese women and men in Mae Sot and Phob Phra has a very different tone from the project of empowering Burmese women to be active citizens in Myanmar. As development and humanitarian industries increasingly regarded displacement and conflict from a gendered perspective, border-based women's rights and women's protection groups in Mae Sot enjoyed increased access to financial support from Northern donor states—namely, the United States, Australia, the United Kingdom, and the European Union—and from philanthropic entities like the Open Society Foundation (OSF). While some funding, especially from OSF, has gone toward expanding women's rights in Myanmar,[15] much of the focus on gender-based violence for Burmese migrants manifests in projects like shelters for survivors of abuse, case management, monthly women's group discussions, workshops on violence against women, gender-transformative approaches on the family

14. For example, in their 2014 and 2016 performance reports and plans, USAID and the US Department of State discuss efforts to support multilevel change in Myanmar, which they refer to as Burma. This includes advocating for the removal of repressive laws and promoting judicial independence, constitutional reform, and democratization. USAID has made women's rights a central component of this effort. See USAID/US Department of State 2015.

15. The Open Society Foundation states: "The Burma Project supports efforts to: address and prevent human rights abuses; promote independent media and access to information; encourage peace and reconciliation; empower women, youth, and ethnic minorities; and encourage an end to discrimination." They prioritize grants to organizations working directly in Myanmar. https://www.opensocietyfoundations.org/grants/burma -project (accessed September 23, 2015).

level, and mobile libraries that bring books and magazines into factories and onto farms for workers. Such work is, by and large, individualized and focused on the body and on the dynamics of intimate relations (Brush and Miller 2019).

Though the Burmese activists with whom I spoke did not generally mention donor pressure as influential in determining their agendas, they described funding competitions and donor-funded "technical support" by "experts" on a wide range of topics related to humanitarian assistance and women's protection.[16] A slew of publications has emerged in the last decade based on these technical visits, which often consist of collaborations between universities, border-based organizations, and donors (e.g., Maung and Belton 2005; Freccero and Seelinger 2013; Hobstetter et al. 2012; Saltsman 2011). These cover topics like "shelter management," "provision of services to survivors of trafficking," "case management system development," and "peaceful families." Such titles indicate a dual focus on professionalizing service provision and addressing migrants' intimate social problems. Navigating between humanitarian reason and their own agendas for change, activists' narratives speak to a kind of biopolitical discipline aimed at extending the bounds of intervention to the lives and bodies of migrant workers; they are as much about self-improvement as healing.

On the level of the body, activists framed programs about reproductive-health assistance as dealing with rights, culture, and personal responsibility. Research and education about reproductive health represent some of the most common humanitarian and development activities in Mae Sot, with multiple organizations running programs on the topic and several participating in an Adolescent Reproductive Health Network. As Naw Htay Paw, an activist from the network, explained: "When we conduct health education, some people are against the idea of teaching how to use condoms. Some people accept it and some people cannot. But there are a lot of negative impacts if they do not use condoms. What we see is women

16. In funding competitions larger Northern NGOs issue requests for proposals from Burmese groups and make strategic decisions about which projects are reliable and support the NGO's agendas.

with unwanted pregnancies who die from unsafe abortions. So we explain to them about this, too. 'If you want to live together with your lover, then use condoms. If you fail to use it, there is also the emergency pill.' We have to give them this knowledge."

While such interventions respond to rates of sexually transmitted infections among the migrant population on the border as well as unwanted pregnancies, Naw Htay Paw also underscores individual culpability resulting from either a lack of education or prejudice rooted in conservative attitudes toward birth control, thus affirming her role and the role of her organization as one of bringing knowledge about self-care to those without. For Naw Htay Paw, "rights and responsibilities must go together": "We must know our rights and we must be responsible. 'This is my right, so I can drink like a man does.' No, no, we are not talking about such things. We want to say we have rights, but at the same time we have the responsibility to maintain our rights. Enjoying our rights at the cost of others is not what we want to be advocating. We must have self-discipline and morality. We share this with women too." In this sense, empowerment and education are, at least in part, about instructing young Burmese women how to be ethical and responsible individuals. Naw Htay Paw operationalizes a concept of rights here as entitlements that fit within a social order built on personal responsibility.

As one of the fundamental principles of women's empowerment in the humanitarian and development lexicon, activists also looked toward economic self-sufficiency as a key goal for migrant women on the border. Staff of local NGOs particularly discussed this as a mission to help women secure their financial independence from husbands. This was in reference, as Ko Reh put it, to "survivors, many women who might need the income-generation project to have some kind of work, and then they are able to take care of the family after getting out of abusive relationships." Organizations in Mae Sot respond to the particular labor demands on the border by providing vocational-training courses on sewing, weaving, and farming. Visiting a labor-rights organization in Mae Sot, I was surprised to step into a room that resembled a factory, full of sewing machines and bags of fabric. By taking this organization's course, women can secure higher-paying jobs or work on their own at home for piece-rate pay.

Another organization maintains several hectares of land in Phob Phra, taking women survivors of sexual abuse there to grow corn.

These projects fit alongside gender-transformative approaches that target migrants' problematic behavior and social problems. One such activity, "Happy Families" (Annan et al. 2017), consists of a series of workshops, trainings, dramatizations, and other collective activities to convey good parenting and relationship skills. In this approach, activities occur alongside multiple rounds of interviews to monitor participants' progress and evaluate the project's impact. The International Rescue Committee runs another program on the border called the "Peaceful Families Initiative," which "involves three-day workshops teaching couples practical skills to strengthen healthy family relationships, manage stress and anger and resolve conflicts peacefully" (Holmes and Bhuvanendra 2014, 8). During interviews with staff who run these types of activities, I learned how such work engenders a paternalistic discourse of individual behavior change. As Soe Soe Mya, who worked for a worker's rights association put it, "We have to show a lot of good examples. Then [workshop participants] will say, 'Aww, [people in the examples] are doing this and living like this and so they are happy.' We give participants the knowledge this way." Ko Min Thu explained this work as an imperative to "change the mindset," saying, "We have to change what migrants already know so that they will be more humane. Then we raise awareness or conduct trainings so that there is less discrimination between men and women." Concerning the question of masculinity and violence, Ko Reh reflected: "We need a lot of awareness raising. Not only for the women but also for the men, so that they also understand. And then education about peaceful families should be provided to the couples. I think if we do the prevention activity a lot and continuously until they understand and absorb that, I think they can control their desires and their feelings, so they can respect each other." The language in these excerpts is permeated with modeling behavior and a disciplinary sense of education, producing an impression of intervention as personal adjustment.

If such accounts describe a biopolitics of empowerment as individual bodily repair and self-improvement, there is also a civilizing discourse seething not so deeply under the surface. On one level, this reflects the infiltration of market logic into the humanitarian and development language of empowerment mentioned above, which promotes a particular package of values and, as some scholars put it, constitutes a backtracking on earlier development goals related to gender equality (Pittman 2014; Wilson 2011). As noted earlier, such values are distributed along the topology of humanitarian borders (Kallio et al. 2019). But on another level, a vocation to "fix" or "adjust" behavior as part of an intervention speaks to the imperial effects present within Northern humanitarianism (Stoler 2016). In fact, this is an all-too-familiar dynamic that resembles the colonial vocation to save through civilizing regimes of order and the neocolonial development mentality of modernization (Scully 2011; Stoler 2002; Syed and Ali 2011). Works like Fanon's *Black Skin, White Masks* (1967), which critique this perspective, consider how the violence of colonial representation, which reifies historically situated and complex social forms, can result in forms of internalization and psychological trauma for the subaltern. Others focus on the transnationality of racialized and gendered hierarchies, which resonate back and forth between multiple locales, influencing local perception and dominant narratives (Magubane 2004). To what extent were these activists—and I—reproducing such gendered and racialized hierarchies as our discussions included reforming deviant female and male bodies, and as we sought to make our work legible to our donors?

Also resonating with this question was the treatment of "culture" and "tradition" as abstract and objective categories culpable for the prevalence of violence in migrant families and neighborhoods. This contrasts with references made by community leaders and mediators to culture as a resource for order and survival, highlighting the multiple gendered meanings of the term "culture" that different actors can employ at various moments. Here, among activists, culture and tradition are at fault, or at least at odds with women's empowerment. To exemplify this, Soe Soe Mya speaks metaphorically to explain the need for "cultural change" in her work: "There is a curry pot. If we cook curry in it a few times, the pot will get stained. We will have to clean it until all the stains are gone. If this pot has been used for a long time, we will need a new technique to clean it. Same is true [for migrants]. The traditional belief comes along with them, a belief such as their own country's law or their own culture and norms, and they practice this in their daily lives."

The image of cleansing migrants of their outdated traditions, like a pot being scoured, is a striking one. A staffer from a women's welfare group reiterated this sentiment, saying, "It is hard to remove conservative thinking and gender discrimination based on religious beliefs and culture." Similar comments featured in most participants' interviews, though I had not thought to explicitly ask about it. Activists described culture in general as "strict," "discriminatory," and the reason why women might be blamed for the sexual abuse they experience. Ma Myo Kyin, a trainer from a labor-rights organization, explained that one of her goals in providing training on "sex and gender" is to respond to "Myanmar culture," where "women have faced discrimination for many years." She continued: "This opinion is accepted everywhere. So during trainings we explain that men and women are different only in terms of sex organs. We're all the same otherwise. Then we discuss individual traditions. For example, women cannot go to pagodas or cannot be monks or cannot be Buddha, and men have more prestige. All these are gender stereotypes that are not related to sex. Sex is inborn. We explain the difference between sex and gender." Within this context, empowerment consists of challenging beliefs seen as "traditional" or "cultural" to create discursive space for the recognition of women as leaders.

An interrogation of culture as static and culpable was especially common when migrant activists discussed social problems in majority-Muslim neighborhoods like Kyuwe Kyan. San, who works at a women's health association located adjacent to the Kyuwe Kyan neighborhood, considered the question of empowerment with her constituency of Muslim women, noting an assessment run by the International Organization for Migration (2011) about community justice in the primarily Muslim neighborhoods of Mae Sot: "Earlier, there was some research carried out with the Muslims. And from interviewing the women, we know about their culture. What their cultural practices are. How their religion controls them. They are not like Burmese. For them, their culture limits women's movement. Cultures are different, so the method for giving them information must also be different. However, since computers are commonly used now, children who go to school can access more information through the internet. But their culture limits them a little." Culture assumes a disciplinary and controlling nature here, a force responsible for the gendered hierarchies in which migrants find themselves. The underlying idea here is that normative gender roles for Burmese people can be oppressive to women and that these roles are fundamentally unmoving. At the same time, as San slips into a "racialized" script, it is clear that such uses of culture can overlap with mechanisms to essentialize ethnic and religious identity in Myanmar.

While Islamophobia among non-Muslim Burmese migrants links to complex political histories and their contemporary manifestation in Myanmar, staffers' treatment of culture as oppositional and static adheres to a set of binaries commonly found within the language of women's empowerment—that is, rights is to culture as liberation is to repression (Avishai et al. 2012). A notion of culture as fixed temporally and spatially features heavily in this discourse about women's rights and gender-based violence, primarily as a negative force (Hodgson 2011). Part of this has to do with the language of international law, which links particular concepts of culture with various forms of gender-based violence (Merry 2006; Susskind 2008).[17] "Humanitarian organizations," write Abramowitz and Moran (2012, 123), "carry into" their work "preconceived notions about the meaning of culture as a determinant of human behaviors" that require "certain forms of intervention." Within this paradigm, culture is indirectly a cause for women's suffering, a complex and yet reified set of beliefs that can be overcome by the introduction of rights. Rights, then, "are weapons

---

17. Article 2(f) of CEDAW explains that state parties must "take all appropriate measures, including legislation, to modify or abolish existing laws, regulations, customs and practices which constitute discrimination against women." Article 5(a) requires state parties "to modify the social and cultural patterns of conduct of men and women, with a view to achieving the elimination of prejudices and customary and all other practices which are based on the idea of the inferiority or the superiority of either of the sexes or on stereotyped roles for men and women." In addition the CEDAW Committee General Recommendation Three describes prejudice against women "owing to socio-cultural factors" and urges "all States parties effectively to adopt education and public information programs, which will help eliminate prejudices and current practices."

that push against intractable culture" to relieve this suffering and liber-
ate women who will be free to realize their own potential as social actors
(Levitt and Merry 2011, 81).[18]

Gendered assumptions tied to concepts of culture such as these are
ever-present but all too often invisible to the very actors who implement
the policies and practices, as are the neoliberal undertones that filter into
articulations of empowerment and influence the nature of intervention.
Nevertheless, they constitute a manifestation of social violence in the
borderlands alongside the other constraints on migrant lives. This violence "haunts" the discourse of humanitarianism and development as it
renders visible migrants' social problems and erases layers of hierarchy
and structural inequality (Gordon 2008). The emphasis on knowledge,
control, and change in the service of producing an ethical subject evokes
an image of deviant men and subjugated women, while simultaneously
overlooking the colonial legacies and conditions of economic exploitation
that are so prominent in migrants' lives in Thailand. The targets of these
interventions are the very same precarious workers and actors of resistance
in the factories and farmlands of the Thailand-Myanmar border. At the
same time as they are so encumbered in the exploitative conditions in
which they live and work, these individuals are under immense pressure
to change and better themselves. Without being linked to the intersecting
levels of oppression and resistance that both men and women experience
on the border, as well as to the complex political histories ever-present in
their lives, behavioral-change activities risk reproducing discourses that
are at once colonial and neoliberal. As we see in the next section, migrants'
varied conceptions of humanitarian intervention reflect some of these
dynamics but also demonstrate the extent to which, for them, humanitarianism constitutes yet another set of opportunities and constraints to

18. A static interpretation of culture also serves to aid strategies that target women
as "ideal" and "trustworthy" recipients of development assistance because of their deficit
of power as women in "traditional" societies and their "natural" instinct to care for their
families (Buvinic and King 2007; Escobar 2012; Wilson 2011). Designating women as a
"smart investment" for aid in effect reproduces the unequal burden of social reproduction on women by glossing over their role in hierarchies of capital (Elias 2010).

be navigated, appropriated, and sometimes contested alongside the others that I discussed in previous chapters.

Interpreting Intervention: Security and Deviance

During interviews and focus groups, activist co-researchers and migrants engaged in conversations about how best to prevent and respond to violence against women. While the intention was to elicit ideas among residents of Phob Phra labor camps and Mae Sot neighborhoods about what role different actors could play in supporting grassroots informal tactics, discussions often revealed quite different understandings of exactly what NGOs were trying to accomplish on the border, and what they should be doing instead. Absent were notions of empowerment, whether individual or collective, neoliberal or politically transformative. Present instead were views largely centered on security, discipline, and bodily care. Only one participant mentioned training or support for livelihoods. Residents of the Mae Sot neighborhoods Kyuwe Kyan and Htone Taung were more likely to see NGOs as a possible source of shelter or rescue, while over all, the most frequent mention of organizations had to do with their role (aspirational or existing) in making or keeping order. This was followed closely by participants' calls for various types of self-improvement workshops.

In considering how to best address violence in and around the community, migrants often noted the need for NGOs to step in to fill gaps in governance. For example, a woman in her late thirties in Htone Taung stressed the need for organizations to play a comprehensive role in the neighborhood, saying, "Organizations should prove that they can also handle *ma dane mu* (rape) cases. If something happens, I think organizations can handle it. Whatever, even if a vehicle hits somebody, I think organizations can handle it." This was also a theme in discussions in Romklao Sahamit, where a thirty-eight-year-old woman who works part time as a community-health volunteer said, "I think we should have—or we must have—an organization to solve problems such as the violation of women, health, marriage troubles, stealing, and so on. Now we just live with fear even though we do not do any wrong." A fifty-three-year-old woman in Kyuwe Kyan specified that NGOs could help strengthen local-level order-enforcement mechanisms by providing "security guards to handle violence." Another resident of Kyuwe Kyan, a thirty-five-year-old woman, expanded on this idea, suggesting, "Organizations should solve the problem. They should arrest those guys. Here in this section people are arrested a lot in that way. People take the wife of another, the husband of another. Happens a lot in this section." Such calls for local groups to keep order (including an ethical sense of order), resolve conflict, and for more aggressive responses to intimate social conflicts prevalent in neighborhoods resonate with the formal and informal roles that NGOs and other cross-border groups play in governance and security.

For some, this had to do with an idea of NGOs as intermediaries between migrants and the Thai government. NGO staff are more likely to speak Thai, and this represents a significant asset and form of power. As participants explained, some groups, like those mentioned in previous chapters, are more involved in adjudicating conflict, but in many other cases, individual staffers of NGOs are the ones who carry out the "security" and "safety" work. Two women in a focus-group discussion in Htone Taung recalled:

> PARTICIPANT 1: The staff give their name cards after they provide us trainings.
>
> PARTICIPANT 2: And then if somebody reports abuse to us, we refer them to the relevant organization. A husband and a wife from Htone Taung fought and then came to us. We directed them where to go to report their case. Phone numbers and cards were given. When we call the organizations, they come and solve the problems.

This suggests an ad hoc arrangement as well as an emphasis on border-based humanitarianism. The work of resolving problems and making order might be more significant in the lives of migrants than are the planned activities usually funded by Northern agencies and designed to empower migrants by equipping them with knowledge of ethical, healthy, and productive living. It was, in fact, not uncommon for Burmese NGO staff based in Mae Sot to spend their time after work fielding phone calls from migrants who had experienced abuse and who were reaching out for help, though when managers at Northern NGOs became aware of this "extra" work, they sometimes regarded it as a problem since these staff-ers were not properly trained to do case management. During one visit to a Phob Phra labor camp with NGO staff there to organize a workshop the following week, I noticed that Naw Klo spent most of her time off to the side, conferring and coordinating with individual women, sometimes briefly examining their bodies or that of their babies. Later in the car, she was on the phone to help find a solution for one of the women who had disclosed an abusive encounter with her husband. Switching seamlessly between Karen and Burmese from one phone call to the next, Naw Klo reached out to a range of contacts, from comrades at border-based organi-zations to local Burmese teachers whose expansive network in the district made them invaluable resources as organizers. When I asked her later if her supervisors knew about her work "on the side," her face cracked into a wide, knowing smile. "They want me to just do my job, but all my life I worked as a midwife, and the migrants trust me."

Despite their emphasis on security, migrants in all four assessment sites also clearly received and interpreted humanitarians' biopolitical and moralizing messages. Whether due to the language abilities or pro-fessional skills of border humanitarians, or perhaps also because of their greater mobility and more secure legal status, a distinct maternal/pater-nal relationship with farm and factory workers was apparent. Explaining how essential these activists and service providers are in helping migrants grapple with social dislocation, a Burmese community leader in Htone Taung stressed that organizations "should bring together young girls once a quarter. They came here for work and they are away from their parents, so they need to know about prevention." Residents of both rural and urban areas noted that violence in their communities might be reduced with reg-ular trainings from NGOs that help impart important reproductive-health knowledge, model good relationships, educate young men and women about appropriate ways to behave, and target men's beliefs and behaviors. Describing the "Happy Families" project, a forty-one-year-old woman in Pyaung Gyi Win explained that the project staff "give us rice and *mohinga* (Burmese fish noodle soup), share information about reproductive protec-tion, social systems, and how to create a happy marriage and family life. They also share how to take care of a child, instructing us in this way: 'To train your child to be polite you should never say rude words to your child, you should use polite words, you should say things politely instead of beating your child.'"

With an explanation that closely mirrors the language of gender transformative approaches, this participant describes her labor camp using the same social-problem lexicon that NGOs use. A thirty-three-year-old woman who has been living in Romklao Sahamit for eight years and who does domestic work there for a wealthier household, noted that, in her view, "cases of violence are less frequent because the people are organized and taught. They now understand how to handle violence when it happens. On the other hand, organizations tell them how to live and what to do. So people are aware and avoid those behaviors." Both excerpts seem to implicitly suggest that before humanitarian and development intervention on the border, migrants lacked proper knowledge to care for themselves and their families. Another way of putting this would be to say that these participants' words reflect a disparagement of their own life knowledge as they call for more expert assistance. Deepening this sense, a man in his forties who lives in the Rim Nam labor camp and who works as a teacher sought to explain why humanitarian interventions in the area tended not to always be successful:

> The problem is that we are only trying to improve things from our side—from the CBO side. Improvement must happen from both sides. If somebody from the community is interested in these issues, we can pick him up to collaborate with the organization. It will make it better to teach about any issue, like sex and gender. I think you must have done a lot of counseling in the village, so you know what I mean. Most of the villagers here only think about the difference between sex when you talk about sex and gender. They don't know that it is more complicated than that and that there are so many issues under the topic of "sex and gender." I think we need a committee that can actually help people. For example, one time I had a problem with someone who came to the village to build latrines for the villagers. The latrines was broken after one or two days so I was really mad at the guy who built them, and I went to his place and asked him what happened. He said the villagers are not using water or tissue in the toilet but they use wooden sticks and the

toilets broke. That is a reason why we need to educate the villagers first. We cannot do one side only.

This teacher bemoans NGO activities that make only superficial changes (i.e., build toilets without teaching people how to use them, or provide trainings on sex and gender without real commitment from community members). But he is also making a secondary point that locates blame for social problems in migrants' lack of knowledge and effort to improve their well-being.

The themes of deviance and discipline are penetrating in these excerpts and they raise serious questions: Do participants really believe they don't know how to behave properly or take care of their children? Do they attribute the violence in their neighborhood to their own personal failings as spouses and partners? Certainly, many of the humanitarian studies of which these migrants are subjects—including our assessment— seem to support such perspectives.[19] These questions invoke the possibility of stigma—that is, internal conflicts of individuals who see themselves through the eyes of a narrative that has labeled them as "deviant" (Blaine 2000). Affirming Erving Goffman's (1963) assertion that stigma creates great uncertainty in the lives of individuals who fall within devalued social categories, humanitarian agencies implementing a Northern agenda appear to acknowledge broader structural violence but focus attention on individual social problems rather than systemic realities. This places the onus of change onto the individual who is problematized to, for example, internalize and/or reject the multiple manifestations and effects of inequality.

Nevertheless, perhaps migrants' articulations of intervention do not reflect their own self-indictments—and by extension the affirmation of intervention—but rather the filtered repetitions of messages transmitted to them by the many different aid projects on the border. This may be a way of responding to an assumption among humanitarian actors that

19. See, for example, results from the "Happy Families" study that suggest that as a result of the intervention, adults improve their capacity as parents and decreased their (self-reported) reliance on harsh disciplinary methods (Sim 2014).

they are the solution-makers, that they are needed. In either case, between the well-funded and coordinated projects to "provide contraceptive pills, measure blood pressure, check body weight, measure heart rates and also provide medicine for hypertension and other heart diseases," and efforts to craft migrants into ethical subjects, NGOs ultimately emerge as another set of patrons amid the many patron-client relationships prevalent on the border. Whether or not this is an unanticipated effect of intervention, migrants render NGOs—including the Burmese staff working for them—practical resources for surviving dispossession. However, while migrants do appear to find ways to make use of humanitarian intervention that serve their particular concerns for safety, security, and mobility, a significant dialectic is also playing out. Between the knowledge accumulated through lived experiences of migration, displacement, violence, poverty, and community life on the one hand, and the professionalized expert knowledge of intervention, on the other.

A Transformative Moment?

It is this dialectic of knowledge that brings me back to the topic of ambivalence, which is present on multiple imbricated levels within the context of aid and displacement. Much of this chapter offers a critique of the subtle politics of humanitarian reason on the border, tracking the proliferation of an ethopolitics of biowelfare that threatens to limit a feminist analysis of interpersonal and structural violence. But I have also outlined the fluid nature of the social field in which intervention takes place, pointing to various moments in which migrants and activists appropriate the language of humanitarian reason for their own agendas, and in ways that make sense according to their own political and social histories, whether as subversive acts of resistance to the Burmese state, efforts to make order, or other practices.

Many of the Global North scholars who write about women's rights groups on the Thailand-Myanmar border seize upon the topic of localized rights' discourses and tend to frame the relationship between local women's organizing and global women's rights activism as a transformative moment for the Burmese women's rights movement in exile, and as the impetus for Burmese women's critical consciousness-raising about gender

(Belak 2002; Harriden 2012; Norsworthy 2017; O'Kane 2006; Snyder 2011). This view identifies humanitarian intervention—and by extension, displacement—as a resource whereby local activists may "vernacularize" transnational discourses on rights to fit their situated concerns, norms, and relational systems, a process on which the legal anthropologist Sally Merry wrote a great deal (2009).[20] Based on this analytical perspective, Jessica Harriden (2012) identifies an ambivalence to displacement for women who "faced new challenges as refugees and migrants with limited legal, social, economic and political rights," but who "were also exposed to new ideas about human rights and gender equality through the media and their interaction with international organizations" (271).

However, the idea of the "transformative moment" appears rather linear and reductionist, implying a progression from oppression in Myanmar to liberation in exile, where women encounter the North as manifested in humanitarian intervention's articulation of women's rights. While this formulation resonates on some level with the stories of activists who arrived in Mae Sot, received trainings, and started social-welfare organizations, it also renders transnational women's rights work the focal point, rather than decades of activism for the rights and welfare of Burmese women, activism that often made use of—and did not necessarily eschew—cultural and religious themes to carve out space for women's power and agency (see, for example, Ho 2015; Ikeya 2012; Ma Ma Lay 1991; Maber 2014; Thin Lei Win 2014). Moreover, seeing intervention as a transformative moment overlooks the extent to which humanitarian

---

20. In putting local adaptations of rights center stage, the "vernacularization" literature argues that culture and rights are not oppositional but can often complement each other in fitting the goals and language of human rights to situated norms as a tactic to render them more effective. Key here, though, is a view of culture as fluid and dynamic (Hodgson 2011; Levitt and Merry 2011; Merry 2006). The interweaving of transnational rights' discourse with cultural knowledge systems suggests neither a prompt rejection nor acceptance of either situated norms or the universalist discourse of transnational human rights institutions. It just means reframing the language or the principles in a way that speaks to situated priorities, experiences, and values (Goodale 2007; Levitt and Merry 2011; Speed 2007).

reason's ethopolitical and biopolitical approach actually assists "in the preparation of young women bound for the flexible migrant labor markets" (Ong 2011, 36).

So instead of talking about a transformative moment, I choose instead to emphasize a multiplicity of humanitarianisms that at times complement and at times contradict one another. This includes the neoliberal logic of Northern intervention focused on individual empowerment, efficient rationality, and biowelfare; the translocal humanitarianism of border-based groups' order-making tactics of governance (such as those discussed in the previous chapter); and the many other manifestations of care and service, including the work of activists in Mae Sot who translate their years of armed struggle into social-welfare programs. This also includes a whole range of actors not discussed here but who ground their aid work in cultural and religious institutions, such as those who perform funeral services as acts of solidarity-building and those who rely on Buddhist narratives of social change or spirit worship to assert subjectivities that transgress "normative scripts of heteropatriarchy and the dominance of abusive centralized authority" (Ho 2009, 277; see also Brac de la Pièrre 2007).[21] These latter manifestations reflect the rich histories and varied articulations of Burmese feminist activism. Each of the above is its own sort of humanitarianism because they represent different political and social visions of change and well-being. Each also represents its own concept of the migrant subject, including the subject as economic actor, transnational citizen, or ethnic or religious constituent, categories that are not mutually exclusive but that overlap and coalesce on the border.

This expanded analysis of intervention and agency creates space to incorporate a more nuanced interpretation of the social impact of humanitarianism, including the various ways in which migrants make meaning of such practices and incorporate them into the everyday politics of survival. Put another way, this analysis allows us to see how humanitarianisms

---

21. Hindstrom (2014), for example, notes the important gender work in the movement to restore the *bhikkhunī* line of Theravāda Buddhist monastics in Sri Lanka and Thailand.

are ambivalent, as they are embedded within the power relations of the border, and in migrants' tactics, which do not necessarily comply with the agendas of the various technologies of governance circulating there. Whether in the workplace or in the spaces of social reproduction, as I discuss in this book, migrants' modes of social organization are simultaneously generated from and subversive to the conditions of precarity in which they live and work.

This kind of analysis also sheds light on another form of ambivalence that the idea of the "transformative moment" threatens to obfuscate. This is the ambivalence I sensed in the gender-based violence training at the start of the chapter. It relates to the double-edged impact of Global North humanitarian action, which offers to heal the wounded at the same time as it advocates a neoliberal framework for conceiving of the gendered self. However, this not only reflects the ambivalence of intervention, from a psychoanalytical perspective it also appears to inspire the subject's ambivalence (see, for example, Butler 1997). As each logic of humanitarianism materializes its own subject-governance relationship, with various interpretations of gender, ethnicity, culture, agency, and change, activists and migrants must struggle with the privileging of certain aspects of their identity and the suppression of others amid racialized and gendered relations of power (Butler 1997). Given that subjectivation always entails internal acts of subordination and privileging and that both are iterative processes, "the subject cannot quell the ambivalence by which it is constituted" (Butler 1997, 17–18). To Butler, the subject is always already in a state of production, reproduction, loss, and power. Taking this framework into consideration, migrants, to the extent they are subject to multiple different humanitarianisms—and to the extent to which they also constantly navigate a variety of other technologies of governance—are involved in an ongoing struggle with the underlying assumptions and influences of these interventions, some of which advocate the ethical subject as a remedy for stigmatized social problems, and others of which affirm dominant "traditional" gender identities. The social violence of humanitarianism's ideology is that it operates on the level of subjectivation to affirm dominant interpretations of gender and culture while denying the diversity of other logics or manifestations of agency.

As humanitarian practitioners, we were, of course, peddling different assumptions about gender, gender violence, and cultural identity in our work with the migrant population. As this chapter has shown, these relations haunt the dialogue and discourse between activists, migrants, and me, pushing, I suggest, for the privileging of certain ideas about what it means to be displaced and what it means to "be empowered," while overlooking others. But as a site of struggle, there is nothing inevitable about humanitarian reason. Analyzing the resonance of relations of power between the global and the local, and how these, in turn, resonate with migrants' everyday politics can show how the violence and ambivalence of humanitarian intervention, not unlike the violence discussed in previous chapters, do not foreclose migrant subjectivity but materialize as resources to be appropriated for survival across multiple gendered border positionalities. As the ideas of intervention interact with migrants' situated ethics, histories, and lived realities, new possibilities open up to problematize gender and offer new paths forward.

7

Conclusion

Erasure

When I started the research for this book, there were eighty-six homes and over four hundred residents in the Kyuwe Kyan settlement. As I conclude no houses remain. During raids in June 2014, as part of the new military government's promise to crack down on unauthorized migration, the Thai landlord of Kyuwe Kyan, reacting to pressure from local authorities, gave his residents 24 hours to get off his property. Despite an intervention by the Thai-Muslim council of Mae Sot to stay their removal, on June 12 at 4:30 am Tak immigration officials and soldiers from the Thai army swept into the settlement and picked up dozens of people while the rest fled into nearby fields. This was not the first time Mae Sot authorities had raided the settlement. Only a year before, Thai security forces arrested a number of residents, threatening to deport them all. But while the authorities in the previous raid relented and allowed migrants to return home, albeit in a state of uncertainty, in June 2014 the new military government was eager to show a firm response to unauthorized migration. Security forces watched over, making sure Kyuwe Kyan residents disassembled their homes, clearing the lot. Of the eighty-nine migrants arrested, immigration officials separated families according to those with children in school and those without. They allowed twelve adults and their thirty-four school-going children to remain but deported forty-three people, including those kids not in school on that day (Migrant Rights Promotion Working Group 2014). Precluded from rebuilding, the rest of the population who fled during the raid—about three hundred people—found themselves homeless.

In the months that followed this raid, migrants rebuilt a handful of houses, but these too were gone by 2016. With each disassembly and reassembly the homes looked less stable, more hastily put together, as if residents knew that they need not bother constructing something that would last. Without the houses of Kyuwe Kyan, the fields behind the buffalo enclosure look empty, just another dusty pasture in the peri-urban desakota. Prior to the establishment of the Tak Special Economic Zone, we could have expected a cyclical pattern of settlement and dispossession in Kyuwe Kyan, a pendular movement between migrants building homes and local authorities wrecking them to make an example of a poor Burmese Muslim slum in response to the state's concerns about unlawful activity. However, mirroring Mae Sot's own transformation in regional imaginaries from a peripheral frontier town to an important transport node in the newly realized ASEAN Economic Community, the buffalo enclosure on the edge of this town is now adjacent to a new highway built in 2019–20 to create another access point to the Moei River and Myanmar beyond. Like other similar spaces, it is probably only a matter of time before the field morphs into part of the SEZ infrastructure of warehouses, condos, and transport services.

Kyuwe Kyan is scarred by the erasure of a place and a people that represented a "threat" for authorities and even for many other Burmese in Mae Sot. Looking at Kyuwe Kyan now, one cannot tell, aside from the scattering of materials and household objects in the grass, that it was full of homes a few years ago. Perhaps this community will easily fade from the town's collective memory—if it had ever been part of its consciousness. Even if it gets rebuilt, the ease with which Kyuwe Kyan disappeared and with which it is possible to forget about the people who lived there, the social ties that might have made this a community to some, and the experiences they faced together, all reflect the violence of this erasure. It is, in fact, the partial absence of this place—the rubble—that exerts a force by reminding others in slums and labor camps along the border that their presence in Thailand is precarious. "Rubble," writes Gordillo (2014, 11), "is constitutive of the spatiality of living places," but is "more often than not disregarded in mainstream sensibilities." As many of the interlocutors who were given a voice in this book have noted, Mae Sot is riddled with sites of physical and social rubble, with erasure and suffering; it is a geography of oppression for those experiencing it, only visible to those who know to look.

Incidents like the raid are reminders of not only the instability of houses that are easy to take apart but also the precarity of the social relations that helped people get through their daily lives together, resolve conflicts, and maintain some level of peace and order. However, like homes unbuilt and rebuilt and people who have separated into other sites, it is likely that elements of social networks and social ties discussed in the preceding pages have not disappeared but have adapted and shifted again, under the duress of repeated displacement. The continual disruption of social forms among Burmese who are on the move and navigating exploitative work and living conditions is both a manifestation of a structurally violent environment and generative of new ways of being and seeing the world and oneself in it. This is part of what makes the positionalities discussed in this book unique to dispossession and borderlands. It is here, in spaces shaped by imperial durabilities, multiple mobilities, and logics of capital, among other forces, that migrants strive for order and safety. Their strategies to perform labor, to produce and reproduce households and social ties, and to organize modes of assistance for their communities and comrades have the potential to subvert dominant technologies of governance at the same time they reflect practices of everyday bordering. That is, the social practices and discourses I shared in this book, just like the construction and forced demolition of Kyuwe Kyan, are part of the work of differentiation, containment, and exposure that defines and redefines this borderscape as a space of hierarchy, precarity, and possibility.

Kyuwe Kyan's erasure also brings the village cleanup and my observations at the start of this book into stark relief with the reality of people's lives. In some ways, like much of what this book discusses, the settlement's demolition demands affective reactions like outrage, compassion, or solidarity before an academic response can be formulated. Nevertheless, reflection pushes me to ask what the imperatives of a written work are when so many of its subjects continue to face abuse and when the space they inhabited during the course of this research has been eradicated. In one sense, the violence of the act speaks to the urgency of work on migration and displacement in places like Mae Sot and the Thailand-Myanmar border. But it also raises uncomfortable questions that I must reconcile: What does the work humanitarian actors do mean in the face of a raid that wiped out an entire community? Or many such raids? What can NGOs like the one conducting the cleanup learn from this violence and from the apparent futility of their work? Can moments like this be used to call into question the political "anti-politics" of Global North humanitarian agencies? Among the many assemblages of power and solidarity discussed in this book, where might one locate the potential for scalable resistance to the violent manifestations of state securitization and capital accumulation? As I bring this book to a close, the dispossession of Kyuwe Kyan's residents places the intellectual exercise of writing into perspective and pushes me to ask reflexively what the implications of my findings might be.

Migration in a Changing Context of Shifting Territory and Borders

As this book has been concerned with the multiplication of borders through the performative reproduction of migrant precarity, it is important to consider some of the ways that these hierarchies might relate to social and political change on a broader level in Thailand and Myanmar and beyond. As noted throughout, while I regard the lines of difference and homogeneity imposed on migrants to be, in many ways, a product of the Thai-Burmese borderlands and its history of socio-spatial hierarchization, it is also increasingly the case that articulations of boundaries are enacted on migrant bodies in ways that correspond to the demands of industry. The structural violence discussed in this book is not limited to the territory of the Thailand-Myanmar boundary; the notion of migrant disposability and flexibility is reproduced every time migrants encounter social actors who see them as alien "others" for whom inhumane treatment or conditions are normal, appropriate, or inevitable. In this sense, migrants carry borderland spaces of exception on their backs wherever they happen to be in Thailand, whether inside or outside specially designated locales such as Export Processing Zones (EPZs) or refugee camps. Indeed, migrant labor and migrant bodies are yoked to imaginaries of industrial profitability in many parts of Southeast Asia and elsewhere (Chang 2009).

This includes the Burmese migrants in Samut Sakhon, the heart of Thailand's vast fishing and seafood industry. More than three hundred thousand Cambodian and Burmese migrants work in this industry that has become, in recent years, notorious for links to human trafficking and forced labor (Human Rights Watch 2018). One can draw numerous parallels between the experiences of Burmese farm and factory workers in Mae Sot and Phob Phra, on the one hand, and on the other hand, those working in fisheries and on fishing boats without legal status or labor contracts, where employers are known to hold captive their documents as well as their pay (Supavadee et al. 2019). Scholars have documented a similar kind of multifaceted exclusion for Burmese workers in this area, most notably in the Mahachai neighborhood of Samut Sakhon, which Puttaporn (2020) describes as both a "cultural safe-haven" and an ethnic enclave that "others" the migrants living there. This was the neighborhood where, as mentioned at the start of chapter 2, local authorities set up a barbed-wire parameter around migrant housing in a display of securitizing the space identified as the source of a COVID-19 outbreak.

In fact, across Thailand one can find Burmese, Laotian, and Cambodian migrant workers fulfilling low-wage jobs with limited protections, encountering similar kinds of labor-regulation regimes that leave them precarious. The revolving door and ad hoc nature of Thailand's immigration policies effectively ensures this reality for the estimated 3.9 million migrant workers there, or 10 percent of the Thai labor force (Smith et al. 2019). Arnold and Campbell (2018) explain that policies like this reflect state and market forces in Mekong Southeast Asia investing in the economic possibilities of low value-added industrial sectors that can feed into global supply chains. The Thai government's 2015 SEZ policy, marking the start of a multiyear project to build the infrastructure to house geographically segregated low-wage labor sectors along the country's frontiers, is part of this trajectory. What this suggests is that the kinds of practices and governance technologies the state and capital have deployed in and around Mae Sot are in fact at the center of how Thailand, and other states in the region, are structuring aspects of their economies looking forward.

Indeed, there are over one hundred SEZs in the Mekong region, part of a global increase in recent decades (Thame 2017). During Myanmar's window of intensive liberalization in the 2010s, investors poured billions of dollars into the country to build up production and transport infrastructure, including for SEZs and highways that are part of the Mekong region's economic corridors (Bahree 2021). The possibility of labor-intensive sectors in Myanmar is particularly attractive to capital, which has built up a US $6 billion garment and footwear industry there (Turton 2021). Burmese labor, whether at home in Myanmar or abroad as a migrant workforce, must grapple with their subjectivation by states and capital as a population for which precarity and low wages are an acceptable reality, a characterization that appears to be at the heart of trajectories for regional development. What technologies of governance are we likely to see as centers of production shift within the region? What role will migrants' social and political networks play in furthering or inhibiting efforts to make these spaces profitable? And what kind of gendered positionalities will these forces combine to produce and reproduce? Such questions point the way for future research on migration, borders, gender, and labor in Southeast Asia.

As this book has shown, frontiers for capitalist accumulation can also double as humanitarian borders, and the discourses and practices of aid and assistance are part of the constellation of governing technologies that migrants must navigate. Intervention by Global North agencies to save displaced Burmese bodies and families is an important site for migrants' political subjectivation as workers, activists, aid recipients, mothers, fathers, and more. In its focus on the suffering individual, the biopolitics and ethopolitics of humanitarian action advocates for a certain kind of entrepreneurial and hard-working subject without questioning the structural violence of the borderlands and its labor regimes (Ticktin 2011b). At the same time, this book has demonstrated that humanitarian interventions on the level of the family and focused on gender-based violence are instrumental to the contours of social reproduction among the migrant population. It is not just that humanitarian care for a few vulnerable beneficiaries can justify the state subjecting the rest of the migrant population to exclusionary and violent practices (as we see in Ticktin 2011a and Williams 2015). Rather, I have shown that humanitarian action is itself a set of discourses that offer and circulate ideas about how to see oneself and others in the world and how to perform selfhood. This includes an industry that produces and reproduces knowledge hierarchies, and gender programing that targets individual migrant and family behavior as a site for change at the expense of a politics of feminist anti-capitalist struggle. While not every site for spatially-determined low-wage production doubles as a zone of humanitarian action at the scale of the Thai-Burmese borderlands, states and NGOs are increasingly intertwined in regions like Mekong Southeast Asia, where the profitability of labor-intensive sectors depends on flexible and precarious labor excluded from regimes of social protection. It is in such places where "care increasingly functions as a technology of border enforcement that extends the reach of the state to govern more bodies" (Williams 2015, 12).

Agency and the Possibilities for Change and Struggle

Imbricated with Global North humanitarian action are what I have referred to as "border humanitarians," in reference to the heterogenous collection of networks, organizations, and individual actors that play a role in mutual aid, order-making, and community organizing among the migrants that live and work along the Thai-Burmese border. If gendered migrant positionalities involve the violence of state actors and employers, they are also made up of transnational and situated political and social networks, which assert their own ordering practices and discourses, as this book has shown through its analysis of the resolution of social conflict and intimate-partner violence. The rise of informal leaders, their tactics for handling disputes among Burmese workers, and the narratives of home, tradition, custom, and gender that arise from these processes play a significant role, both to help migrants make meaning of their experiences and as a form of governance that has emerged amid an assemblage of Burmese mobilities, regional imaginaries, and state (in)security practices. One of the significant findings of this book is that there is no single technology of discipline in spaces of exclusion or for excluded populations. Rather, collective and individual life that has been rendered precarious finds order in a diversity of fractured, partial, or mutated sources, some of which support the aims of capital and some of which assert alternative modes of social organization—that is, some of which can be attributed to the state or the market, and some of which come from elsewhere, whether it be a retired neighborhood police officer or actors affiliated with an ethnic armed group. That these relations materialize in a geography shaped by mobilities, iterations of dispossession, and narratives of exclusion remind us to ground our analysis in the social forms of the borderscape. This can help us deepen our understanding of how diverse assemblages coalesce to produce and reproduce the border as well as provide us with a lens for thinking about how borderland politics is situated within both local and global political economy.

In the wake of the February 2021 coup in Myanmar, for example, as the Tatmadaw intensified its aerial bombardment of Karen villages and displaced tens of thousands of residents, including many over the border into Thailand, border-based Karen humanitarian groups were, at least initially, some of the only ones able to access this population (Panu 2021). The relationships and cross-border aid networks forged through agency, mobility, and faith-based ethno-nationalism—including those that incorporate a growing Karen diaspora—mean that groups like the Karen Peace Support Network had the ability to fundraise on a global scale through social media and deliver much-needed assistance to those displaced in Myanmar and on the Thai side of the border, amid conflict that prevented access by Global North humanitarian agencies (Peck 2021). As well, the low-wage labor sector in Myanmar played a central role in resisting the military takeover in the early weeks following the coup (Haack and Hlaing 2021). This includes trade union leaders from Myanmar's emergent garment industry, many of whom are women and many of whom have experience working across the border in Thailand. These activists' histories of organizing, both in Myanmar, and in Thailand, even under conditions when such mobilization was (or is) banned, reflect a significant site for conceiving of ways that precarious labor conditions have generated their own forms of resistance and order-making. Gendered border positionalities are embedded within the texture of worker resistance in Myanmar, part of the many sets of experiences and ways of knowing that are present among the hundreds of thousands whose life trajectories have brought them back to Myanmar, at least for now.

Yet, as this book shows, it does a disservice to code these alternative forms of order-making as resistance and stop there. This is because while such situated mechanisms for maintaining social order can foster a kind of solidarity in the face of pressure to accept unjust conditions, they can sometimes reproduce their own kind of biopolitical management of workers, and of women in particular. As we have seen, the gendered discourse of such disciplinary practices often affirms dominant ideas of femininity and masculinity that displace the challenges and pressures of life in precarious conditions to the roles of men and women in migrant-worker households. Many of the explanations among border humanitarians for the violence of everyday life link to ideas about how men and women should behave. And the strategies to manage conflicts, including intimate-partner violence, sometimes involve an invocation of "traditional" and "customary" gender identities to avoid trouble and to combat the ways that precarious life corrodes social mores. Migrant activists' narratives about conflict resolution tell us something about how gender, violence, governance, and culture are contested concepts integral in various ways to surviving displacement. The ways in which these practices and discourses produce "gender" as a concept show us the complexity of what one might otherwise call "resistance" by reminding us to ask: Resistance for whom and to what? And at whose expense?

Borderland Positionalities on the Move

In addition to thinking about how these broader-level shifts relate to the dynamics of migrant spaces and collectivities, this book raises a number of questions about how violence and precarity interact with agency in the lives of migrants navigating displacement. I show that in migrants' narratives about violent life outside and inside the home are gendered ideas about why abuse takes place and how women and men should live their lives. While scholars have looked at the way perpetrators can use acts of sexual violence to strip individuals of their humanity, I show that for those participants in this study who are surrounded by but may not always directly experience such acts, the result is not an erasure of their humanity but rather its gendered reconstitution in a space of dispossession. Migrants' narratives are useful mechanisms to help explain the nature of life in places like Mae Sot and Phob Phra. Precarious life is often violent and there are specific ways men and women can look to their masculinity and femininity in hopes of avoiding trouble. That is, precarity, violence, and gender are mutually constitutive. This suggests that the particular gendered positionalities with which migrants grapple in spaces of dispossession can constitute resources for navigating the visible and invisible brutality of these spaces, even as they sometimes also signify sources of restriction. On a more general level, this set of findings calls for a scholarship on displacement and migration that conceives of movement as contingent not only on tangible costs and benefits but on more nuanced calculations based on gendered perceptions of how to get by.

This is not to say that gendered strategies for explaining violence and making order are necessarily forms of constraint on men and women. They can also manifest themselves as tactics for security as well as the organization of collective efforts and the expression of certain solidarities. I illustrated this point in two different places. First, in activists' recollections of how they developed their political consciousness and mutual-aid work in Mae Sot or elsewhere on the border, one sees how individuals' particular responses to the violence they experienced or witnessed in the process of being uprooted from their homes in Myanmar, or amid the conditions of life in displacement, led to particular social-change agendas and efforts to organize people around them in the name of social and gender justice. And second, the tactics of migrants to respond to gender violence that involve forms of mutual aid, as opposed to authoritative leadership, are important moments for the articulation of agency and the formation of social ties, including in ways that are sometimes subversive of extant power structures. I show, however, that at the same time, these sites for the articulation of relationships and identities that embody expressions of resistance must also be considered for the way they may privilege certain knowledges over others and reproduce power-laden sets of ethics.

By pointing to the double-edged nature of these border positionalities, I show the ambiguity in the "critical border thinking" that helps surface discourses, affect, gestures, and practices that appropriate and redefine the terms of dispossession. Continuing from here, further research is needed to consider what these kinds of gendered exertions of agency in spaces of dispossession could mean for women's rights organizing in Thailand as well as in Myanmar. Rather than assuming that gender-justice work on the Thailand-Myanmar border offers a more globally integrated version of a women's movement than that which is taking place now and in the past in Myanmar, subsequent studies might look to the way that particular solidarities, logics, and networks resonate back and forth between the peripheries and the center, between the borderlands and the polity.

Such a lens is especially relevant given the number of Thai-Burmese border-based activists who relocated to Myanmar, during the 2010s. Several of my co-researchers from the gender-based violence assessment in Mae Sot and Phob Phra, and other interlocutors from this project, moved back to Myanmar when they felt it was safe to do so; many went to pursue activist agendas and to follow the funding as Global North donor agencies shifted their priorities from the Thai-Burmese border to development and humanitarian work in Myanmar. Catching up with them in Yangon in 2019, I could see how their border-based experiences informed their perspective and approach to doing gender-justice work in Myanmar. Ko Reh, who has continued to work with Global North NGOs but was, at the time of our conversation, focused on gender-based violence in western Myanmar, saw her role as one of translation—taking "global concepts" from her organization's "technical unit" and doing what she called "contextualized translation" to fit the cultural dynamics of the communities where she worked. In her new role, it was important to proliferate the kinds of GBV case-management skills that her organization had deployed in the Thai-Burmese borderlands. She also expressed an interest in incorporating the women's empowerment and gender-transformative work she learned from her Global North humanitarian NGO into gender-justice work in Myanmar. In her opinion, "best practices to respond to gender-based violence [in Myanmar] is still a new area," suggesting a need for the import of these "global" tools that she had initially learned about on the border.

By contrast, Naw Htay Paw, who I also met up with in Yangon in 2019 and who works with the same ethnic women's organization as when she was in Thailand, explained that while her group mostly focused on GBV response and prevention in Thailand, including case-management activities, her main emphasis since moving to Myanmar was on organizing, advocacy, and women's leadership on multiple levels of government.

She described "community consultations" to document villagers' social problems and provide "updates about the peace process," and then noted that she conducts advocacy with both ethnopolitical organizations and representatives of the state government, advising women in leadership positions. For the peace process, Naw Htay Paw shared, "we demand of the stakeholders that at least 30 percent of the participants at all levels be women."[1] In this case, Naw Htay Paw was in no way signaling a rejection of the kinds of Global North humanitarian logics with which she engaged when in Thailand, but her work in Myanmar was more overtly political and focused on broader-level governance.

The diverse logics and narratives that border-based activists like Naw Htay Paw and Ko Reh deploy when they move to Myanmar are indicative of the heterogeneity of positionalities within the borderland's matrix of social hierarchies, variegated governance, and multiple expressions of humanitarianism. Their approaches resonate with contemporary transformations that were in place in Myanmar prior to the coup, including campaigns for national legislation to specifically address domestic violence as well as violence against women more broadly (Sadeque 2020).[2] As well, Naw Htay Paw's advocacy work is part of a much broader effort among women's rights organizations to push Myanmar to adhere to UN Security Council resolutions 1325 and 1889, which speak to the involvement of women in peacebuilding and post-conflict recovery. In the aftermath of the February 2021 coup, representation and gender justice were at the fore of resistance efforts and discussions around the National Unity Government formed as an alternative to military rule. Such moments in Myanmar's political and social landscape constitute important opportunities for the kinds of feminist organizing and activism we saw on the Thai-Burmese border; organizing that sought to frame women's individualized political subjectivation within a broader struggle for rights and democracy

---

1. I have not been able to reach Naw Htay Paw since the February 2021 coup and am not sure if she continues to do this work.

2. Though passage of this legislation would be a step toward ending violence against women, many anti-GBV advocates have been critical, pointing to anachronistic definitions of rape that come from an 1861 colonial law.

in Myanmar (see also Maber 2014). Examples like those shared here signal the need for a more in-depth analysis of how resonance can happen among the modes of social organization and the personal perceptions of gender and gender justice in Mae Sot and various movements for social change in Myanmar. Such a line of inquiry would be useful to deepen our sense of how border positionalities interact with broader political and social forces that migrants encounter elsewhere—that is, how the afterlife of precarious work in borderlands represents a durable force.

Turning Analysis into Action

Although this book is rooted in a collaborative action research project that informed the activities of border-based organizations operating in Mae Sot and Phob Phra, the urgency of the context and the sense of insufficiency that comes in the aftermath of incidents of mass violence such as the raid mentioned above engender reflection of what else can be done. On the one hand, findings from this research certainly reflect that migrants' everyday lives could be improved with certain changes to Thai policy, such as the establishment of a more permanent and stable legal status for migrants, obtainable more easily at no expense to migrants; the extension of social protections to migrants in a way that improves access to healthcare and education; stricter enforcement of pay and labor conditions; and the right for migrants to move freely, form unions, and collectively bargain, to name a few.

But on the other hand, with this book's focus on the more nuanced level of discourse, gendered subjectivation, and knowledge production, the stories included here underscore the importance of subtler and more localized changes. As the social actors in this context who have the explicit aim of bettering migrants' lives through concepts of "empowerment," "participation," and improving their access to basic human rights, I look to humanitarian and human-rights agencies—both border-based and Global North—as responsible for certain reforms. Though it will not stop raids and deportations, there are a number of practices among NGOs and border-based groups that could help make their work more supportive of the struggles in migrant collectivities for safer and more just lives. This includes agencies being more in tune with the multiple lines of difference that intersect labor camps and result in hierarchies that are not always immediately visible to some. Outsiders looking to effect positive change might strive for greater awareness of ongoing practices in migrant spaces that enhance security and solidarity. It is crucial to distinguish between these initiatives, which are often less visible, and those interventions that ultimately maintain order by imposing gendered hierarchies. There may be ways for outsiders to support the subtle forms of solidarity-making and care in migrant sites, or perhaps the greater need is to understand when *not* to get involved, in recognition of the fact that situated tactics to subvert or circumvent unjust systems sometimes need to be left alone rather than professionalized.

In regard to the work of many humanitarian organizations striving to empower women, this book stresses the importance of a broader gender analysis that takes into consideration not only family dynamics but also the nature of life in displacement, and the political and economic structures of power that are built on and perpetuate gender injustice. This broader analysis would include the ways in which aid agencies tend to project the dilemmas of displacement onto social and cultural forms in ways that reflect and affirm patriarchal structures and the relations of capital. This means making space within conceptions of humanitarianism for ways of doing aid work that are rooted in anti-capitalist or pro-labor solidarity and not in the reaffirmation of liberal or neoliberal values. Such an analysis would also relate to the fluidity of culture and gender categories—that is, how rather than adhering to static structures, migrants are in fact engaged in the work of producing and reproducing cultural forms and gendered subjectivities as they find ways to navigate the violence of displacement. Among humanitarian agencies, a dynamic and constructivist perspective like this could help ensure that project goals are more commensurate with participants' needs and not overly concerned with upholding neoliberal gender values.

Finally, this book has pointed to the importance of interrogating the diverse and sometimes invisible hierarchies that are pervasive in humanitarian and development work. This implies the need for greater reflexivity in the work of NGOs to go beyond the analysis of whether they are "harming" their service users and to examine how the power and privilege of their institution and staff influence the production of knowledge and hierarchies, even during efforts to promote "empowerment" and "participation." Though these comments essentially call for humanitarian agencies to slow down their work, embrace a more nuanced analysis of the context, and localize their goals in order to fit situated needs over donor demands, such recommendations are not all new and echo some of the critiques to which humanitarian actors have been attempting to respond for some time.

Knowledge Production and the Imperatives of Research in Contexts of Displacement

A central theme of this book has been the importance of reflexivity and praxis in research on displacement and violence. At the core of my analysis of migrant practices and discourse in Mae Sot and Phob Phra is the question of how discourse translates into material realities and consequences. This includes asking how the knowledges and agendas of the collaborative action research project that informed this book circulate as a form of power that interacts alongside other relations to reproduce or to challenge inequalities. My analysis, and that of the co-researcher group, was part of the construction of knowledge about migrants' lives that not only risked essentialization but in fact led to tangible projects and interventions designed to affect those same lives. The contours of such activities were informed by our collaborative assessment of the particular dimensions of need. A reflexive approach has helped to point me in the direction of the subtle or not-so-subtle ways that the knowledge and privilege that directly and indirectly informed the research might have seeped into participants' daily lives and self-conceptions. As noted elsewhere, contexts of dispossession are often sites of not only flexible labor and precarity but also biopolitical interest, whether in terms of humanitarian intervention or in the focus of researchers, government agencies, or other sources of neoliberal and bureaucratic authority. If this book makes a methodological contribution, it is to insist that a reflexive approach is key to research on displacement because it enables an analysis of contingent social forces that resonate between the situated and transnational and that, in some cases, operate in subtle ways.

This means that praxis is necessary, not only when focusing primarily on the impacts that research or the institutions supporting research have but on any work in sites of dispossession and violence. This approach signifies an insistence on focusing on difference, the production of hierarchy, and the perspectives that come from the interstices between what appear to be seamless categories. To do this is to use a feminist approach to interrogate scholarly approaches in order to assess the extent to which they overlook particular voices or knowledges and the way inquiry and analysis are structured. This is important not only because it may provide for a more nuanced study of process, discourse, and practice, but also because it offers researchers from the Global North a way to engage the power they bring to the context, interrogate it for how it contributes to the production and reproduction of certain hierarchies, and identify how it reflects the broader flow of discourse between global and local spaces. Such a perspective enables researchers to be more mindful of their relationship to the social violence inflicted upon dispossessed peoples.

But a call for reflexivity in researching displacement is about more than trying not to further inflict forms of invisible violence on participants. It is also a way to navigate a course of what Lykes (2013, 776) calls "informed empathy and passionate solidarity." An emphasis on thinking *with* and not just *about* participants relates to this and is what enables one to more fully be an activist-scholar who "accompanies" participants' journeys as they find their way amid the immense violence of dispossession and precarity.

References · Index

References

Abramowitz, Sharon, and Mary H. Moran. 2012. "International Human Rights, Gender-Based Violence, and Local Discourses of Abuse in Postconflict Liberia: A Problem of 'Culture'?" *African Studies Review* 55 (2): 119–46. doi:10.1353/arw.2012.0037.

Afifi, Rima A., et al. 2020. "Implementing Community-Based Participatory Research with Communities Affected by Humanitarian Crises: The Potential to Recalibrate Equity and Power in Vulnerable Contexts." *American Journal of Community Psychology* 66 (3–4): 381–91.

Agence France-Presse (AFP). 2020. "Thai PM Blames Migrant Workers for Market Coronavirus Outbreak". December 21.

Ager, Alastair, et al. 2014. "Strengthening the Evidence Base for Health Programming in Humanitarian Crises." *Science* 345 (6202): 1290–92.

Agier, Michel. 2002. "Between War and City: Towards an Urban Anthropology of Refugee Camps." *Ethnography* 3 (3): 317–41.

———. 2016. *Borderlands: Towards an Anthropology of the Cosmopolitan Condition*. Translated by David Fernbach. Cambridge: Polity Press.

Al-Abdeh, Maria, and Champa Patel. 2019. "'Localising' Humanitarian Action: Reflections on Delivering Women's Rights-Based and Feminist Services in an Ongoing Crisis." *Gender & Development* 27 (2): 237–52.

Alarcón, Norma. 1989. "Traddutora, Traditora: A Paradigmatic Figure of Chicana Feminism." *Cultural Critique* 13: 57–87.

Amnesty International. 2005. Thailand: The Plight of Burmese Migrant Workers. London.

Anderson, Benedict. 1991. *Imagined Communities: Reflections on the Origin and Spread of Nationalism*. London: Verso.

Andrijasevic, Rutvica. 2007. "Beautiful Dead Bodies: Gender, Migration and Representation in Anti-Trafficking Campaigns." *Feminist Review* 86 (1): 24–44.

Angkana Boonsit, Ron Claasen, and Suwatchara Piemyat. 2004. "Restorative Justice and Domestic Violence Resolution in Thailand." *Connections* 17 (1): 9–16.

Annan, Jeannie, et al. 2017. "Improving Mental Health Outcomes of Burmese Migrant and Displaced Children in Thailand: A Community-Based Randomized Controlled Trial of a Parenting and Family Skills Intervention." *Prevention Science* 18 (7): 793–803.

Anurak Panthuratana. 1998. *Mae Sot: One Hundred Years*. Mae Sot: Sunwathanatham Amphur Mae Sot.

Arendt, Hannah. 2013 [1958]. *The Human Condition*. 2nd ed. Chicago: Univ. of Chicago Press.

Arnold, Dennis. 2013. "Burmese Social Movements in Exile: Labour, Migration, and Democracy." In *Social Activism in Southeast Asia*, edited by M. Ford, 89–103. New York: Routledge.

Arnold, Dennis, and Kevin Hewison. 2005. "Exploitation in Global Supply Chains: Burmese Workers in Mae Sot." *Journal of Contemporary Asia* 35 (3): 319–40.

Arnold, Dennis, and John Pickles. 2011. "Global Work, Surplus Labor, and the Precarious Economies of the Border." *Antipode* 43 (5): 1598–624.

Arnold, Dennis, and Stephen Campbell. 2018. "Capitalist Trajectories in Mekong Southeast Asia." *European Journal of East Asian Studies* 17 (2): 181–91.

Asian Development Bank. 2010. *Strategy and Action Plan for the Greater Mekong Subregion East–West Economic Corridor*. Mandaluyong. https://www.adb.org/sites/default/files/publication/27496/gms-action-plan-east-west.pdf (accessed May 25, 2021).

———. 2011. *The Greater Mekong Subregion Economic Cooperation Program Strategic Framework: 2012–2022*. Mandaluyong. https://www.adb.org/sites/default/files/institutional-document/33422/files/gms-ec-framework-2012-2022.pdf (accessed May 25, 2021).

Assawin Pinitwong. 2019. "Kokko Chinatown Project Sparks Concerns in Tak." *Bangkok Post*, June 23. https://www.bangkokpost.com/business/1700208/kokko-chinatown-project-sparks-concerns-in-tak (accessed May 3, 2021).

Attanapola, Chamila T., Cathrine Brun, and Ragnhild Lund. 2013. "Working Gender after Crisis: Partnerships and Disconnections in Sri Lanka after the Indian Ocean Tsunami." *Gender, Place and Culture* 20 (1): 70–86.

Aung, Soe Lin. 2014. "The Friction of Cartography: On the Politics of Space and Mobility among Migrant Communities in the Thai-Burma Borderlands." *Journal of Borderlands Studies* 29 (1): 27–45.

Aung, Zaw. 2010. *Burmese Labor Rights Protection in Mae Sot*. Bangkok: Center for Social Development Studies, Chulalongkorn Univ.

Avishai, Orit, Lynne Gerber, and Jennifer Randles. 2012. "The Feminist Ethnographer's Dilemma." *Journal of Contemporary Ethnography* 42 (4): 394–426.

Bahree, Megha. 2021. "For Foreign Investors in Myanmar, Coup Adds New Uncertainties." *Al-Jazeera*, February 18. https://www.aljazeera.com/economy /2021/2/18/for-foreign-investors-in-myanmar-coup-adds-new-uncertainties (accessed May 24, 2021).

Bangkok Post. 2021. "Myanmar Coup Means Huge Losses," February 2. https:// www.bangkokpost.com/business/2060839/myanmar-coup-means-huge -losses (accessed February 4, 2022).

Barnett, Michael. 2011. *Empire of Humanity: A History of Humanitarianism*. Ithaca, NY: Cornell Univ. Press.

———. 2013. "Humanitarian Governance." *Annual Review of Political Science* 16 (1): 379–98.

Barron, Sandy. 2004. *Twenty Years on the Border*. Bangkok: Burmese Border Consortium.

Batliwala, Srilatha. 1994. "The Meaning of Women's Empowerment: New Concepts from Action." In *Population Policies Reconsidered: Health, Empowerment and Rights*, edited by Gita Sen, Adrienne Germain, and Lincoln C. Chen, 127–38. Cambridge: Harvard Univ. Press.

———. 2007. "Taking the Power out of Empowerment—an Experiential Account." *Development in Practice* 17 (4–5): 557–65.

Belak, Brenda. 2002. *Gathering Strength: Women from Burma on Their Rights*. Chiang Mai: Images Asia.

Bell, David, Jon Binnie, Julia Cream, and Gill Valentine. 1994. "All Hyped Up and No Place to Go." *Gender, Place and Culture* 1 (1): 31–47.

Bello, Walden. 1997. "Siamese Twins: The Currency Crisis in Thailand and the Philippines." *Focus on the Global South*, September 24. https://focusweb .org/siamese-twins-the-currency-crisis-in-thailand-and-the-philippines/ (accessed May 26, 2021).

Bello, Walden, Shea Cunningham, and Kheng Po Li. 1998. *A Siamese Tragedy: Development and Disintegration in Modern Thailand*. London: Zed Books.

Benjamin, Walter. 1998. *Understanding Brecht*. London: Verso.

Bernal, Victoria, and Inderpal Grewal, eds. 2014. "The NGO Form: Feminist Struggles, States, and Neoliberalism." In *Theorizing NGOs: States, Feminisms, and Neoliberalism*, edited by Victoria Bernal and Inderpal Grewal, 1–18. Durham: Duke Univ. Press.

Bishop, David, and Kimberly Bowman. 2014. "Still Learning: A Critical Reflection on Three Years of Measuring Women's Empowerment in Oxfam." *Gender & Development* 22 (2): 253–69.

Blaine, Bruce E. 2000. *The Psychology of Diversity: Perceiving and Experiencing Social Difference*. Mountain View, CA: Mayfield.

Blanchet, Karl, et al. 2017. "Evidence on Public Health Interventions in Humanitarian Crises." *The Lancet* 390 (10109): 2287–96.

Board of Investment. 2016. *A Guide to the Board of Investment*. Bangkok: Office of the Board of Investment.

———. 2018. *A Guide to Investment in the Special Economic Development Zones (SEZ)*. Bangkok: Office of the Board of Investment.

The Border Consortium. 2012. *Changing Realities, Poverty and Displacement in Southeast Burma/Myanmar*. Bangkok: The Border Consortium.

———. 2021. *Refugee and IDP Camp Populations: May 2021*. Bangkok: The Border Consortium.

Bourdieu, Pierre. 1999. *The Weight of the World: Social Suffering in Contemporary Society*. Stanford, CA: Stanford Univ. Press.

Bowles, Edith. 1998. "From Village to Camp: Refugee Camp Life in Transition on the Thailand-Burma Border." *Forced Migration Review* 2: 11–14.

Boyer, Kate. 2006. "Reform and Resistance: A Consideration of Space, Scale, and Strategy in Legal Challenges to Welfare Reform." *Antipode: A Journal of Radical Geography* 38 (1): 22–40.

Brac de la Pièrre, Bénédicte. 2007. "To Marry a Man or a Spirit: Women, the Spirit Possession Cult, and Domination in Burma." In *Women and the Contested State: Religion, Violence, and Agency in South and Southeast Asia*, edited by Monique Skidmore and Patricia Lawrence, 208–28. Notre Dame, IN: Univ. of Notre Dame Press.

Brambilla, Chiara. 2015. "Exploring the Critical Potential of the Borderscapes Concept." *Geopolitics* 20: 14–34.

Brambilla, Chiara, and Reece Jones. 2020. "Rethinking Borders, Violence, and Conflict: From Sovereign Power to Borderscapes as Sites of Struggles." *Environment and Planning D: Society and Space* 38 (2): 287–305.

Brees, Inge. 2009. "Livelihoods, Integration, and Transnationalism in a Protracted Refugee Situation: Case Study: Burmese Refugees in Thailand." PhD diss., Ghent Univ.

Brenner, David. 2019. *Rebel Politics: A Political Sociology of Armed Struggle in Myanmar's Borderlands.* Ithaca, NY: Cornell Univ. Press.

Brown, Wendy. 2008. "Porous Sovereignty, Walled Democracy." Paper presented at Roma Tre Univ., March 27.

———. 2014. *Walled States, Waning Sovereignty.* New York: Zone Books.

———. 2015. *Undoing the Demos: Neoliberalism's Stealth Revolution.* New York: Zone Books.

Brush, Lisa D., and Elizabeth Miller. 2019. "Trouble in Paradigm: 'Gender Transformative' Programming in Violence Prevention." *Violence against Women* 25 (14): 1635–56.

Bryan, Dick, Randy Martin, and Mike Rafferty. 2009. "Financialization and Marx: Giving Labor and Capital a Financial Makeover." *Review of Radical Political Economics* 41: 458–72.

Buchanan, John. 2016. "Militias in Myanmar." *The Asia Foundation* (blog). https://asiafoundation.org/publication/militias-in-myanmar/ (accessed February 12, 2021).

Bunnag, Tej. 1977. *The Provincial Administration of Siam, 1892–1915: The Ministry of Interior under Prince Damrong Rajanubhab.* Oxford: Oxford Univ. Press.

Butler, Judith. 1993. *Bodies That Matter.* New York: Routledge.

———. 1997. *The Psychic Life of Power: Theories in Subjection.* Stanford, CA: Stanford Univ. Press.

Butler, Judith, and Athena Athanasiou. 2013. *Dispossession: The Performative in the Political.* Cambridge: Polity Press.

Buvinic, Mayra, and Elizabeth M. King. 2007. "Smart Economics." *Finance and Development* 44 (2): 7–12.

Cabot, Heath. 2016. "'Refugee Voices': Tragedy, Ghosts, and the Anthropology of Not Knowing." *Journal of Contemporary Ethnography* 45 (6): 645–72.

Callahan, Mary. 2007. *Political Authority in Burma's Ethnic Minority States: Devolution, Occupation and Coexistence.* Policy Studies, no. 31 (Southeast Asia). Washington, DC: East-West Center Washington; Singapore: Institute of Southeast Asian Studies.

Callister, Ronda Roberts, and James A. Wall. 2004. "Thai and U.S. Community Mediation." *Journal of Conflict Resolution* 48 (4): 573–98.

Campbell, Stephen. 2012. "Cross-Ethnic Labor Solidarities among Myanmar Workers in Thailand." *Sojourn: Journal of Social Issues in Southeast Asia* 27 (2): 260–84.

———. 2013. "Solidarity Formations under Flexibilization: Workplace Struggles of Precarious Migrants in Thailand." *Global Labour Journal* 4 (2): 134–51.

———. 2018a. *Border Capitalism, Disrupted: Precarity and Struggle in a Southeast Asian Industrial Zone.* Ithaca, NY: ILR Press.

———. 2018b. "Migrant Waste Collectors in Thailand's Informal Economy: Mapping Class Relations." *European Journal of East Asian Studies* 17 (2): 263–88.

Caouette, Therese and Mary E. Pack. 2002. *Pushing Past Definitions: Migration from Burma to Thailand.* Washington D.C.: Refugees International and Open Society Institute.

Carr, Stuart C., Ishbel McWha, Malcolm MacLachlan, and Adrian Furnham. 2010. "International–Local Remuneration Differences across Six Countries: Do They Undermine Poverty Reduction Work?" *International Journal of Psychology* 45 (5): 321–40.

Castro-Gomez, Santiago, and Desiree A Martin. 2002. "The Social Sciences, Epistemic Violence, and the Problem of the 'Invention of the Other.'" *Nepantla: Views from South* 3 (2): 269–85.

Chang, Dae-oup. 2009. "Informalising Labour in Asia's Global Factory." *Journal of Contemporary Asia* 39 (2): 161–79.

Cheesman, Nick. 2017. "How in Myanmar 'National Races' Came to Surpass Citizenship and Exclude Rohingya." *Journal of Contemporary Asia* 47 (3): 461–83.

Chitruedee Weerawess. 2006. "Restorative Justice in Thai Court: The Study of Appropriate Model Relating to Domestic Violence." PhD diss., Mahidol Univ., Bangkok.

Chuthatip Maneepong. 2006. "Regional Policy Thinking and Industrial Development in Thai Border Towns." *Labour and Management in Development* 6 (4): 3–29.

Chuthatip Maneepong, and Chung-Tong Wu. 2004. "Comparative Borderland Developments in Thailand." *ASEAN Economic Bulletin* 21 (2): 135–66.

Couvy, Pierre-Araud, ed. 2013. *An Atlas of Trafficking in Southeast Asia: The Illegal Trade in Arms, Drugs, People, Counterfeit Goods and Natural Resources in Mainland Southeast Asia.* London: IB Taurus.

Comaroff, Joshua. 2007. "Ghostly Topographies: Landscape and Biopower in Modern Singapore." *Cultural Geographies* 14 (1): 56–73.

Comaroff, John L., and Jean Comaroff, eds. 2006. *Law and Disorder in the Postcolony.* Chicago: The Univ. of Chicago Press.

———. 2006. "Law and Disorder in the Postcolony: An Introduction." In *Law and Disorder in the Postcolony*, 1–56.

Cooper, Robert G. 1979. "The Tribal Minorities of Northern Thailand: Problems and Prospects." *Southeast Asian Affairs* 6: 323–32.

Cornwall, Andrea, and Maxine Molyneux. 2006. "The Politics of Rights—Dilemmas for Feminist Praxis: an Introduction." *Third World Quarterly* 27 (7): 1175–91.

Cornwall, Andrea, and Althea-Maria Rivas. 2015. "From 'Gender Equality' and 'Women's Empowerment' to Global Justice: Reclaiming a Transformative Agenda for Gender and Development." *Third World Quarterly* 36 (2): 396–415.

Crosby, Alison, and M. Brinton Lykes. 2011. "Mayan Women Survivors Speak: The Gendered Relations of Truth Telling in Postwar Guatemala." *The International Journal of Transitional Justice* 5: 456–76.

Daley, Patricia. 2013. "Rescuing African Bodies: Celebrities, Consumerism and Neoliberal Humanitarianism." *Review of African Political Economy* 40 (137): 375–93.

Daley, Patricia, Eugene McCann, Alison Mountz, and Joe Painter. 2017. "Re-Imagining Politics & Space: Why Here, Why Now?" *Environment and Planning C: Politics and Space* 35 (1) : 3–5.

DARA. 2011. The Humanitarian Response Index 2011: Addressing the Gender Challenge. Madrid: DARA.

Das, Veena. 2007. *Life and Words: Violence and the Descent into the Ordinary.* Berkeley: Univ. of California Press.

———. 2008. "Violence, Gender, and Subjectivity." *Annual Review of Anthropology* 37: 283–99.

Das, Veena, and Arthur Kleinman. 2000. "Introduction." In *Violence and Subjectivity*, edited by Veena Das, Arthur Kleinman, Mamphela Ramphele, and Pamela Reynolds, 1–19. Berkeley: Univ. of California Press.

Das, Veena, and Deborah Poole. 2004. *Anthropology in the Margins of the State.* Santa Fe, NM: School of American Research Press.

Davids, T. W. Rhys. 1932. "Buddhist Law." *Encyclopedia of Religion and Ethics.* Edited by James Hastings and John A. Selbie. Edinburgh: T & T Clark.

De Certeau, Michel. 1984. *The Practice of Everyday Life.* Translated by Steven F. Rendall. Berkeley: Univ. of California Press.

Decha Tangseefa. 2015. "Illegality and Alterity: Preliminary Notes on SEZ, Civil Society, and the Thai-Burmese Borderland." *The Journal of Territorial and Maritime Studies* 2 (2): 53–72.

Deleuze, Gilles. 1988. *Spinoza: Practical Philosophy.* Translated by Robert Hurley. San Francisco: City Light Books.

Deleuze, Gilles, and Felix Guattati. 1987. A *Thousand Plateaus: Capitalism and Schizophrenia.* Translated by Brian Massumi. Minneapolis: Univ. of Minnesota Press.

Denney, Lisa, William Bennett, and Khin Thet San. 2016. *"Making Big Cases Small and Small Cases Disappear": Experiences of Local Justice in Myanmar.* London: MyJustice, British Council.

De Waal, A. 2007. "Humanitarianism Reconfigured: Philanthropic Globalization and the New Solidarity." In *In Nongovernmental Politics,* edited by M. Feher, G. Krikorian, and Y. McKee, 183–99. New York: Zone Book.

Dewsbury, John-David. 2000. "Performativity and the Event: Enacting a Philosophy of Difference." *Environment and Planning D: Society and Space* 18: 473–96.

Deyo, Frederic C. 2012. *Reforming Asian Labor Systems: Economic Tensions and Worker Dissent.* Ithaca, NY: Cornell Univ. Press.

Dodson Lisa, Deborah Piatelli, and Leah Schmalzbauer. 2007. "Researching Inequality through Interpretive Collaborations: A Discussion of Methodological Efforts to Include the Interpretive Voices of Participants in Research Findings" *Qualitative Inquiry* 13 (6): 821–43.

Dogra, Nandita. 2011. "The Mixed Metaphor of 'Third World Woman': Gendered Representations by International Development NGOs." *Third World Quarterly* 32 (2): 333–48.

Dominguez, Silvia, and Cecilia Menjívar. 2014. "Beyond Individual and Visible Acts of Violence: A Framework to Examine the Lives of Women in Low-Income Neighborhoods." *Women's Studies International Forum* 44: 184–95.

Edwards, Penny. 2007. *Cambodge: The Cultivation of a Nation, 1860–1945.* Honolulu: Univ. of Hawaii Press.

Elias, Juanita. 2010. "Making Migrant Domestic Work Visible: The Rights Based Approach to Migration and the 'Challenges of Social Reproduction.'" *Review of International Political Economy* 17 (5): 840–59.

Englund, Harri. 2006. *Prisoners of Freedom: Human Rights and the African Poor.* Berkeley: Univ. of California Press.

EPW. 1976. "Fighting Insurgency." *Economic & Political Weekly* 11 (47): 1,822–23.

Escobar, Arturo. 2012. *Encountering Development: The Making and Unmaking of the Third World.* 2nd ed. Princeton, NJ: Princeton Univ. Press.

Falk, Monica. 2010. "Feminism, Buddhism, and Transnational Women's Movements in Thailand." In *Women's Movements in Asia: Feminisms and Transnational Activism,* edited by Mina Roces and Louise Edwards, 110–23. Oxon: Routledge.

Fanon, Frantz. 1967. *Black Skin, White Masks.* Translated by Charles Lam Markmann. New York: Grove Press.

Fassin, Didier. 2008. "The Humanitarian Politics of Testimony: Subjectification through Trauma in the Israeli-Palestinian Conflict." *Cultural Anthropology* 23 (3): 531–58.

———. 2011. "Policing Borders, Producing Boundaries: The Governmentality of Immigration in Dark Times." *Annual Review of Anthropology* 40: 213–26.

———. 2012. *Humanitarian Reason: A Moral History of the Present.* Translated by Rachel Gomme. Berkeley: Univ. of California Press.

Feingold, David A. 2013. "Trafficking, Trade and Migration: Mapping Human Trafficking in the Mekong Region." In Chouvy, *An Atlas of Trafficking in Southeast Asia,* 53–88.

Felbab-Brown, Vanda. 2013. "The Jagged Edge: Illegal Logging in Southeast Asia" In Chouvy, *An Atlas of Trafficking in Southeast Asia,* 111–32.

Ferguson, James. 1994. *The Anti-Politics Machine: "Development," Depoliticization, and Bureaucratic Power in Lesotho.* Minneapolis: Univ. of Minneapolis Press.

Fink, Christina. 2009. *Living Silence in Burma: Surviving under Military Rule.* 2nd ed. London: Zed Books.

Fisher, William F. 1997. "Doing Good? The Politics and Antipolitics of NGO Practices." *Annual Review of Anthropology* 26 (1): 439–64.

Foucault, Michel. 1977. *Discipline and Punish: The Birth of the Prison.* Translated by Alan Sheriden. New York: Vintage Books.

———. 1988. "The Political Technology of Individuals." In *Technologies of the Self: A Seminar with Michel Foucault,* edited by Luther H. Martin, Huck Gutman, and Patrick H. Hutton, 145–62. Amherst: Univ. of Massachusetts Press.

———. 1991. "Governmentality." In *The Foucault Effect: Studies in Governmentality, with Two Lectures by and an Interview with Michel Foucault,* edited by

Graham Burchell, Colin Gordon, and Peter Miller, 87–104. Chicago: The Univ. of Chicago Press.

———. 2008. The Birth of Biopolitics: Lectures at the College de France 1978–1979. Translated by Graham Burchell. New York: Picador.

Fowle, E. 1860. "Translation of a Burmese Version of the Niti Kyan, a Code of Ethics in Pali." *Journal of the Royal Asiatic Society of Great Britain and Ireland* 17: 252–66.

Freccero, Julie, and Kim Thuy Seelinger. 2013. *Safe Haven: Sheltering Displaced Persons from Sexual and Gender-Based Violence (Case Study: Thailand)*. Berkeley: Human Rights Center, Univ. of California, Berkeley.

Freire, Paulo. 2000. *Pedagogy of the Oppressed*. Translated by Myra Bergman Ramos. New York: Bloomsbury.

Fujimatsu Rin, and Alex Moodie. 2015. "Japan's Misadventures in Burma," *Wall Street Journal*, January 6. https://www.wsj.com/articles/rin-fujimatsu-and-alex -moodie-japans-misadventures-in-burma-1420566359 (accessed June 8, 2021).

Furnivall, John S. 2014 [1948]. Colonial Policy and Practice: A Comparative Study of Burma and Netherlands India. Cambridge: Cambridge Univ. Press.

Ghoddousi, Pooya, and Sam Page. 2020. "Using Ethnography and Assemblage Theory in Political Geography." *Geography Compass* 14 (10): e12533.

Gjerdingen, Erick. 2009. "Suffocation Inside a Cold Storage Truck and Other Problems with Trafficking as "Exploitation" and Smuggling as "Choice" along the Thai-Burmese Border." *Arizona Journal of International and Comparative Law* 26: 699–737.

Glassman, Jim. 2007. "Recovering from Crisis: The Case of Thailand's Spatial Fix." *Economic Geography* 83 (4): 349–70.

———. 2010. *Bounding the Mekong: The Asian Development Bank, China, and Thailand*. Honolulu: Univ. of Hawaii Press.

Goffman, Erving. 1963. *Stigma: Notes on the Management of Spoiled Identity*. London: Penguin.

Goodale. Mark. 2007. "The Power of Right(s): Tracking Empires of Law and New Modes of Social Resistance in Bolivia (and Elsewhere)." In *The Practice of Human Rights: Tracking Law between the Global and the Local*, edited by Mark Goodale and Sally Engle Merry, 130–62. Cambridge: Cambridge Univ. Press.

Gordon, Avery F. 2008. *Ghostly Matters: Haunting and the Sociological Imagination*. Minneapolis: Univ. of Minnesota Press.

Gramsci, Antonio. 1971. *Selections from the Prison Notebooks*. Edited and Translated by Quintin Hoare and Geoffrey Nowell Smith. New York: International Publishers.

Gray, Denis. 2015. "From Backwater to Boomtown—Thailand's Mae Sot." *Nikkei Asia*, February 15. https://asia.nikkei.com/Economy/From-backwater-to-boomtown-Thailand-s-Mae-Sot (accessed June 11, 2021).

Gray, James. 1886. *Ancient Proverbs and Maxims from Burmese Sources; or the Nîti Literature of Burma*. London: Trubner.

Green, Margaret, Karen Jacobsen, and Sandee Pyne. 2008. "Invisible in Thailand: Documenting the Need for International Protection for Burmese." *Forced Migration Review* 30: 31–32.

Grundy-Warr, Carl, and Elaine Wong Siew Yin. 2002. "Geographies of Displacement: The Karenni and the Shan across the Myanmar-Thailand Border." *Singapore Journal of Tropical Geography* 23 (1): 93–122.

Gupta, Avijit. 2005. *The Physical Geography of Southeast Asia*. Oxford: Oxford Univ. Press.

Haack, Michael, and Nadi Hlaing. 2021. "Workers in Myanmar Are Launching General Strikes to Resist the Military Coup." *Jacobin Magazine*. https://jacobinmag.com/2021/03/myanmar-burma-general-strike-coup/ (accessed May 22, 2021).

Häkli, Jouni, Elisa Pascucci, and Kirsi Pauliina Kallio. 2017. "Becoming Refugee in Cairo: The Political in Performativity." *International Political Sociology* 11 (2): 185–202.

Han, Naw Betty. 2019. "Shwe Kokko: A Paradise for Chinese Investment." *Frontier Myanmar*, September 5. https://www.frontiermyanmar.net/en/shwe-kokko-a-paradise-for-chinese-investment/ (accessed June 10, 2021).

Han, Naw Betty, and Thomas Kean. 2020. "On the Thai-Myanmar Border, COVID-19 Closes a Billion-Dollar Racket." *Frontier Myanmar*, June 6. https://www.frontiermyanmar.net/en/on-the-thai-myanmar-border-covid-19-closes-a-billion-dollar-racket/ (accessed June 10, 2021).

Harkins, Benjamin, ed. 2019. *Thailand Migration Report 2019*. Bangkok: International Organization for Migration.

Harms, Eric. 2011. *Saigon's Edge: On the Margins of Ho Chi Minh City*. Minneapolis: Univ. of Minnesota Press.

Hardt, Michael, and Antonio Negri. 2000. *Empire*. Cambridge: Harvard Univ. Press.

Harkins, Benjamin, and Anas Ali. 2017. *Evidence or Attitudes? Assessing the Foundations of Thailand's Labour Migration Policies*. Bangkok: International Organization for Migration. http://un-act.org/publication/evidence-attitudes -assessing-foundations-thailands-labour-migration-policies (accessed June 14, 2021).

Harrell-Bond, Barbara. 2002. "Can Humanitarian Work with Refugees Be Humane?" *Human Rights Quarterly* 24 (1): 51–85.

Harriden, Jessica. 2012. *The Authority of Influence: Women and Power in Burmese History*. Copenhagen: NIAS Press.

Harrisson, Annika Pohl, and Helene Maria Kyed. 2019. "Ceasefire State-Making and Justice Provision by Ethnic Armed Groups in Southeast Myanmar." *Sojourn: Journal of Social Issues in Southeast Asia* 34 (2): 290–326.

Harvey, David. 2006. *Spaces of Global Capitalism: Towards a Theory of Uneven Geographical Development*. London: Verso.

Herzfeld, Michael. 2002. "The Absent Presence: Discourses of Crypto-Colonialism." *The South Atlantic Quarterly* 101 (4): 899–926.

Heynen, Nik, Peter Hossler, and Andrew Herod. 2009. "Surviving Uneven Development: Social Reproduction and the Persistence of Capitalism." *New Political Economy* 16 (2): 239–45.

Hilhorst, Dorothea. 2003. *The Real World of NGOs: Discourses, Diversity, and Development*. London: Zed Books.

Hindstrom, Hanna. 2014. "The Rise of Buddhist Feminism?" *The Diplomat*, May 18. http://thediplomat.com/2014/05/the-rise-of-buddhist-feminism/ (accessed January 22, 2015).

Hirsch, Philip. 1992. "State, Capital and Land in Recently Cleared Areas of Western Thailand." *Pacific Viewpoint* 33 (1): 36–57.

———. 2009. "Revisiting Frontiers as Transitional Spaces in Thailand." *The Geographical Journal* 175 (2): 124–32.

Hla Aung. 1968. "The Effect of Anglo-Indian Legislation on Burmese Customary Law." In *Family Law and Customary Law in Asia: A Contemporary Legal Perspective*, edited by David C. Buxbaum, 67–88. The Hague: Martinus Nijhoff.

Ho, Tamara C. 2009. "Transgender, Transgression, and Translation: A Cartography of Nat Kadaws Notes on Gender and Sexuality within the Spirit Cult of Burma." *Discourse* 31 (3): 273–317.

———. 2015. *Romancing Human Rights: Gender, Intimacy, and Power between Burma and the West*. Honolulu: Univ. of Hawaii Press.

Hobsbawm, Eric. 1983. "Introduction: Inventing Tradition." In *The Invention of Tradition*, edited by Eric Hobsbawm and Terence Ranger, 1–14. Cambridge: Cambridge Univ. Press.

Hobstetter, Margaret, et al. 2012. *Separated by Borders, United in Need: An Assessment of Reproductive Health on the Thailand-Burma Border*. Cambridge, MA: Ibis Reproductive Health.

Hochschild, Arlie R., and Anne Machung. 2012. *The Second Shift*. New York: Avon.

Hodgson, Dorothy L. 2011. "Introduction: Gender and Culture at the Limit of Rights." In *Gender and Culture at the Limit of Rights*, edited Dorothy L. Hodgson, 1–16. Philadelphia: Univ. of Pennsylvania Press.

Holmes, Rebecca, and Dharini Bhuvanendra. 2014. *Preventing and Responding to Gender-Based Violence in Humanitarian Crises*. London: Humanitarian Practice Network.

Hondagneu-Sotelo Pierrette, and Michael A. Messner. 1994. "Gender Displays and Men's Power: The 'New Man' and the Mexican Immigrant Man." In *Theorizing Masculinities*, edited by Harry Brod and Michael Kaufman, 200–218. London: Sage.

Hopkins, Peter. 2018. "Feminist Geographies and Intersectionality." *Gender, Place & Culture* 25 (4): 585–90.

Horst, Cindy. 2006. *Transnational Nomads: How Somalis Cope with Refugee Life in the Dadaab Camps of Kenya*. Oxford: Berghahn Books.

Horstmann, Alexander. 2011. "Sacred Networks and Struggles among the Karen Baptists across the Thailand-Burma Border." *Moussons* 17 (1): 85–104.

———. 2014. "Stretching the Border: Confinement, Mobility and the Refugee Public among Karen Refugees in Thailand and Burma." *Journal of Borderlands Studies* 29 (1): 47–61.

———. 2015. "Uneasy Pairs: Revitalizations of Karen Ethno-Nationalism and Civil Society across the Thai-Burmese Border." *The Journal of Territorial and Maritime Studies* 2 (2): 55–75.

———. 2018. "Humanitarian Assistance and Protestant Proselytizing in the Borderlands of Myanmar: The Free Burma Rangers." In *Routledge Handbook of Asian Borderlands*, edited by Alexander Horstmann, Martin Saxer, and Alessandro Rippa, 349–60. Oxon: Routledge.

Human Rights Watch. 2010. *From the Tiger and the Crocodile: Abuse of Migrant Workers in Thailand*. New York: Human Rights Watch.

————. 2012. *Ad Hoc and Inadequate: Thailand's Treatment of Refugees and Asylum Seekers*. New York: Human Rights Watch.

————. 2018. Hidden Chains: Rights Abuses and Forced Labor in Thailand's Fishing Industry. New York: Human Rights Watch.

Hyndman, Jennifer. 2000. *Managing Displacement: Refugees and the Politics of Humanitarianism*. Minneapolis: Univ. of Minnesota Press.

————. 2002. "Business and Bludgeon at the Border: A Transnational Political Economy of Human Displacement in Thailand and Burma." *GeoJournal* 56 (1): 39–46.

Hyndman, Jennifer, and Wenona Giles. 2017. *Refugees in Extended Exile: Living on the Edge*. New York: Routledge.

Ikeya, Chie. 2012. *Refiguring Women, Colonialism, & Modernity in Burma*. Chiang Mai: Silkworm Books.

Ilcan, Suzan, and Kim Rygiel. 2015. "'Resiliency Humanitarianism': Responsibilizing Refugees through Humanitarian Emergency Governance in the Camp." *International Political Sociology* 9 (4): 333–51.

Inda, Jonathan Xavier. 2006. *Targeting Immigrants: Government, Technology, and Ethics*. Malden, MA: Blackwell Publishing.

Inter-Agency Standing Committee. 2006. *Women, Girls, Boys, and Men: Different Needs—Equal Opportunities*. Geneva: IASC.

International Commission of Jurists. 2012. *Women's Access to Justice: Identifying the Obstacles and Need for Change—Thailand*. Bangkok: International Commission of Jurists and Justice for Peace Foundation.

International Labor Organization. 2013. *Employment Practices and Working Conditions in Thailand's Fishing Sector*. Bangkok: International Labor Organization and Asian Research Center for Migration.

International Organization for Migration (IOM). 2011. *An Assessment of the Provision of Health and Social Services to Burmese Muslims in Mae Sot, Thailand*. Bangkok: IOM.

International Rescue Committee. 2006. *Assessment of Protection Issues, with a Focus on Access to Justice and the Rule of Law*. Bangkok: International Rescue Committee.

————. 2010. *Legal Assistance Center (LAC): Mid-term Assessment, October 2010*. Bangkok: International Rescue Committee.

————. 2011. *Participatory Assessment of the Protection Needs of Women and Girls in Mae La Refugee Camp*. Bangkok: International Rescue Committee.

Isin, Engin F. 2012. *Citizens without Frontiers*. New York: Bloomsbury.

Jackson, M. 2013. *The Politics of Storytelling: Variations on a Theme by Hannah Arendt.* Copenhagen: Museum Musculanum Press.

Jacobsen, Karen. 2005. *The Economic Life of Refugees.* Bloomfield: Kumarian Press.

Janes, Julia E. 2016. "Democratic Encounters? Epistemic Privilege, Power, and Community-Based Participatory Action Research." *Action Research* 14 (1): 72–87.

Jardine, John. 1882. *Notes on Burmese Law,* vol. 1, *Marriage.* Rangoon: Office of the Superintendent, Burma.

Jessop, Bob. 2012. "Cultural Political Economy, Spatial Imaginaries, Regional Economic Dynamics." CPERC Working Paper, 2012–02. Cultural Political Economy Research Centre, Lancaster Univ. http://www.lancaster.ac.uk /cperc/docs/Jessop% 20CPERC% 20Working% 20Paper, 202, 012–02.

Johnston, Lydia. 2017. "Gender and Sexuality III: Precarious Places." *Progress in Human Geography* 42 (6): 928–36.

Jolliffe, Kim. 2014. Ethnic Conflict and Social Services in Myanmar's Contested Regions. Yangon: The Asia Foundation.

Kabachnik, Peter, et al. . 2013. "Traumatic Masculinities: The Gendered Geographies of Georgian IDPs from Abkhazia." *Gender, Place & Culture* 20 (6): 773–93.

Kaiser, Robert J. 2014. "Performativity, Events, and Becoming Stateless." In *Performativity, Politics, and the Production of Social Space,* edited by Michael R. Glass and Reuben Rose-Redwood, 121–45. New York: Routledge.

Kaiser, Peter, Marie T. Benner, and Kai Pohlmann. 2020. "Prolonged Humanitarian Crises – Mental Health in a Refugee Setting at the Thai-Myanmar Border." *Athens Journal of Health and Medical Sciences* 7 (2): 105–26.

Kallio, Kirsi P, Jouni Häkli, and Elisa Pascucci. 2019. "Refugeeness as Political Subjectivity: Experiencing the Humanitarian Border." *Environment and Planning C: Politics and Space* 37 (7): 1258–76.

Karen Human Rights Group. 2009. *Cycles of Displacement: Forced Relocation and Civilian Responses in Nyaunglebin District.* N.p.: Karen Human Rights Group.

———. 2010. *Self-Protection under Strain: Targeting of Civilians and Local Responses in Northern Karen State.* N.p.: Karen Human Rights Group.

Katz, Cindi. 2004. *Growing Up Global: Economic Restructuring and Children's Everyday Lives.* Minneapolis: Univ. of Minnesota Press.

Keck, Margaret E., and Kathryn Sikkink. 1998. *Activists beyond Borders: Advocacy Networks in International Politics.* Ithaca, NY: Cornell Univ. Press.

Kerkvliet, Benedict J. Tria. 2009. "Everyday Politics in Peasant Societies (and Ours)." *Journal of Peasant Studies* 36 (1): 227–43.

Keyes, Charles F. 1979. "The Karen in Thai History and the History of the Karen in Thailand." In *Ethnic Adaptation and Identity: The Karen on the Thai Frontier with Burma*, edited by Charles F. Keyes, 25–62. Philadelphia: Institute for the Study of Human Issues.

———. 2002. "'The Peoples of Asia'—Science and Politics in the Classification of Ethnic Groups in Thailand, China and Vietnam." *Journal of Asian Studies* 61 (4): 1163–203.

———. 2008. "Ethnicity and the Nation-State of Thailand and Vietnam." In *Challenging the Limits: Indigenous Peoples of the Mekong Region*, edited by Prasit Leepreecha, Don Mccaskill, and Kwanchewan Buadaeng, 13–53. Chiang Mai: Mekong Press.

Kittipong Kittayarak. 2003. "Restorative Justice: The Thai Experience." Paper presented at UNAFEI International Seminar on Victim Rights Protection and Restorative Justice Approaches, January 8–February 14.

Klein, Naomi. 2007. *Shock Doctrine: The Rise of Disaster Capitalism*. New York: Picador.

Kritaya Archavanitkul. 2007. *The Thai State and the Changing AIDS and Reproductive Health Policies on Migrant Workers* (In Thai). IPSR Publication no. 327. Nakhon Pathom: Institute for Population and Social research, Mahidol Univ.

———. 2010. *Thai State Policy to Manage Irregular Migration from Neighboring Countries*. Bangkok: Institute for Population and Social Research.

Kritaya Archavanitkul and Kulapa Vajanasara. 2008. *Employment of Migrant Workers under the Working of Aliens Act 2008 and the List of Occupations Allowed to Foreigners*. Bangkok: International Organization for Migration.

Kudo, Toshihiro. 2013. "Border Development in Myanmar: The Case of the Myawaddy-Mae Sot Border." In *Border Economies in the Greater Mekong Subregion*, edited by Masami Ishida, 186–205. New York: Palgrave Macmillan.

Kusakabe, Kyoko, and Ruth Pearson. 2010. "Transborder Migration, Social Reproduction and Economic Development: A Case Study of Burmese Women Workers in Thailand." *International Migration* 48 (6): 13–43.

Kyed, Helene Maria. 2018. "Introduction to the Special Issue on Everyday Justice." *Independent Journal of Burmese Scholarship* 1 (2): 1–26.

———, ed. 2020. *Everyday Justice in Myanmar: Informal Resolutions and State Evasion in a Time of Contested Transition*. Copenhagen: NIAS Press.

———. 2020. "Introduction: Everyday Justice in a Contested Transition." In Kyed, *Everyday Justice in Myanmar*, 1–42.

Lang, Hazel. 2002. *Fear and Sanctuary: Burmese Refugees in Thailand*. Ithaca, NY: Southeast Asia Program Publications.

Lang, Sabine. 2012. *NGOs, Civil Society, and the Public Sphere*. Cambridge: Cambridge Univ. Press.

Lawi Weng. 2012. "Rights Groups Say Migrants Blocked from Leaving Mae Sot." *The Irrawaddy*, October 2. https://www.irrawaddy.com/news/burma /rights-groups-say-migrants-blocked-from-leaving-mae-sot.html (accessed June 24, 2021).

Leach, Edmund R. 1954. *Political Systems of Highland Burma*. London: Athlone Press.

———. 1960. "The Frontiers of 'Burma.'" *Comparative Studies in Society and History* 3 (1): 49–68.

Lefebvre, Henri. 1991. *The Production of Space*. Translated by Donald Nicholson-Smith. Malden, MA: Blackwell.

Leiter, Karen, et al. 2006. "Human Rights Abuses and Vulnerability to HIV/ AIDS: The Experiences of Burmese Women in Thailand." *Health and Human Rights* 9 (2): 88–111.

Lems, Annika. 2020. "Phenomenology of Exclusion: Capturing the Everyday Thresholds of Belonging." *Social Inclusion* 8 (4): 116–25.

Levitt, Peggy, and Sally Engle Merry. 2011. "Making Women's Human Rights in the Vernacular: Navigating the Culture/Rights Divide." In *Gender and Culture at the Limit of Rights*, edited by Dorothy L. Hodgson, 81–100. Philadelphia: Univ. of Pennsylvania Press.

Li, Tania Murray. 2007. *The Will to Improve: Governmentality, Development, and the Practice of Politics*. Durham: Duke Univ. Press.

Lindorfer, Simone. 2009. "In Whose Interest Do We Work? Critical Comments of a Practitioner at the Fringes of the Liberation Paradigm." *Feminism & Psychology* 19 (3): 354–67.

Lintner, Bertil. 1999. *Burma in Revolt: Opium and Insurgency since 1948*. 2nd ed. Boulder, CO: Westview Press.

———. 2013. "The Trade in Counterfeit Goods and Contraband in Mainland Southeast Asia." In Couvy, *An Atlas of Trafficking in Southeast Asia*, 136–57.

Loos, Tamara. 2006. *Subject Siam: Family, Law, and Colonial Modernity in Thailand*. Ithaca, NY: Cornell Univ. Press.

Lunet de La Jonquière, Étienne. 2001 [1906]. *Siam and the Siamese: Travels in Thailand and Burma in 1904*. Bangkok: White Lotus Press.

Lwin Lwin Mon. 2020. "Dispute Resolution and Perceptions of Security among Urban Karen: The Role of Religious and Ethnic Identity." In Kyed, *Everyday Justice in Myanmar*, 163–88.

Lykes, M. Brinton. 2013. "Participatory and Action Research as a Transformative Praxis: Responding to Humanitarian Crises from the Margins." *American Psychologist* 68 (8): 774–83.

Lykes, M. Brinton, and Alison Crosby. 2014. "Feminist Practice of Action and Community Research." In *Feminist Research Practice: A Primer*, edited by Sharlene Nagy Hesse-Biber, 145–81. Thousand Oaks, CA: Sage.

Ma Ma Lay. 1991. *Not Out of Hate: A Novel of Burma*. Translated by Margaret Aung-Thwin. Athens: Ohio Univ. Press.

Maber, Elizabeth. 2014. "(In)Equality and Action: The Role of Women's Training Initiatives in Promoting Women's Leadership Opportunities in Myanmar." *Gender & Development* 22 (1): 141–56.

Mac Ginty, Roger. 2015. "Where Is the Local? Critical Localism and Peacebuilding." *Third World Quarterly* 36 (5): 840–56.

Magubane, Zine. 2004. *Bringing the Empire Home: Race, Class, and Gender in Britain and Colonial South Africa*. Chicago: Univ. of Chicago Press.

Malkki, Liisa H. 1992. "National Geographic: The Rooting of Peoples and the Territorialization of National Identity among Scholars and Refugees." *Cultural Anthropology* 7 (1): 24–44.

———. 1995. *Purity and Exile: Violence, Memory, and National Cosmology among Hutu Refugees in Tanzania*. Chicago: Univ. of Chicago Press.

———. 1996. "Speechless Emissaries: Refugees, Humanitarianism, and Dehistoricization." *Cultural Anthropology* 11 (3): 377–404

Marks, Thomas A. 1994. *Making Revolution: The Insurgency of the Communist Party of Thailand in Structural Perspective*. Bangkok: White Lotus Press.

Massey, Doreen. 1994. *Space, Place, and Gender*. Cambridge: Polity Press.

Matthews, Bruce. 2006. "Myanmar's Human and Economic Crisis and Its Regional Implications." *Southeast Asian Affairs* 2006: 208–23.

Maung, Cynthia, and Suzanne Belton. 2005. *Working Our Way Back Home: Fertility and Pregnancy Loss on the Thai-Burma Border*. Mae Sot: Mae Tao Clinic.

Maung Aung Myo. 2009. *Building the Tatmadaw: Myanmar Armed Forces since 1948*. Singapore: Institute of Southeast Asian Studies.

Maung Maung. 1963. *Law and Custom in Burma and the Burmese Family.* The Hague: M. Nijhoff.

McCartan, Brian, and Kim Jolliffe. 2016. *Ethnic Armed Actors and Justice Provision in Myanmar.* San Francisco: The Asia Foundation.

McConnachie, Kirsten. 2014. *Governing Refugees: Justice, Order and Legal Pluralism.* Oxon: Routledge.

———. 2020. "Everyday Justice in Karen Refugee Camps." In Kyed, *Everyday Justice in Myanmar,* 284–304.

McGeachy, Hilary. 2002. "The Invention of Burmese Buddhist Law: A Case Study in Legal Orientalism." *The Australian Journal of Asian Law* 4 (1): 30–52.

McGee, Terry. 1991. "The Emergence of *Desakota* Regions in Asia: Expanding a Hypothesis." In *The Extended Metropolis: Settlement Transition in Asia,* edited by Norton Ginsburg, Bruce Koppel, and Terry G. McGee, 3–25. Honolulu: Univ. of Hawaii Press.

McGuffey, C. Shawn. 2005. "Engendering Trauma: Race, Class, and Gender Reaffirmation after Child Sexual Abuse." *Gender and Society* 19 (5): 621–43.

———. 2008. "'Saving Masculinity': Gender Reaffirmation, Sexuality, Race, and Parental Responses to Male Child Sexual Abuse." *Social Problems* 55 (2): 216–37.

McNabb, Scott F. 1983. "The Hill Areas Education Project of Northern Thailand: Constraints and Prospects for Hill Tribe Participation." *Crossroads: An Interdisciplinary Journal of Southeast Asian Studies* 1 (2): 17–29.

Merriam, Sharan B., et al. 2001. "Power and Positionality: Negotiating Insider/Outsider Status within and across Cultures." *International Journal of Lifelong Education* 20 (5): 405–16.

Merry, Sally Engle. 1988. "Legal Pluralism." *Law & Society Review* 22 (5): 869–96.

———. 2006. "New Legal Realism and the Ethnography of Transnational Law." *Law and Social Inquiry* 31 (4): 975–95.

———. 2009. *Gender Violence: A Cultural Perspective.* Sussex: Wiley-Blackwell.

Meyer, Sarah R., et al. 2019. "Gender Differences in Violence and Other Human Rights Abuses among Migrant Workers on the Thailand-Myanmar Border." *Violence against Women* 25 (8): 945–67.

Mezzadra, Sandro, and Brett Neilson. 2013. *Border as Method, or, the Multiplication of Labor.* Durham, NC: Duke Univ. Press.

Mignolo, Walter D., and Madina V. Tlostanova. 2006. "Theorizing from the Borders: Shifting to Geo- and Body-Politics of Knowledge." *European Journal of Social Theory* 9: 205–21.

Migrant Rights Promotion Working Group. 2014. "Fact Sheet: Forced Removal of Migrant Workers from Kok Kwai Community." June 11. Mae Sot: Migrant Rights Promotion Working Group.

Millán, Márgara. 2016. "The Traveling of 'Gender' and Its Accompanying Baggage: Thoughts on the Translation of Feminism(s), the Globalization of Discourses, and Representational Divides." *European Journal of Women's Studies* 23 (1): 6–27.

Mills, Mary Beth. 1999. *Thai Women in the Global Labor Force: Consuming Desires, Contested Selves*. New Brunswick, NJ: Rutgers Univ. Press.

Mohanty, Chandra Talpade. 2016. "Anti-Globalization Pedagogies and Feminism." In *Gender through the Prism of Difference*, edited by Maxine Baca Zinn, Pierrette Hondagneu-Sotelo, Michael A. Messner, and Amy M. Denissen, 60–66. Oxford: Oxford Univ. Press.

Morris, Rosalind C. 2006. "The Mute and the Unspeakable: Political Subjectivity, Violent Crime, and the 'Sexual Thing' in a South African Mining Community." In Comaroff and Comaroff, *Law and Disorder in the Postcolony*, 57–101.

Morse, Stephen, and Nora McNamara. 2006. "Analysing Institutional Partnerships in Development: A Contract between Equals or a Loaded Process?" *Progress in Development Studies* 6 (4): 321–36.

Mouffe, Chantal. 2005. *On the Political*. New York: Routledge.

Mountz, Alison. 2004. "Embodying the Nation-State: Canada's Response to Human Smuggling." *Political Geography* 23 (3): 323–45.

———. 2018. "Political Geography III: Bodies." *Progress in Human Geography* 42 (5): 759–69.

Mya Maung. 1991. *The Burma Road to Poverty*. New York: Praeger.

Myanmar Development Research, and Susanne Kempel. 2012. *Village Institutions and Leadership in Myanmar: A View from Below*. Yangon: UN Development Program.

Nagar, Richa, Victoria Lawson, Linda McDowell, and Susan Hanson. 2002. "Locating Globalization: Feminist (Re)readings of the Subjects and Spaces of Globalization." *Economic Geography* 78: 257–84.

Natenapha Wailerdsak. 2008. "Companies in Crisis." In Pasuk Phongpaichit and Baker, *Thai Capital after the 1997 Crisis*, 17–57.

National Statistics Office–Thailand. 2014. *The 2010 Population and Housing Census: Changwat Tak*. Bangkok: National Statistics Office.

New Light of Myanmar. 2003. "Rehabilitation Centre for Women Inspected." *New Light of Myanmar*, April 5.

Nitta, Yuichi. 2018. "Myanmar's Not-So-Underground Casinos in Line for Legalization." *Nikkei Asia*, April 1. https://asia.nikkei.com/Politics/Myanmar-s-not-so-underground-casinos-in-line-for-legalization (accessed June 24, 2021).

Nobpaon Rabibhadana and Yoko Hayami. 2013. "Seeking Haven and Seeking Jobs: Migrant Workers' Networks in Two Thai Locales." *Southeast Asian Studies* 2 (2): 243–83.

Norsworthy, Kathryn L. 2017. "Mindful Activism: Embracing the Complexities of International Border Crossings." *American Psychologist* 72 (9): 1035–43.

Norsworthy, Kathryn L., and Ouyporn Khuankaew. 2004. "Women of Burma Speak Out: Workshop to Deconstruct Gender-Based Violence and Build Systems of Peace and Justice." *The Journal for Specialists in Group Work* 29 (3): 259–83.

O'Kane, Mary. 2006. "Gender, Borders and Transversality: The Emerging Women's Movement in the Burma-Thailand Borderlands." In *Gender, Conflict, and Migration*, edited by Navnita Chadha Behera, 227–54. Sherman Oaks, CA: Sage.

Oh, Su-Ann. 2010. *Education in Refugee Camps in Thailand: Policy, Practice, and Paucity.* Paris: UNESCO.

———. 2018. "The Moral Economy of the Myawaddy-Mae Sot Border." In *Routledge Handbook of Asian Borderlands*, edited by Alexander Horstmann, Martin Saxer, and Alessandro Rippa, 361–75. Oxon: Routledge.

Ong, Aihwa. 2011. "Translating Gender Justice in Southeast Asia: Situated Ethics, NGOs, and Bio-Welfare." *Hawwa: Journal of Women in the Middle East and Islamic World* 9: 26–48.

Ormel, Ilja, et al. 2020. "Key Issues for Participatory Research in the Design and Implementation of Humanitarian Assistance: A Scoping Review." *Global Health Action* 13: 1–15.

Pallister-Wilkins, Polly. 2019. "Im/mobility and Humanitarian Triage." In *Handbook on Critical Geographies of Migration*, edited by Katharyne Mitchell, Reece Jones, and Jennifer L. Fluri, 372–83. Cheltenham, UK: Edward Elgar Publishing.

Paasi, Anssi. 2011. "Geography, Space and the Re-Emergence of Topological Thinking." *Dialogues in Human Geography* 1 (3): 299–303.

Panu Wongcha-um. 2014. "Mae Sot to Be Thailand, Myanmar's New Special Economic Zone," *Chanel News Asia*, October 10.

———. 2021. "Thousands of Myanmar Villagers Poised to Flee Violence to Thailand, Group Says." *Reuters*. April 29. https://www.reuters.com/world/asia-pacific/thousands-myanmar-villagers-poised-flee-violence-thailand-group-says-2021-04-30/ (accessed on February 10, 2022).

Pasuk Phongpaichit, and Christopher John Baker. 2008. *Thai Capital after the 1997 Crisis*. Chiang Mai: Silkworm Books.

Pearson, Elaine, et al. 2006. *The Mekong Challenge—Underpaid, Overworked and Overlooked*. Bangkok: International Labor Organization.

Pearson, Ruth, and Kyoko Kusakabe. 2012a. *Thailand's Hidden Workforce: Burmese Migrant Women Factory Workers*. London: Zed Books.

———. 2012b. "Who Cares? Gender, Reproduction, and Care Chains of Burmese Migrant Workers in Thailand." *Feminist Economics* 18 (2): 149–75.

———. 2013. "Cross-Border Childcare Strategies of Burmese Migrant Workers in Thailand." *Gender, Place & Culture: A Journal of Feminist Geography* 20 (8): 960–78.

Peeradej Tanruangporn. 2011. "Booming Mae Sot Eagerly Waits to Become Special Administrative Zone." *The Nation*, August 15.

Peck, Grant. 2021. "UN Says Conflict in Myanmar Impedes Its Humanitarian Aid." *AP News*. https://apnews.com/article/united-nations-myanmar-race-and-ethnicity-f5024a4b4aadcc55aecc5022d44277c3 (accessed May 22, 2021).

Pinkaew Laungaramsri. 2003. "Constructing Marginality: The 'Hill Tribe' Karen and Their Shifting Locations within Thai State and Public Perspectives." In *Living at the Edge of Thai Society: The Karen in the Highlands of Northern Thailand*, edited by Claudio O. Delang, 21–42.

Pitch Pongsawat. 2007. "Border Partial Citizenship, Border Towns, and Thai-Myanmar Cross-Border Development: Case Studies at the Thai Border Towns." PhD diss., Univ. of California, Berkeley.

Pittman, Alexandra. 2014. "Fast-Forwarding Gender Equality and Women's Empowerment? Reflections on Measuring Change for UNDP's Thematic Evaluation on Gender Mainstreaming and Gender Equality 2008–2013." Occasional Paper, United Nations Development Program.

Piya Pangsapa. 2007. *Textures of Struggle: The Emergency of Resistance among Garment Workers in Thailand*. Ithaca, NY: Cornell Univ. Press.

———. 2009. "When Battlefields become Marketplaces: Migrant Workers and the Role of Civil Society and NGO Activism in Thailand." *International Migration* 53(3): 1-26.

Pollard, Jane. 2012. "Gendering Capital: Financial Crisis, Financialization and (an Agenda for) Economic Geography." *Progress in Human Geography* 37 (3): 403–23.

Pollock, Jackie, and Soe Linn Aung. 2010. "Critical Times: Gendering Implications of the Economic Crisis for Migrant Workers From Burma/Myanmar in Thailand." *Gender and Development* 18 (2): 213–27.

Puttaporn Areeprachakun. 2020. "The Construction of Othering: The Study of Migrant Workers from Myanmar in Samut Sakhon Province, Thailand." PhD diss., Univ. of Wisconsin, Madison.

Quijano, Anibal. 2000. "Coloniality of Power, Eurocentrism and Latin America." *Nepantla* 1 (3): 533–80.

Rajaram, Prem Kumar, and Carl Grundy-Warr, eds. 2007. *Borderscapes: Hidden Geographies and Politics at Territory's Edge.* Minneapolis: Univ. of Minnesota Press.

Rancière, Jacques. 2010. *Dissensus: On Politics and Aesthetics.* Translated by Steven Corcoran. London: Continuum.

Raquiza, Antoinette R. 2012. *State Structure, Policy Formation, Economic Development in Southeast Asia.* New York: Routledge.

Razack, Sherene. 2005. "How Is White Supremacy Embodied? Sexualized Racial Violence at Abu Ghraib." *Canadian Journal of Women and the Law* 17 (2): 341–63.

Renard, Ronald D. 2000. "The Differential Integration of Hill People into the Thai State." In *Civility and Savagery: Social Identity in Tai States,* edited by Andrew Turton, 63–83. Richmond: Curzon Press.

———. 2006. "Creating the Other Requires Defining Thainess against Which the Other Can Exist: Early-Twentieth-Century Definitions." *Southeast Asian Studies* 44 (3): 295–320.

Reyes, Victoria. 2020. "Ethnographic Toolkit: Strategic Positionality and Researchers' Visible and Invisible Tools in Field Research." *Ethnography* 21 (2): 220–40.

Rhoads, Elizabeth. 2020. "Informal (Justice) Brokers: Buying, Selling, and Disputing Property in Yangon." In Kyed, *Everyday Justice in Myanmar,* 283–314.

Richey, Lisa Ann. 2018. "Conceptualizing 'Everyday Humanitarianism': Ethics, Affects, and Practices of Contemporary Global Helping." *New Political Science* 40 (4): 625–39.

Robertson, Philip S., and Federation of Trade Unions–Burma, eds. 2006. *The Mekong Challenge: Working Day and Night—The Plight of Migrant Child Workers in Mae Sot, Thailand.* Bangkok: International Labor Organization.

Roepstorff, Kristina. 2020. "A Call for Critical Reflection on the Localisation Agenda in Humanitarian Action." *Third World Quarterly* 41 (2): 284–301.

Rose. Nikolas. 1999. *Powers of Freedom: Reframing Political Thought.* Cambridge: Cambridge Univ. Press.

Rose-Redwood, Reuben, and Michael R. Glass. 2014: "Introduction: Geographies of Performativity." In *Performativity, Politics, and the Production of Social Space,* edited by Michael R. Glass and Reuben Rose-Redwood, 1–35. New York: Routledge.

Rössel, Jorg, and Randall Collins. 2001. "Conflict Theory and Interaction Rituals: The Microfoundations of Conflict Theory." In *Handbook of Sociological Theory,* edited by Jonathan H Turner, 509–32. New York: Kluwer/ Plenum.

Ryan, Louise. 2015. "'Inside' and 'Outside' of What or Where? Researching Migration through Multi-Positionalities." *Forum Qualitative Sozialforschung / Forum: Qualitative Social Research* 16 (2): n.p.

Sadeque, Samira. 2020. "Myanmar's Protection Bill Falls Short of Address Violence against Women." *Interpress Service,* July 28. http://www.ipsnews.net /2020/07/myanmars-protection-bill-falls-short-of-addressing-violence-against -women/ (accessed June 1, 2021).

Sai Silp. 2007. "Mae Sot Metropolis Plan." *The Irrawaddy,* June 5. http://www2 .irrawaddy.org/print_article.php?art_id=7379 (accessed November 7, 2014).

Saltsman, Adam. 2011. *Developing a Profiling Methodology for Displaced People in Urban Areas: Case Study—Mae Sot, Thailand.* Medford, MA: Feinstein International Center.

———. 2012. *Surviving or Thriving on the Thai-Burma Border: Vulnerability and Resilience in Mae Sot, Thailand.* Bangkok: International Rescue Committee.

———. 2014. "Beyond the Law: Power, Discretion and Bureaucracy in the Management of Asylum Space in Thailand." *Journal of Refugee Studies* 23 (3): 457–76.

Saltsman, Adam and Nassim Majidi. 2021. "Storytelling in Research with Refugees: On the Promise and Politics of Audibility and Visibility in Participatory Research Contexts of Forced Migration." *Journal of Refugee Studies* 34 (3): 2522–38.

Saratsawadi Ongsakun. 1996. *Prawattisat Lanna* [History of Lanna]. Bangkok: Amarin.

Schaffer, Kay, and Sidonie Smith. 2004. *Human Rights and Narrated Lives: The Ethics of Recognition.* New York: Palgrave.

Schmid, Alex P., and Albert J. Jongman. 2005. *Political Terrorism: A New Guide to Authors, Actors, Concepts, Data Bases, Theories, and Literature.* 2nd ed. New Brunswick, NJ: Transaction Publishers.

Sciortino, Roberta, and Sureephorn Punpuing. 2009. *International Migration in Thailand 2009.* Bangkok: International Organization for Migration.

Scott, James C. 1972. "Patron-Client Politics and Political Change in Southeast Asia." *American Political Science Review* 66 (1): 91–113.

———. 1985. *Domination and the Arts of Resistance.* New Haven, CT: Yale Univ. Press.

———. 2009. *The Art of Not Being Governed: An Anarchist History of Upland Southeast Asia.* New Haven, CT: Yale Univ. Press.

Scully, Pamela. 2011. "Gender, History, and Human Rights." In *Gender and Culture at the Limit of Rights*, edited by Dorothy L. Hodgson, 17–31. Philadelphia: Univ. of Pennsylvania Press.

Sein Tu. 1962. *Lokanīti.* Mandalay: Tetnaylin Press.

Sharples, Rachel. 2020. *Spaces of Solidarity: Karen Activism in the Thailand-Burma Borderlands.* New York: Berghan Books.

Sidaway, James D. 2007. "Spaces of Post-Development." *Progress in Human Geography* 31 (3): 345–61.

Sim, Amanda. 2014. *Building Happy Families: Impact Evaluation of a Parenting and Family Skills Intervention for Migrant and Displaced Burmese Families in Thailand.* New York: International Rescue Committee.

Simmel, Georg. 1955. *Conflict and the Web of Group Affiliations.* Translated by Reinhard Bendix. New York: Free Press.

Sinatti, Giulia. 2014. "Masculinities and Intersectionality in Migration: Transnational Wolof Migrants Negotiating Manhood and Gendered Family Roles." In *Migration, Gender and Social Justice Perspectives on Human Insecurity*, edited by Thanh-Dam Truong, Des Gasper, Jeff Handmaker, and Sylvia I. Bergh, 215–26. Heidelberg: Springer.

Smith, Harry, Reuben Lim, and Benjamin Harkins. 2019. "Thailand Migration Profile." In *Thailand Migration Report 2019*, edited by Benjamin Harkins, 9–25. Bangkok: International Organization for Migration.

Smith, Martin. 1991. *Burma: Insurgency and the Politics of Ethnicity*. London: Zed Books.

———. 2007. *State of Strife: The Dynamics of Ethnic Conflict in Burma*. Washington DC: East-West Center.

Snyder, Anna. 2011. "Developing Refugee Peacebuilding Capacity: Women in Exile on the Thai-Burmese Border." In *Critical Issues in Peace and Conflict Studies: Theory, Practice, and Pedagogy*, edited by Thomas Matyók, Jessica Senehi, and Sean Byrne, 177–98. Plymouth, MA: Lexington Books.

South, Ashley. 2008. *Ethnic Politics in Burma: States of Conflict*. London: Routledge.

———. 2011. *Burma's Longest War: Anatomy of the Karen Conflict*. Amsterdam: Transnational Institute.

Spangaro, Jo, et al. 2015. "Mechanisms Underpinning Interventions to Reduce Sexual Violence in Armed Conflict: A Realist-Informed Systematic Review." *Conflict and Health* 9 (1): 1–14.

Spangaro, Jo, Chinelo Adogu, and Geetha Ranmuthugala. 2013. "What Evidence Exists for Initiatives to Reduce Risk and Incidence of Sexual Violence in Armed Conflict and Other Humanitarian Crises? A Systematic Review." *Plos One* 8 (5): 1–13.

Speed, Shannon. 2007. "Exercising Rights and Reconfiguring Resistance in the Zapatista Juntas de Buen Gobierno." In *The Practice of Human Rights: Tracking Law between the Global and the Local*, edited by Mark Goodale and Sally Engle Merry, 163–92. Cambridge: Cambridge Univ. Press.

Sphere. 2011. *Humanitarian Charter and Minimum Standards in Humanitarian Response*. 3rd ed. London: Sphere.

Spivak, Gayatri Chakravorty. 1993. *Outside in the Teaching Machine*. New York: Routledge.

Springer, Simon. 2011. "Violence Sits in Place? Cultural Practice, Neoliberal Rationalism, and Virulent Imaginative Geographies." *Political Geography* 30: 90–98.

Sternbach, Ludwik. 1963. "The Pāli 'Lokanīti' and the Burmese 'Nīti Kyan' and Their Sources." *Bulletin of the School of Oriental and African Studies* 26 (2): 329–45.

Stoakes, Emanuel, Chris Kelly, and Annie Kelly. 2015. "Revealed: How the Thai Fishing Industry Trafficks, Imprisons and Enslaves." *The Guardian*, July 20. http://www.theguardian.com/global-development/2015/jul/20/thai-fishing -industry-implicated-enslavement-deaths-rohingya (accessed May 20, 2021).

Stoler, Ann Laura. 2002. *Carnal Knowledge and Imperial Power: Race and the Intimate in Colonial Rule.* Berkeley: Univ. of California Press.

———. 2016. *Duress: Imperial Durabilities in Our Times.* Durham, NC: Duke Univ. Press.

Supavadee Chotikajan, Jason Judd, Susana Siar, and Tomomi Ishida. 2019. "Working Conditions for Migrants and Illegal, Unreported and Unregulated Fishing in Thailand's Fishing Sector." In *Thailand Migration Report 2019.* Bangkok: International Organization for Migration.

Susskind, Yifat. 2008. "Indigenous Women's Anti-Violence Strategies." In *Violence and Gender in the Globalized World: The Intimate and the Extimate,* edited by Sanja Bahun-Radunović and V. G. Julie Rajan, 11–24. Hampshire: Ashgate.

Sutatip Chavanavesskul, and Giuseppe T. Cirella. 2020. "Land Use Change Model Comparison: Mae Sot Special Economic Zone." In *Sustainable Human–Nature Relations,* edited by Giuseppe T. Cirella, 123–38. Singapore: Springer Singapore.

Syed, Jawad, and Faiza Ali. 2011. "The White Woman's Burden: From Colonial Civilization to Third World Development." *Third World Quarterly* 32 (2): 349–65.

Takamuri, Saburo, and Suguru Mouri. 1984. *Border Trade: The Southeast Asian Black Market.* Tokyo: Koubundo Publishers.

Tapp, Nicholas. 1989. *Sovereignty and Rebellion: The White Hmong of Northern Thailand.* Oxford: Oxford Univ. Press.

Teubner, Gunther. 1997. "Global Bukowina: Legal Pluralism in the World Society." In *Global Law without a State,* edited by Gunther Teubner, 3–28. Brookfield, VT: Dartmouth Publishing.

Thai News Service. 2015. "Thailand: Tak Province to Map out Plans to Prevent Land Price Speculation." January 23.

Thame, Charlie. 2017. "SEZs and Value Extraction from the Mekong: A Case Study on the Control and Exploitation of Land and Labour in Cambodia and Myanmar's Special Economic Zones." Bangkok: Focus on the Global South.

The Nation. 2020. "Tak Chamber Seeks Opening of Border Checkpoints to Revive Trade with Myanmar." May 8. https://www.nationthailand.com/news/30387563 (accessed June 25, 2021).

Thin Lei Win. 2014. "Burma Activists Demand Law to Ban Violence against Women." *The Irrawaddy,* October 1.

Thongchai Winichakul. 1994. *Siam Mapped: A History of the Geo-Body of a Nation*. Honolulu: Univ. of Hawaii Press.

———. 2000a. "The Others Within: Travel and Ethno-Spatial Differentiation of Siamese Subjects, 1885–1910." In Turton, *Civility and Savagery*, 38–62.

———. 2000b. "The Quest for 'Siwilai': A Geographical Discourse of Civilization Thinking in the Late-Nineteenth and Early-Twentieth-Century Siam." *Journal of Asian Studies* 59 (3): 528–49.

Thornton, Phil. 2006. *Restless Souls: Rebels, Refugees, Medics, and Misfits on the Thai-Burma Border*. Bangkok: Asia Books.

Ticktin, Miriam. 2011a. *Casualties of Care: Immigration and the Politics of Humanitarianism in France*. Berkeley: Univ. of California Press.

———. 2011b. "The Gendered Human of Humanitarianism: Medicalising and Politicizing Sexual Violence." *Gender & History* 23 (2): 250–65.

Tol, Wietse A., et al. 2013. "Sexual and Gender-Based Violence in Areas of Armed Conflict: A Systematic Review of Mental Health and Psychosocial Support Interventions." *Conflict and Health* 7 (16): 1–9.

Tomsa, Dirk, and Andreas Ufen. 2013. *Party Politics in Southeast Asia: Clientelism and Electoral Competition in Indonesia, Thailand and the Philippines*. New York: Routledge.

Torre, María Elena, Brett G. Stoudt, Einat Manoff, and Michelle Fine. 2018. "Critical Participatory Action Research on State Violence: Bearing Wit(h)ness across Fault Lines of Power, Privilege, and Dispossession." In *The Sage Handbook of Qualitative Research*, edited by Norman K. Denzin and Yvonna S. Lincoln, 492–515.

Tsing, Anna L. 2005. *Friction: An Ethnography of Global Connection*. Princeton, NJ: Princeton Univ. Press.

Tunon, Max, and Nilim Baruah. 2012. "Public Attitudes towards Migrant Workers in Asia." *Migration and Development* 1 (1): 149–62.

Turton, Andrew, ed. 2000. *Civility and Savagery: Social Identity in Tai States*. Richmond: Curzon Press.

———. "Introduction to *Civility and Savagery*." In Turton, *Civility and Savagery*, 3–31.

Turton, Shaun. 2021. "Myanmar Coup Clouds Future of Country's Crucial Garment Industry." *Nikkei Asia*, February 10. https://asia.nikkei.com/Spotlight/Myanmar-Coup/Myanmar-coup-clouds-future-of-country-s-crucial-garment-industry (accessed June 25, 2021).

United Nations. 2016. "Secretary General, at Round Table, Commits to Making Humanitarian Action 'Local as Possible, International as Necessary.'" UN Press Release, May 23. https://www.un.org/press/en/2016/sgsm17778.doc.htm (accessed June 25, 2021).

UN High Commissioner for Refugees. 2006. *Analysis of Gaps in Refugee Protection Capacity—Thailand*. Bangkok: UNHCR.

UN Women. 2014. *Humanitarian Strategy 2014–2017*. Geneva: UN Women.

USAID/US Department of State. 2015. *FY 2014 Performance Report, FY 2016 Performance Plan*. https://www.usaid.gov/sites/default/files/documents/1868/State-USAID_FY16_APP_FY%2014_APR.pdf (accessed October 8, 2021).

Valentine, Gill. 2002. "Queer Bodies and the Production of Space." In *Handbook of Lesbian and Gay Studies*, edited by Diane Richardson and Steven Seidman, 145–60. London: Sage.

Vandergeest, Peter, and Nancy Lee Peluso. 1995. "Territorialization and State Power in Thailand." *Theory and Society* 24 (3): 385–426.

Vichit Sukaviriya. 1966. *Facts about Community Development Programs*. Bangkok: Ministry of Interior.

Vitit Muntarbhorn. 2007. *Refugee Law and Practice in the Asia and Pacific Region: Thailand as a Case Study*. Bangkok: UNHCR.

Wagner-Pacifici, Robin, and Meredith Hall. 2012. "Resolution of Social Conflict." *Annual Review of Sociology* 38: 181–99.

Wahyu Kuncoro. 2018. *Burmese-Muslim Social Networks in the Borderland: A Case Study of Islam Bamroong Muslim Community in Mae Sot, Tak, Thailand*. Chiang Mai: Chiang Mai Univ. Press.

Walker, Andrew, and Nicholas Farrelly. 2008. "Northern Thailand's Specter of Eviction." *Critical Asian Studies* 40 (3): 373–97.

Walters, William. 2011. "Foucault and Frontiers: Notes on the Birth of the Humanitarian Border." In *Governmentality: Current Issues and Future Challenges*, edited by Ulrich Bröckling, Susanne Krasmann, and Thomas Lemke, 138–64.

Wanchai Watanasap. 2010. "The Community Justice History in Northeast Thailand." Paper presented at BITEC Ban Nga, Bangkok, September 9.

Williams, Jill M. 2015. "From Humanitarian Exceptionalism to Contingent Care: Care and Enforcement at the Humanitarian Border." *Political Geography* 47 (July): 11–20.

Wilson, Kalpana. 2011. "'Race,' Gender and Neoliberalism: Changing Visual Representations in Development." *Third World Quarterly* 32 (2): 315–31.

World Health Organization. 2012. *Understanding and Addressing Violence against Women*. Geneva: WHO.

Wright, Melissa W. 2006. *Disposable Women and Other Myths of Global Capitalism*. New York: Routledge.

Yuval-Davis, Nira, Georgie Wemyss, and Kathryn Cassidy. 2019. *Bordering*. Cambridge: Polity Press.

Index

Photos, figures, and table are indicated by italicized page numbers.

251

Adam P. Saltsman is an assistant professor and director of the Urban Action Institute in the Department of Urban Studies at Worcester State University in Worcester, Massachusetts. His research and teaching focus on borderlands and the politics of belonging and urban exclusion among refugees and others who are on the move or displaced. He lived and worked in Thailand and Cambodia for a number of years doing research and working for human-rights and humanitarian organizations before becoming a professor in the United States.